Macmillan Building and Surveying Series
Series Editor: IVOR H. SEELEY
        Emeritus Professor, The Nottingham Trent University

Advanced Building Measurement, second edition Ivor H. Seeley
Advanced Valuation Diane Butler and David Richmond
An Introduction to Building Services Christopher A. Howard
Applied Valuation Diane Butler
Asset Valuation Michael Rayner
Building Economics, third edition Ivor H. Seeley
Building Maintenance, second edition Ivor H. Seeley
Building Maintenance Technology Lee How Son and George C. S. Yuen
Building Procurement Alan E. Turner
Building Project Appraisal Keith Hutchinson
Building Quantities Explained, fourth edition Ivor H. Seeley
Building Surveys, Reports and Dilapidations Ivor H. Seeley
Building Technology, fourth edition Ivor H. Seeley
Civil Engineering Contract Administration and Control, second edition
        Ivor H. Seeley
Civil Engineering Quantities, fifth edition Ivor H. Seeley
Civil Engineering Specification, second edition Ivor H. Seeley
Commercial Lease Renewals Philip Freedman and Eric F. Shapiro
Computers and Quantity Surveyors Adrian Smith
Construction Contract Claims Reg Thomas
Contract Planning and Contractual Procedures, third edition
        B. Cooke
Contract Planning Case Studies B. Cooke
Cost Estimation of Structures in Commercial Building Surinder Singh
Design-Build Explained David E. L. Janssens
Development Site Evaluation N. P. Taylor
Environmental Science in Building, third edition R. McMullan
Greener Buildings Stuart Johnson
Housing Associations Helen Cope
Housing Management: Changing Practice Christine Davies (editor)
Information and Technology Applications in Commercial Property
        Rosemary Feenan and Tim Dixon (editors)
Introduction to Valuation D. Richmond
Marketing and Property People Owen Bevan
Principles of Property Investment and Pricing, second edition
        W. D. Fraser
Property Valuation Techniques David Isaac and Terry Steley
Public Works Engineering Ivor H. Seeley
Quality Assurance in Building Alan Griffith
Quantity Surveying Practice Ivor H. Seeley
Recreation Planning and Development Neil Ravenscroft
Resource Management for Construction M. R. Canter
Small Building Works Management Alan Griffith
Structural Detailing, second edition P. Newton
Urban Land Economics and Public Policy, fourth edition
        P. N. Balchin, J. L. Kieve and G. H. Bull
Urban Renewal – Theory and Practice Chris Couch
1980 JCT Standard Form of Building Contract, second edition
        R. F. Fellows

STRUCTURAL DETAILING

For Architecture, Building and Civil Engineering

Peter H. Newton

C Eng, FICE

Second Edition

MACMILLAN

First published 1985 by
THE MACMILLAN PRESS LTD
Houndmills, Basingstoke, Hampshire RG21 2XS
and London
Companies and representatives
throughout the world

ISBN 0–333–55471–X

A catalogue record for this book is available
from the British Library.

Second edition 1991
Reprinted 1993, 1994

Printed in Hong Kong

Series Standing Order

If you would like to receive future titles in this series as they are published, you can
make use of our standing order facility. To place a standing order please contact your
bookseller or, in case of difficulty,write to us at the address below with your name
and address and the name of the series. Please state with which title you wish to
begin your standing order. (If you live outside the United Kingdom we may not have
the rights for your area, in which case we will forward your order to the publisher
concerned.)

Customer Services Department, Macmillan Distribution Ltd
Houndmills, Basingstoke, Hampshire RG21 2XS, England

CONTENTS

PREFACE TO THE FIRST EDITION

Structural detailing consists of transforming the work of a structural engineer into working drawings for the use of the builder. It sounds quite simple. That it is not is evidenced by the many 'bog-ups' and even failures, that are constructed. The author has spent half a lifetime working for consulting engineers, contractors and government organisations, at home and abroad, and writes from experience. He has spent the last decade instructing young people in, among other things, the art of detailing.

In the first place, not all designers have enough knowledge of how things are done, and in the second, not all contractors appreciate the reasons behind the design. It is for the detailer to bring these two together and to produce working drawings that do not frustrate the intentions of the designer and are easy for the contractor to follow, simply and economically.

The detailer should, ideally, have a good understanding of both design and construction. But the intended reader of this book is often young and inexperienced and has not yet mastered bending moments and shearing forces, principal stresses and limit states, areas of steel and equivalent lengths. For this reason the book has been written for the reader with little or no prior knowledge of structural mechanics and simple explanations are given of the behaviour of structural components in service.

Similarly it is assumed that the reader will have had little or no site experience and, in any case, will have little real understanding of the processes that are going on (don't worry, some of the older hands haven't either!). Here, again, an attempt has been made to describe the construction process, insofar as it affects the work of the detailer. At the same time, the reader should lose no opportunity to visit sites of construction, watch steelwork being erected, reinforcement fixed, concrete placed and roofs constructed — all, of course, with the permission of the agent and /or engineer.

Detailing is a game played to rules. In the first place the materials are standard — standard steel sections, standard reinforcement, standard timber sizes, standard quality. Non-standard materials can be used, but they are not readily available and usually cost a lot more.

In the second place methods are standard — standard projections, standard scales, standard symbols and notation, standard scheduling and listing. Standard methods are understood by all parties to the process, so reducing the risk of error due to faulty communication.

Finally the techniques are standard — standard hole sizes and spacings, standard edge distances and cover, to name but a few. These have evolved from decades of practical experience to ensure adequate standards of construction and, hence, good service and safety.

It may all sound rather boring, but think how difficult God would have found it making a man from a Picasso.

The rules are contained in a number of documents. Some are British Standards, some proprietary handbooks and others are reports and recommendations of learned bodies. The practising detailer will need to be in possession of up-to-date copies of all the documents pertaining to the discipline in which he or she works. It is unlikely that it will include structural steelwork, reinforced concrete and timber simultaneously, but the cost of the documents will still be considerable.

For the student of all three, this book provides sufficient reference information (with the approval of the copyright holders) for a start to be made with detailing. Throughout the text appropriate clauses and tables are quoted and, in part III, extracts are given, which will enable the reader to practise detailing other structures in steel, concrete and timber, following the examples given in each chapter.

The assumption has been made throughout the book that the design considerations have been made — the sizes of the sections have been determined; the number and sizes of nails, bolts and welds have been calculated; the types, sizes and distribution of reinforcement are known. This is not a reference book and it is not exhaustive. It is a textbook leading the reader, with little prior knowledge, gently through the art of basic detailing, not architectural detailing, but structural detailing.

It is hoped that students following the book assiduously will acquit themselves with distinction in the B/TEC units of Structural Detailing II and III and so endear themselves to their employers.

Lastly, the author has met women engineers and technicians, both as colleagues and students, and looks forward to their numbers increasing in the future. He begs the forbearance of female readers for the occasional use of the male pronoun to cover both genders.

PETER H. NEWTON

PREFACE TO THE SECOND EDITION

Since the publication of the first edition there have been changes to some British Standards. While these do not affect the detailer greatly, it would be wrong to ignore them.

BS 449 is still valid at the time of going to press, but *BS 5950 The structural use of steelwork in building, Parts 1 and 2,* is intended to supersede BS 449 and both are currently in use. BS 449 has been retained for this edition of *Structural Detailing,* but extracts from BS 5950 are included in Part III for the student to make comparisons.

CP 110 has been replaced by BS 8110 and references to the former have been removed from the book. The basic design concept of CP 114 has however failed to die and a new 'code' has been published by the Institution of Structural Engineers. Presently known as *Recommendations for the permissible stress design of reinforced concrete for building structures,* appropriate extracts have been included in Part III.

CP 112 Part 2 has been replaced by BS 5268 Part 2, similarly with Part 3. As in the first edition, the author refers the reader to the widespread use of proprietary prefabricated timber roof trusses as making detailing unnecessary.

BS 4466 has been changed with the introduction of new shapes and the omission of others. Tailor-made steel fabric reinforcement to BS 4483 is now being made and supplied already bent.

The increasing use of computer-aided design in all the structural fields has been the main motive for changes in codes of practice. This poses a problem for the author, as most students will be studying the subject without reference to computers. This edition continues to emphasise the 'manual' ways of detailing of the kind that could be carried out in a small office. Students will find practice in the real world rather different.

PETER H. NEWTON

ACKNOWLEDGEMENTS

The author would like to acknowledge the help he has received from the following.

Braithwaite & Company Structural Limited, Neptune Works, Newport, Gwent, for explaining the use of numerically controlled machines and their effect on the detailing of steelwork connections, and for supplying examples.

Robert Watson & Company (Steelwork) Ltd, Filton, Bristol, for explaining current practice in the fabrication of welded portal frames, and for supplying examples.

Extracts from British Standards are reproduced by permission of the British Standards Institution, 2 Park Street, London, W1A 2BS, from whom complete copies of the standards can be obtained.

Details of the steel sections and dimensions included in part III have been taken from the *Structural Steelwork Handbook* and are reproduced in this publication by permission of the British Constructional Steelwork Association Ltd and Steel Construction Institute. Copies of this complete publication, which contains the Safe Load Tables, can be obtained from the BCSA Ltd, 35 Old Queen Street, London, SW1H 9HZ, or Steel Construction Institute, Silwood Park, Ascot, Berks., SL5 7PY (hereinafter referred to as the SCI). The copyright of these extracts belongs to the BCSA and the SCI, and they may not be re-copied in any form or stored in a retrieval system without their permission.

The Concrete Society for permission to the use the material contained in *Technical Report No. 2 Standard method of detailing reinforced concrete*, being a report of a joint committee of the Concrete Society and the Institution of Structural Engineers.

The British Cement Association for permission to base some of the detailing examples on *Designed and Detailed* by J. B. Higgins and M. R. Hollington. Copies of both the last two publications can be obtained from the BCA, Wexham Springs, Slough SL3 6PL. The Concrete Society is at Devonshire House, 12/15 Dartmouth Street, London, SW1H 9BL. Hunter Timber Engineering Ltd, The Legger, Bridgwater, Somerset, and Gang-Nail Systems Limited, Christy Estate, Ivy Road, Aldershot, Hants GU12 4XG for permission to use the software, Concept 2000, an example of a computer-designed roof truss.

Metal Sections Ltd, Oldbury, West Midlands, for permission to reproduce their tables of Metsec purlins.

Ward Brothers (Sherburn) Ltd, Sherburn, North Yorkshire, for permission to reproduce illustrations and tables of their Multibeam purlin and rail system.

The Institution of Structural Engineers for permission to reproduce parts of their *Recommendations for the permissible stress design of reinforced concrete building structures*.

A. N. Beale, BSc CEng MICE MIStructE, for advising on revisions for the second edition.

Every effort has been made to trace the copyright holders but, if any have been inadvertently overlooked, the publisher will be pleased to make the necessary arrangements at the first opportunity.

Part I

This part covers the aims and objectives in B/TEC unit *Structural Detailing II* and is suitable as a first year of study for students of architecture, building and civil engineering

1. THE CONSTRUCTION PROCESS

DESIGN

In the beginning there is a client, the person or group that wants a building erected and who will pay the total cost of that building. The client usually knows in broad terms what he wants — a factory or warehouse, a block of offices or flats, a school or hospital, of a certain size. He may often have ideas about its shape and appearance and what form of construction should be used. Planning controls and environmental considerations will also be factors.

It is the designer's job to prepare drawings that will meet the client's requirements and those of the regulating authorities. In many instances this work will be performed entirely by an architect, but frequently it involves the design skills of a structural engineer. This is usually the case if a structural steel or reinforced concrete framework is called for.

In the design of the structural framework the structural engineer will use his knowledge of structural mechanics, of bending moments and shearing forces, of loadings and moments of resistance. He will work out the sizes of members required in every position and the nature of the connections between them. For reasons of economy the structural needs may affect the shape and appearance of the finished structure. It is a skilled art, upon which the safety of many people, as well as the client's investment, may depend. It is an art which is not the subject of this book.

DETAILING

Once the design has been agreed, it is necessary for detailed drawings to be prepared to enable the framework to be fabricated. In the case of a steel structure, this is always done off site in a factory. Reinforced concrete structures may be manufactured on site (*in situ*) or in a factory (precast).

Detailing consists of breaking the structure down into its component parts and making drawings of each that will tell the fabricator precisely how each is to be made, of what materials and in what quantity. The parts must be detailed so that they will fit together and be erected in the most economical way. This is no mean task and it does require the detailer to know how the structure is going to be manufactured and erected. The budding detailer should visit construction sites whenever possible to ensure familiarity with the problems that arise in fabrication and erection.

THE MANUFACTURE OF STRUCTURAL STEELWORK

Structural steelwork is an assemblage of standard steel sections (dealt with in chapter 3), connected by welding or bolting or a combination of both. In the past riveting was used and may still be found in the alteration of existing buildings.

Welding has, until recently, been the preferred method of jointing, but, with the development of micro-chip technology, there is now a move back to bolting.

Welding is done mainly in the fabricating shop, as it is best carried out with the work lying flat and the welder bending over it. In the fabricating shop the work may be turned over for the other side to be welded from above. This cannot be done on site and more difficult vertical or overhead welding is necessary. Automatic and semi-automatic welding is available in the shop and this is particularly useful for long runs of welding in portal frames and plate girders.

Numerically controlled machines are now in use in fabricating shops. These allow correct lengths to be cut or cropped automatically and holes to be drilled or punched automatically, often in three directions simultaneously. No setting-out is required as the machine is instructed what to do by a prepared punched tape.

It is often more economical to bolt than weld, hence the move back to bolting. There are obvious implications for the steel detailer. In this book the emphasis will be on bolting for beam and column and lattice construction, and welding for portal frames and plate girders.

There are obviously limitations upon the size of the welded assembly. If it will not fit conveniently on a standard lorry, there will be transport problems. If it is too heavy, larger (and more costly) cranes will be required to lift it into position. The aim is to deliver to site conveniently sized pieces that may be connected together with the minimum of effort.

It is possible to weld the pieces together on site and this is what is done in the construction of steel box girder bridges. It is not a convenient way for the structures that are the concern of this book. There is a number of reasons why this is so. It would require the presence of welders, skilled and certificated for the various types of joints that would be needed. It would require access platforms for them and shelter from the weather for the process, and it would require the pieces to be held relative to one another while the joints are being made.

The answer is to bolt the pieces together on site. Some additional steelwork is required, such as gussets (flat plates connecting the pieces of a roof truss together) and cleats (angles connecting beams and columns together). These are usually welded to the piece on one side of the joint, as they are relatively small and could otherwise be lost. There are three types of bolts, which will be dealt with in chapter 3.

THE ERECTION OF STRUCTURAL STEELWORK

Before the steelwork arrives on site the bases, upon which it will stand, must be ready to receive it. These will be constructed of concrete and may take the form of pad foundations or pile caps. Typical foundations are shown in figure 1.1. The bottom of the steel columns are provided with flat plates to spread the forces from the columns over the concrete surface of the foundation. These have holes drilled to receive the holding down bolts (HDBs), which are cast into the foundations using

large steel washers or plates under the bolt head to prevent the HDBs pulling out. A tube of steel, plastic or cardboard is placed around the HDBs before the concrete is placed so that the projecting ends of the bolts may be moved laterally to take up any inaccuracy in their positioning. After the concrete has been placed, but before it has hardened, the builder will wobble the top of the bolts about so as to leave the head free to allow this movement, but not to rotate.

The top of the foundation will be left 25 to 50 mm below the nominal level shown on the drawings. This is because it is difficult for the builder to cast the base at precisely the right level or smoothly enough for the column baseplate to sit snugly on the concrete. By leaving the top low, steel plates, known as shims, may be used to pack the baseplate up to its correct position. Placed at the centre of the base, the shims act as a hinge when the column is plumbed. The space around is then packed firmly with fairly dry concrete made with a small sized aggregate. Sand and cement grout should not be used as it is a source of weakness in a highly stressed area.

Care has to be exercised when the columns are lowered over the HDBs so as not to damage their threads. Washers and nuts are applied to each bolt, but not tightened at this stage. A small group of columns is erected and temporarily guyed or propped, while some of the interconnecting beams or purlins and crossbracing is fixed. This group is then plumbed and all the fixing bolts are tightened to give a rigid structure off which the rest of the building may be supported during erection.

The student is strongly recommended to visit a site where steelwork is being erected to watch the procedure. Even so, it is not difficult to imagine the process — two columns, standing somewhat precariously upon their bases, and a beam to be fixed between them some 3 to 4 metres above the ground. Anything that can be done to make it easier for the connecting bolts to be inserted will be welcomed. One way is to provide a seating cleat, which takes the form of a short length of angle welded to the column on to which the beam can be placed. This ensures that the beam is at least at the right level and all the erector has to do is move the beam sideways until the holes in the projecting leg of the cleat line up with those in the bottom flange of the beam. The erector does this with the aid of a podger spanner (figure 1.2) which has the usual jaws at one end and, at the other, a tapered (rat-tail) end of the same diameter as the shank of the bolt. This can be inserted through the two holes, so aligning them, and is sufficient to hold the beam to the column while the other bolt is being fixed. This is not to say that seating cleats are always provided. There are places where, for example, beams connect with beams, when seating cleats are omitted. The presence of the first beam facilitates the positioning of the second.

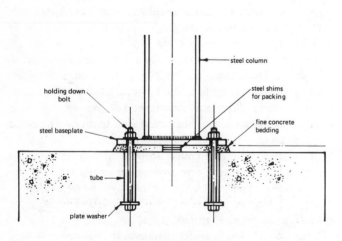

Figure 1.1 Typical connection between steel column and concrete base

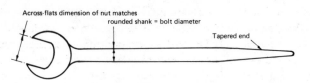

Figure 1.2   Podger or rat-tail spanner

The cleats and gussets are rarely supplied loose, but are fixed by the fabricator to one of the members to be joined. The detailer must know which one is best. Let us consider a beam to column connection further. If it is a large structure it is likely that there will be other cleats joining the web of the beam to the column (figure 1.3). These cleats must arrive on site fixed to the beam. Imagine if they were fixed to the column and the beam web had to be slid in between them!

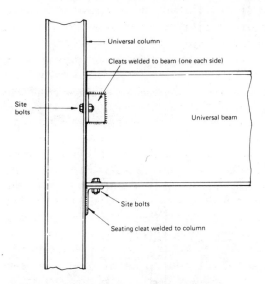

Figure 1.3   Typical connection between beam and column

Always try and arrange for the cleats to provide some support for the joint as soon as possible. Roof trusses or pitched portal frames have their purlin cleats welded to their top surfaces, so that the purlins can rest against them while waiting to be fixed.

THE MANUFACTURE OF REINFORCED CONCRETE STRUCTURES

Like steelwork, reinforced concrete structures start off with a base or pile cap. It is part of the reinforced concrete frame and has to be detailed along with the columns and beams. This book will consider only cast *in situ* concrete frameworks, resting on simple spread foundations as opposed to pile caps.

Spread foundations may take the form of isolated bases supporting one column or strip foundations supporting a wall. They are usually reinforced with steel bars to spread the concentrated load of the column or wall over a larger area of soil. Exactly how large they will have to be is determined by the structural engineer, knowing the bearing capacity of the soil from tests previously taken.

Concrete is not nearly as strong in tension as it is in compression. Unless bases are reinforced they are likely to fail in shear or bending. Figure 1.4 illustrates the nature of the failure that is likely to occur. The reinforcing steel should be placed where it will compensate for the low tensile strength of the concrete, as shown in figure 1.5.

The foundation is cast in a hole in the ground and bears directly on the soil. To keep the area clean while the reinforcing steel is being placed and the formwork fixed in position, a layer of blinding concrete, about 50 to 75 mm thick, is usually laid below the designed bottom of the foundation. The reinforcing steel must be protected from the soil by a minimum

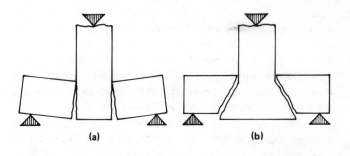

Figure 1.4   Failure modes of a concrete pad foundation: (a) bending, (b) shearing

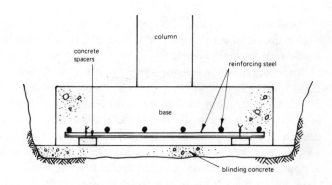

Figure 1.5   Reinforcement of a concrete base

thickness of concrete, known as the cover. This is ensured by the use of spacers or chairs, which support the steel the required distance above the blinding concrete.

The columns are next built on top of the bases. These will be reinforced to counteract bending, shearing and direct compression failures as shown in figure 1.6.

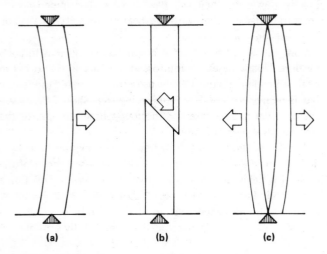

Figure 1.6   *Failure modes of a concrete column: (a) bending, (b) shearing, (c) direct compression*

A column will have at least four longitudinal bars and a series of transverse bars, known as links, which will compensate for the weakness of the concrete (figure 1.7).

It is necessary to tie the column to the base with reinforcement, so starter bars are cast into the base, which project far enough above the surface for the longitudinal column bars to be fixed to them by a process known as lapping. These are shown in figure 1.8. Note that the starter bars are bent through 90°, so that they can lap with the foundation reinforcement, thus ensuring continuity from base through to column.

It might be thought that the column bars could be placed straight away, doing away with the starter bars, but this would involve the use of very long bars that would be cumbersome to handle and difficult to support.

The column will be formed by a wooden or steel box, called formwork or shuttering. This will stand on the base and be strutted with props to keep it vertical while it is concreted. In order to locate the lower end of the box it is usual to construct a very short length of column (about 75 mm), known as a kicker. Not only does this hold the bottom of the box firmly in position, but it also prevents the loss of fines from the concrete, which might otherwise force their way under the box and lead to honeycombing of the concrete and consequent

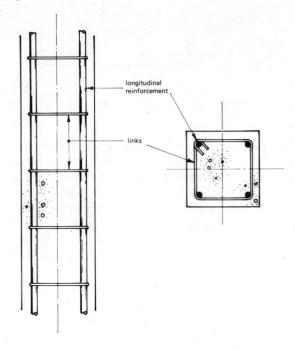

Figure 1.7   *Reinforcement of a concrete column*

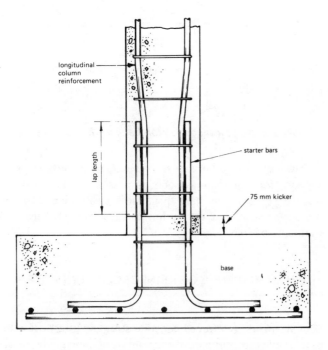

Figure 1.8   *Junction of column with base*

structural weakness. The depth of the kicker has to be taken into account by the detailer when determining the length of the starter bars.

The column will be concreted up to the underside of the first intersecting beam or floor. The joints, between different days' pours of concrete, are known as construction joints and there are recognised places where these should occur, so as not to weaken the structure or make it more difficult to build. The detailer should be aware of these rules, which are summarised in figure 1.9.

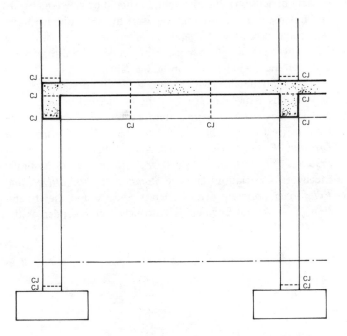

Figure 1.9   Siting of construction joints (CJ)

The column bars have to be made long enough to extend sufficiently far above the top of the column to allow for the depth of the beam and floor, the kicker for the next column and the necessary lap.

The beams and floor slab can often be cast in a single operation, but it is usual to cast larger beams up to the underside of the floor slab first, casting the floor slab on another day. From a strength point of view, the structural engineer has included the full depth of the beam in his calculations, but a horizontal construction joint is permissible here. The vertical construction joints in beams and slabs are best located between the one-third points, but they do not affect the detailing of the reinforcement, other than the general point that the use of excessively long bars, spanning more than one bay, add to the builder's difficulties.

Staircases span from floor to floor and are virtually sloping slabs with steps cast on to them. They are usually built after the floors and starter bars have to be left projecting from the floors at the top and the bottom, to lap with the longitudinal bars in the flight. It is a good idea to precast the flights of stairs and drop them in after the floors have been built.

There are many things the detailer should take into account that will facilitate the construction process. He should know the order in which the bars will be fixed and number them accordingly on the drawings and schedules. He must specify the minimum cover in every situation, so that the builder uses the right spacers and the steel is protected from the elements. He must leave room for the concrete to be placed around the reinforcement — too many bars too close together can prevent this. Most importantly, he must ensure that bars do not occupy the same position. This is particularly liable to happen where floors meet beams and beams meet columns. It must be clear to the steelfixer which bars are outside of which, which bars are over which, and the shape of the bent bars must allow them to be fixed correctly.

The author has seen more than one completed building where there has been a pile of reinforcing steel that did not get fixed in the structure. The consequences could be very serious. Good detailing practice can help the builder to stop this from happening.

STEEL REINFORCEMENT

Steel for reinforced concrete can be ordinary mild steel or high tensile steel. The bars may be plain round or deformed to bond with the surrounding concrete and they may be straight or bent to various shapes. Often the ends are provided with a hook or 90° bend to help anchor the ends in the concrete. All these variations are covered by British Standards and are dealt with in chapter 6.

It used to be the practice to send to site loads of uncut steel bars of different sizes and of maximum rolled length. The builder employed steel benders, whose job it was to cut and bend the bars to the required length and shape, using a simple bar bending machine on a bench. Today, high tensile steel bars are common and these require the use of power benders. Current practice is to order the reinforcing steel required for a job already cut, bent, bundled and labelled, from a specialist supplier. The labelling is important, as it ensures that the bars required for the bases are delivered first, the columns next and so on. The supplier will even load the lorry so that, when the bars are offloaded on site, the bars required first are on the top of the pile.

The processing of orders for reinforcing steel is now largely computerised. When the bars are scheduled, instead of drawing little diagrams to show the steel benders what is required, the shapes are coded and the dimensions are given as a set of standard measurements. Schedules of both kinds are dealt with in chapter 6.

THE ROLE OF THE DETAILER

It is becoming apparent that the detailer is an extremely important person, who can make a considerable contribution to the construction process. He is essentially a communicator and his principal medium is the drawing. Above all he must be a good draughtsman, working in a methodical way to present the fabricator with all the information he requires in a logical order. To do this well he must imagine himself in the position of the man whose task it is to fabricate the piece. Consider the simple example of a steel beam — what does he need to know?

> What type of section is required — is it a universal beam, a joist or a channel?
> What nominal size?
> What mass per metre?

What length is required?
What notches have to be cut and where?
What sized holes have to be drilled and where?
What cleats are required and where are they to be fixed?
How many of such beams are required?
What mark number is to be painted on each?
How should the beam be finished in the factory?

The good detailer will provide all this information in related groups, so that the fabricator does not have to hunt for a missing dimension. The information should be given once only and not repeated in different views of the same piece. Should it become necessary to change a dimension, there is a danger that only one may be changed if it is shown more than once, and then there will be two conflicting values.

The good detailer will adhere to accepted standards and conventions. The fabricator and the builder get used to these and there is less risk of misinterpretation. Practice does vary from office to office, but adherence to *BS 1192: Construction Drawing Practice* (British Standards Institution), *Metric Practice for Structural Steelwork* (British Constructional Steelwork Association) and the *Standard Method of Detailing Reinforced Concrete* (The Concrete Society and the Institution of Structural Engineers) is strongly recommended as the basis for all drawings and schedules.

2. DRAWING OFFICE PRACTICE

EQUIPMENT

It is better to purchase equipment at a shop specialising in drawing office equipment, rather than a chain store that is aiming at the school market. Quality can be very variable and the better quality is more expensive. The student should buy the best quality he can afford, spreading the cost by building up his collection gradually. He should not buy expensive sets of anything, but individual items as they become necessary.

PENCILS AND PENS

There is a superabundance of both available from the shops, in a variety of types. The humble pencil is still the best for the beginner. It is easier to hold, and to draw with, than many of the clutch pencils that are so *chic*. Properly sharpened to a long tapering point and properly used, by trailing it across the paper instead of pushing it, giving it a slight rotation at the same time, a pencil will give excellent results. It is better to use a softer pencil (grade F, H or 2H) rather than a very hard one that scores the surface of the paper and makes erasure difficult. In his early days the student will do a lot of rubbing out!

For the same reason the student should not rush into the use of ink. All the techniques of structural detailing can be learnt with a pencil on cartridge paper. This includes the variations in line thickness that are needed. If ink pens are bought, then they will be required in three different sizes if they are of the stylographic type (0.35, 0.5 and 0.7 mm), or with three interchangeable nibs of similar sizes if they are of the graphos type (nibs that have pivoted blades that are used like the old adjustable blade ruling pen).

SET SQUARES AND PROTRACTORS

A pair of 45° and 30°/60° set squares is essential. An adjustable set square is desirable, but is expensive and easily broken. The set squares should not be too small, say 300 mm long, and the thicker the better. The author prefers plain (square edge) set squares, as their depth enables slight adjustments to be made to the position of the drawn line by a slight inclination of the pencil. Bevel-edged set squares do not allow this and have the annoying habit of slipping underneath the tee square. When used with a pen there is the risk that the ink may run under the set square owing to capillary action. It is possible to obtain set squares with double inking edges. These have a small square rebate along both sides, which prevents the ink running, while retaining the advantages of the square edge.

In the absence of an adjustable set square, a protractor of at least 200 mm diameter, either 180° or 360°, divided into half degrees, should be obtained.

COMPASSES AND CIRCLE TEMPLATES

For the purposes of this book, compasses are hardly required, except perhaps a set of small bows for the drawing of bolt symbols or placing circles around grid letters and numbers. It is easier and less expensive to use a circle template for these purposes. A typical template has 35 circles from 1 to 35 mm diameter and has ink edges. The template enables the same pencil or pen to be used for curves as well as straights, which leads to uniformity of linework.

SCALES

One oval section scale, 300 mm long, with four edges graduated 1:1 & 1:100, 1:20 & 1:200, 1:5 & 1:50 and 1:1250 & 1:2500 respectively, is recommended. These are to BS 1347 and are usually marked 'RIBA appd'. These are all the scales a detailer should use. Any other scales would not be in accordance with standard metric practice, which is not to say that 1:10, 1:1000, 1:500 and similar scales are not permissible. Remember that a scale is not a straight edge and should not be employed as a ruler.

DRAWING BOARDS AND TEE SQUARES

A good drawing board is essential for good draughtsmanship. One with a smooth white melamine face gives an excellent surface upon which to mount the paper or plastic film, and it is easier to keep clean than other types of face. If a plain wooden board is used, it will require a heavy cartridge paper backing sheet under the paper or film. The size of the board will depend upon the nature of the work to be detailed, but it is better if the drawing does not occupy the whole board.

Sizes of drawing boards in millimetres

Classification	Board size	Paper size
A4		297 x 210
A3		420 x 297
A2	650 x 470	594 x 420
A1	920 x 650	841 x 594
A1 ext	1100 x 650	
A1 ext (large)	1200 x 700	
A0	1270 x 920	1189 x 841
A0a	1370 x 920	
A0 ext	1500 x 920	

The standard A-range of papers is based upon the golden square — the longer side is equal to the diagonal of a square formed by the shorter side, that is in the ratio 1 to 1.414. A1 is half of A0, A2 half of A1 and so on to the smallest size of paper. For learning purposes A2 is just large enough. A1 is probably the best size for the detailer, as it is the largest size of paper that can be handled comfortably on site, in the factory or in the office. A0 is cumbersome and gets folded or caught by the wind and is thus more easily damaged.

Various proprietary parallel motion systems are available, but the student will probably start with a simple tee square. The blade can be of wood, provided either with a hard black PVC working edge or a transparent PVC working edge, or the blade may be entirely of transparent acrylic. The stock (the part that slides up the side of the board) is of wood, with a hard black PVC sliding edge.

The blade of a tee square is usually tapered and has only one working edge. The stock is moved by the left hand, leaving the right hand free to hold the pen or pencil. It is not reversible. Left-handed tee squares are available for left-handed people.

ERASERS, ERASING SHIELDS AND SANDPAPER BLOCKS

Good-quality erasers are available in two types for removing pencil lines and ink lines. Ink may also be very carefully scraped off plastic film using a scalpel or razor blade, taking care to remove only the ink. Specially coated transparent paper is available, which makes it easier to erase ink. Ink work on opaque drawing paper can be obliterated with a fast-drying paint, called Snopake, which can then be drawn over as soon as it is dry. This method may be used commercially, where electrostatic copying is employed, for drawings and schedules of A3 size or smaller.

Erasing shields are very thin stainless steel templates that allow part of the drawing to be rubbed out without damaging the surrounding work.

Sandpaper blocks are pads of ten sheets of fine sandpaper for sharpening the points of lead pencils, which should afterwards be polished on smooth paper. They are a source of much graphite dust and must be used carefully to prevent the drawing becoming grubby.

Clean working is essential to successful draughtsmanship. Start off with clean hands and clean equipment and have a soft cloth available to keep everything clean. This is particularly important for the undersides of tee squares and set squares.

DRAWING MEDIA

The principal materials are cartridge paper, detail paper, tracing paper and plastic film. Cartridge paper is cheap and adequate for the student. Detail paper is thinner and semi-transparent; it is tough and has a smooth surface and is useful for preliminary drawings, but it does not provide good prints. Tracing paper is more transparent and will produce good dye-line prints. It is tough and has a good surface suitable for both pencil and ink. It is cheaper than plastic film, which is suitable only for ink drawings.

All drawing materials shrink or stretch under the effects of changing temperature and humidity. The phrase is — they lack dimensional stability. Drawings are never scaled. They should be regarded as vehicles to carry the dimensions to which the work is to be made and illustrate what the finished work is going to look like. Drawings should be covered up each night and tee squares should not be left lying on uncovered drawings, as differential shrinkage will occur, which will make the material cockle and impossible to draw upon.

DRAUGHTING

Drawings should be provided with a border which prints as a clear margin all round. The edges of the printed drawing are susceptible to damage through constant handling and, if details were taken right up to the edges, they would soon become illegible. If the drawings are to be bound, a much larger margin is required on the left hand side. A standard title box should be placed in the lower right-hand corner for ease of reference.

It is a good idea to repeat the drawing number in the upper right-hand corner. Drawing no. 2.1 shows an acceptable layout (to BS 1192). If all the drawings are kept the same size for a particular job, it makes filing and retrieval easier.

The choice of scale is conditioned by the relative sizes of job and paper, but it is not a good idea to use different scales on the same drawing. There are accepted scales for different purposes, which should be adhered to wherever possible as, with experience, one develops a feel for the size of the finished work from the drawing.

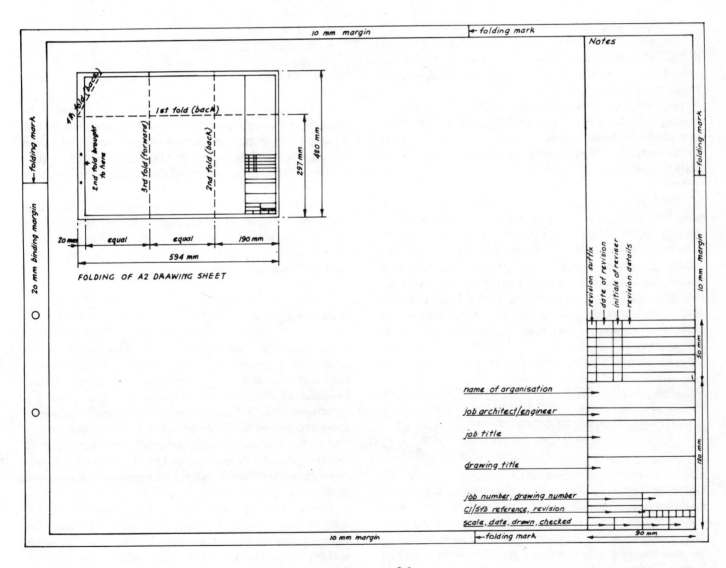

Drawing no. 2.1

Type of drawing	Recommended format		Alternative format	
	Scale	Sheet size	Scale	Sheet size
Site plan	1:200	A1	1:100	A0
			1:500	A2
Location plan				
Sections and elevations	1:100	A1	1:200	A0
Marking plans			1:50	A2
Details	1:20	A1	1:10	A2
			1:5	A3
Schedules	—	A4	—	A3

Figure 2.2 shows lines with the following descriptions:
- 0.7 mm outlines requiring emphasis, section lines and reinforcing steel
- 0.5 mm general outlines, links and stirrups
- 0.35 mm grid lines, dimension lines and leader lines
- 0.35 mm centre lines
- 0.5 mm hidden outlines
- 0.35 mm break or discontinuity lines

Figure 2.2   Types of line used on drawings

The second stage consists of drawing each view lightly with a sharp pencil, carrying the lines well clear of the view to assist with the subsequent drawing of the dimension lines, and even from view to view, when they are projections of one another. These are the construction lines.

The third stage consists of going over those lines that are to feature in the finished drawing, to the appropriate line thickness. If the construction lines are truly light — visible only to the draughtsman — they need not be removed as they are not likely to print.

This third stage can be carried out in pencil or in ink. The latter will produce sharper prints, but takes longer as the ink takes time to dry. The inking-in process can be speeded up by drawing the horizontal lines first, working from the top to the bottom, followed by the vertical lines from left to right. This assumes the correct procedure (for a right-handed person) of drawing vertical lines in an upward direction on the left-hand side of the set square. The tee square should never be held against the top or bottom edge of the drawing board for the purpose of drawing vertical lines, as the board may not be perfectly square.

Lines should be of three different thicknesses:

thin   0.35 mm for centre lines, dimension lines, leader lines and grid lines.
medium   0.50 mm for general outlines.
thick   0.70 mm for outlines requiring emphasis, reinforcing steel and section lines.

Obtaining these accurately with pens is relatively easy but, if stylographic pens are being used, three separate pens are required, or three separate nibs, if graphos pens are being used. More skill is required when pencils are being used, which can be developed only with practice. Figure 2.2 illustrates various types of line used in detailing.

PROJECTION

This is the presentation of plans, elevations and sections of the structure or components, in a manner understood by the builder. Orthographic projection derives from the word 'orthogonal' — at right angles. BS 1192 recommends the system known as first angle orthographic projection, but in large structures this places the view of the left-hand end of the building on the right of the elevation, which can be confusing. The system known as third angle orthographic projection corrects this, but puts the plan above the elevation. A compromise is recommended, combining the best features of both systems. This is illustrated in figure 2.3.

DIMENSIONING

A dimension line consists of a line drawn parallel to the distance being dimensioned, with leader lines at right angles at both ends, indicating the beginning and end of the distance. Examples of dimension lines are shown in figure 2.4. The figures and letters making up the dimension should be written above and parallel to the dimension line, so that they may be read from the bottom or right-hand side of the drawing. They should be placed near the middle of the dimension line, except for running dimensions, which should be placed near the arrow head.

Two kinds of arrow heads are used. Open arrows give dimensions between centres or nominal dimensions of spaces. For dimensions giving the actual sizes of components to which working tolerances will be applied, solid arrows are used. These should be of pleasing proportions, neither too long and

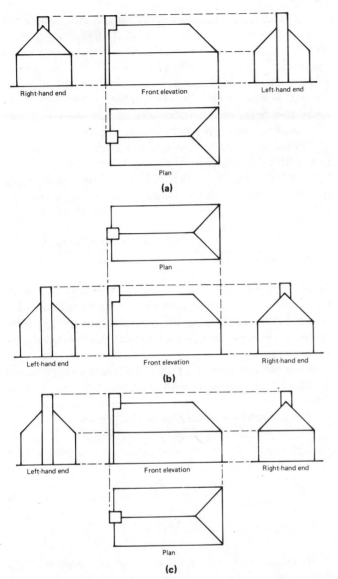

Figure 2.3   *Orthographic projection: (a) first angle projection, (b) third angle projection, (c) combined first and third angle (recommended)*

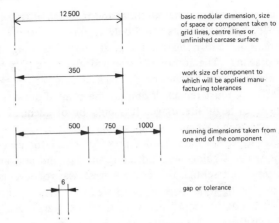

Figure 2.4   *Types of dimension line used on drawings*

thin nor too short and stubby. Solid arrows should also be used for notes.

The positioning of dimension lines with respect to the detail, and with one another, is most important and can mar a drawing if badly done. The lines should not be crowded too closely to the outline or too closely together. This also applies to leader lines and centre lines. When the dimensioning of a beam is considered we shall see that it is necessary to distort

the scale a little so as to space out the leader lines to make the drawing clearer.

The question of which dimensions to give on the drawing will be dealt with later in the book. As a general rule, dimensions should be given only from one end of the component. Owing to working tolerances it is impossible to conform to more than one dimension.

In metric drawing practice, distances are measured in multiples of a thousand. The basic unit of length is the metre (abbreviation m), consisting of 1000 millimetres (mm) and there being one thousand to the kilometre (km). Note that the symbols used are lower case and never plural (mms). The only punctuation allowed is the decimal point. Commas should not be used to mark the thousands, instead a space should be left when more than four digits are involved. One space should also be left after the last digit in the number, before the symbol is written. Fullstops should not be placed after the symbols. The following are examples of correct usage:

300 mm 34 500 mm 7.250 m 11.9 km 1550 m 15 500 m

For large-scale drawings of detail it is usual to note above the title box that 'all dimensions are in millimetres'. Thereafter all symbols may be omitted, except in any notes, where it is desirable for them to be included.

For smaller-scale layout and general arrangement drawings, the dimensions are given in metres, with a decimal point and three places of decimals, even if these are noughts.

LETTERING

There are several ways in which lettering on a drawing may be executed — by hand, by using stencils or by transfers. For the purposes of this book only hand lettering will be considered. It is much quicker than other methods and freehand lettering is a skill that all good draughtsmen should acquire.

Dimensions and notes are the most important things on a detail drawing. (The author has seen a sizable piled jetty built from dimensioned sketches on the back of a cigarette packet.) The lettering must remain legible as the printed drawing deteriorates through site usage. It should be of adequate size (some workmen have poor sight), simple and clear.

We need to go back to our primary school for lettering purposes. Feint guidelines, indicating the top and bottom of the letters, are essential. Figure 2.5 suggests ways of developing a good lettering style. It is not suggested that lettering should be carried out in accordance with the first three lines. The purpose of these is to analyse lower case lettering.

The letters in the first line are all formed out of circles or parts of circles and straight lines — except for s, which is a difficult letter to print well. The letters in the second line are formed of 'walking sticks' and straight lines and those in line three are 'matchstick' letters, formed entirely of straight lines.

Having studied the anatomy of letters, the student is then able to start developing a style which, because it is based on simple forms, has a uniformity that makes it attractive to read.

The author favours a slight slope to his lettering — mainly because any irregularity is less noticeable than it is in upright lettering — and the manuscript alphabet in the fourth and fifth lines is that adopted for the drawings in this book.

The reader must develop a style that is legible, simple and consistent. It should not be too small (2 mm absolute minimum) or too large (5 mm absolute maximum) as larger letters are more difficult to do. The parts of the letters that project above and below should not do so excessively — half the lettering size is about right. Capitals needed to complement the lower case notes are shown in lines six and seven. For titles requiring larger letters it is better to use stencils.

Capitals are used for titles, without punctuation. Lower case is used for dimensions and notes. Underlining is a convention for indicating that a dimension is not true to scale, which should be avoided for other purposes, except major headings/titles.

DRAWING LAYOUT

Before commencing with a drawing it is necessary to plan its layout. The overall size of each view should be calculated and a sketch prepared showing the views correctly projected. At this stage decisions about the scale and size of the drawing can be taken.

A few minutes spent planning the drawing will ensure that the space available is used with advantage and no part of the drawing is unduly cramped. A typical layout sketch is shown in figure 2.6, prepared for a general arrangement drawing.

Figure 2.5   Freehand lettering

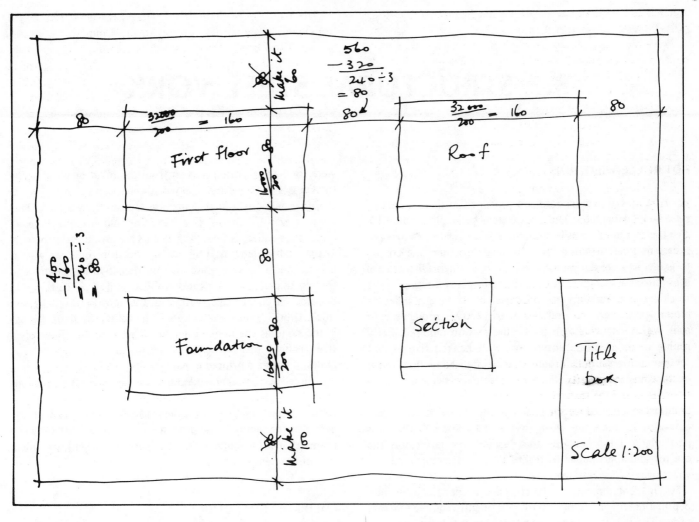

Figure 2.6   Roughing out a drawing layout

3.   STRUCTURAL STEELWORK

HOT ROLLED SECTIONS

Standard hot rolled sections are produced in three grades of steel — 43, 50 and 55. These numbers, when multiplied by 10, give the maximum tensile strength of the steel in newtons per square millimetre (N/mm^2). By adding chromium and copper to grade 50 steel during manufacture, a weather-resistant steel is produced, which does not require a protective coating.

Hot rolled sections are produced by passing a billet or bloom (large ingot) of steel, heated to 1200°C, through sets of rolls which change its shape to the section required. Early rolling methods produced sections with tapered flanges, but the new universal mills produce parallel flanged sections. Wear in the rolls leads to variations in the actual dimensions of sections. British Standard BS 4: part 1, which lists the standard sections rolled, also specifies tolerances to which they must conform. Extracts are given in part III of this book. It is particularly important for the detailer, the fabricator, the erector and the builder to realise that steel sections are not exact sizes or dead straight.

Beams, columns, joists and channels are described by their depth, breadth, mass per metre and length required, in that order. The standard abbreviations used are as follows:

Universal beam	UB
Universal column	UC
Rolled steel joist	RSJ
Rolled steel channel	RSC

The expression 457 × 152 × 60 UB × 7440 would describe a universal beam with a depth of 457 mm, width of 152 mm, weighing 60 kg/metre and 7440 mm long. Reference to the tables in part III of this book will show that the depth is in fact 454.7 mm and the width is 152.9 mm. It will also show that there are five beams having a serial size of 457 × 152 mm, each having a different mass per metre. The serial size is a nominal size and not the actual size.

The difference in mass per metre is achieved by 'raising the rolls', that is by varying the distance between the rolls that were used to form the section from the billet or bloom. The thicknesses of flange and web will also be seen to vary.

Other sections available include tees and angle bars. Tees are usually cut from universal beams or columns, but there are a few sizes rolled as tees. Angles bars are produced with equal or unequal leg lengths. Tees are described in the same way as beams. Angle bars are described by their two leg lengths and the leg thickness. The expression 150 × 150 × 12 L would describe an equal angle, with legs 150 mm long and 12 mm thick. Unlike beams and columns, the actual length of the legs is the same as the nominal length. Angles are the only rolled steel sections to have sensible metric (ISO) dimensions. The tables of sizes are printed in part III.

The reader is recommended to draw the actual cross-sections of rolled steel sections accurately to scale. Not only is this good drawing practice, but it helps to gain familiarity with the details of the sections, the presence of radii, the depth between fillets (that is the length of the flat part of the web), the thickness of the flange of tapered sections, and so on.

COLD ROLLED SECTIONS

Cold rolled sections are formed by folding flat sheet steel into a variety of shapes, the commonest of which are troughing, decking and cladding, zed and channel sections.

Purlins used to be formed from hot rolled steel angles and channels, but these are now considered too costly. Zed and channel sections are now widely used for both roofing purlins and sheeting rails. They have a high strength/weight ratio and can be formed to an accuracy of ± 0.25 mm.

Entire systems have been built up by manufacturers to clad the roofs and sides of industrial and agricultural buildings. Extensive handbooks have been produced that are available for the asking. Extracts of typical product tables have been included in part III, but these represent only a very small proportion of what is available.

The purlins and rails may be fixed to traditional hot rolled angle cleats or to cleats supplied by the manufacturer. The cleats may be bolted or welded to the rafters and columns. If welded they will be fixed in the fabricating shop. Purlins and rails are usually delivered direct to site, already drilled to fix to the cleats and to each other. Their zinc galvanised finish reduces subsequent maintenance costs in a traditionally difficult area.

Figure 3.1 illustrates two types of proprietary purlins.

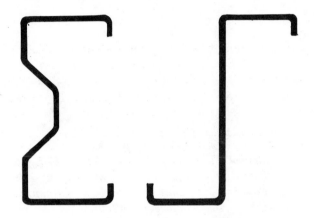

Figure 3.1   Cold rolled steel purlin sections

BOLTED CONNECTIONS

There are three types of bolts used for connecting structural steelwork:

Black bolts — grade 4.6 — to BS 4190
Black bolts — grade 8.8 — to BS 3692
High strength friction grip bolts (HSFG) — to BS 4395

Extracts from the *Steelwork Handbook*, giving details of the sizes and common lengths of these bolts, are reprinted in part III. The decision as to which bolts to use, and how many, will have been taken by the engineer.

The rules for the positioning of bolts come from clause 52 of *BS 449: part 2: Specification for the use of structural steel in building*. The important rules for detailers read as follows.

Minimum pitch — the distance between centres of bolts shall be not less than $2\frac{1}{2}$ times the nominal diameter of the bolt.
Maximum pitch — (i) the distance between centres of any two adjacent bolts connecting together elements of compression or tension members shall not exceed $32t$ or 300 mm, where t is the thickness of the thinner outside

plate; (ii) the distance between the centres of two adjacent bolts, in a line lying in the direction of stress, shall not exceed $16t$ or 200 mm in tension members, and $12t$ or 200 mm in compression members; (iii) the distance between the centres of any two consecutive bolts in a line adjacent and parallel to an edge of an outside plate, shall not exceed 100 mm $+ 4t$ or 200 mm in compression or tension members.
Edge distance — (i) the minimum edge distance from the centre of any hole to the edge of a plate shall be in accordance with table 21, reproduced in part III of this book. (ii) where two or more parts are connected together, a line of bolts shall be provided at a distance of not more than 40 mm $+ 4t$ from the nearest edge, where t is the thickness of the thinner outside plate.

END DISTANCE

When a bolt is preventing the two plates it joins from sliding, the side of the bolt will bear against the side of the hole and the metal may fail if there is insufficient of it. To counter this tendency the distance of the last hole from the end of the plate should not be less than two bolt diameters.

BACK MARK

Holes in angles and channels are drilled along a line parallel to and a set distance from the heel of the section. This distance is known as the back mark and is given in figures 3.3 and 3.4 for angles and channels respectively.

MAXIMUM BOLT SIZE

The recommended diameter of bolt given in figures 3.2, 3.3 and 3.4 should be taken as the maximum bolt size.

These rules are explained diagrammatically in figure 3.5, which also explains edge distance, pitch etc. The reasons for the rules relate to the danger of the plates being buckled, split or burst apart if these dimensions are not adequate, as illustrated in figure 3.6. The reason for the variation in edge distance is that sheared or hand flame cut edges may produce work hardening of the steel or misaligned edges, respectively, both of which are a source of weakness.

Clause 57 says that where black bolts are used, the holes may be made not more than 2 mm greater than the diameter of the bolts, for bolts up to 24 mm diameter, and not more

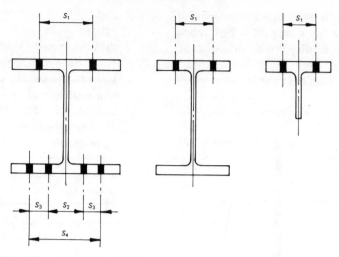

Nominal flange widths (mm)	Spacings (mm)				Recommended dia. of rivet or bolt (mm)	Actual b_{min} (mm)	Nominal flange widths (mm)	Spacing S_1 (mm)	Recommended dia. of rivet or bolt (mm)	Actual b_{min} (mm)
	S_1	S_2	S_3	S_4						
419 to 368	140	140	75	290	24	362	146 to 114	70	20	130
330 to 305	140	120	60	240	24	312	102	54	12	98
330 to 305	140	120	60	240	20	300	89	50		
292 to 203	140				24	212	76	40		
190 to 165	90				24	162	64	34		
152	90				20	150	51	30		

Note that the actual flange width for a universal section may be less than the nominal size and that the difference may be significant in determining the maximum diameter. The column headed b_{min} gives the actual minimum width of flange required to comply with Table 21 of BS 449.
The dimensions S_1 and S_2 have been selected for normal conditions but adjustments may be necessary for relatively large diameter fasteners or for particularly heavy weights in a given serial size.

Figure 3.2   Spacing of holes in columns, beams, joists and tees

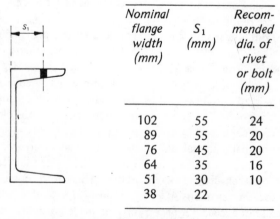

Nominal flange width (mm)	S_1 (mm)	Recommended dia. of rivet or bolt (mm)
102	55	24
89	55	20
76	45	20
64	35	16
51	30	10
38	22	

Figure 3.3   Spacing of holes in channels

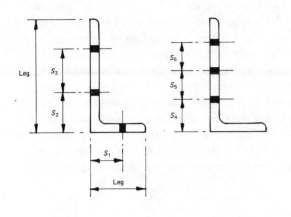

Nominal leg length (mm)	Spacing of holes (mm)						Maximum diameter of bolt or rivet (mm)		
	S_1	S_2	S_3	S_4	S_5	S_6	S_1	S_2 and S_3	S_4, S_5 and S_6
200		75	75	55	55	55		30	20
150		55	55					20	
125		45	50					20	
120		45	50					16	
100	55						24		
90	50						24		
80	45						20		
75	45						20		
70	40						20		
65	35						20		
60	35						16		
50	28						12		
45	25								
40	23								
30	20								
25	15								

Note that HSFG bolts may require adjustments to the backmarks shown owing to the larger nut and washer dimensions.
Inner gauge lines are for normal conditions and may require adjustment for large diameters of fasteners or for thick members.
Outer gauge lines may require consideration in relation to a specific edge distance.

Figure 3.4   *Spacing of holes in angles*

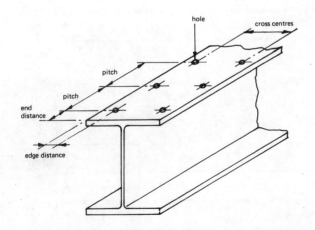

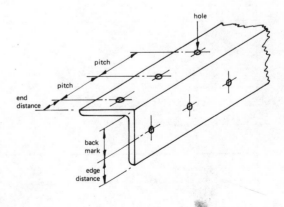

Figure 3.5   *Hole positioning terms*

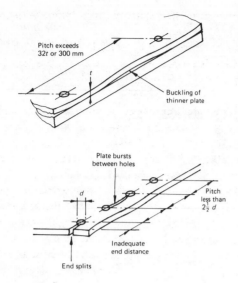

Figure 3.6   Buckling, bursting and splitting

DIMENSIONING OF HOLES

There are two basic methods of dimensioning the positions of holes along the length of a member. In the first, running dimensions are given from one end of the member — the datum. In the second, chain dimensions are given, with each group of holes related to the ends of the member or to the centre-line of a connecting member. Figure 3.7 makes clear the difference between the methods. Both methods will be employed in the examples given in chapters 4 and 7, because either may be appropriate in different circumstances. The running dimension method reduces the danger of errors accumulating when setting out the distances by the chain method.

SYMBOLS

than 3 mm greater than the diameter of the bolt, for bolts over 24 mm diameter, unless otherwise specified by the engineer. Full advantage of this clause is usually taken. The BCSA/SCI publications say that holes for HSFG bolts must be 2 mm and 3 mm larger respectively.

Standard symbols are used on drawings to represent holes, rivets and bolts, which are understood by the fabricator. Many drawing offices use pre-printed drawing sheets on which a table of symbols is printed close to the corner box, so there is no misunderstanding between office and shop. Figure 3.8 illustrates these symbols.

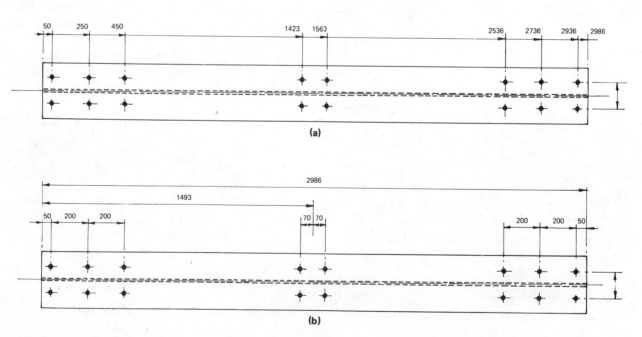

Figure 3.7   Dimensioning of holes along a member: (a) running dimensions, (b) chain dimensions

WELDED CONNECTIONS

Welding is an alternative to shop bolting. Its use is a matter of company policy and whether or not the shop is equipped with numerically controlled machines.

Welded connections have the advantages of the saving in weight of the cleats and splice plates, avoidance of loss of strength of sections by drilling holes in them, and a smoother and more easily maintained profile.

Welding joins two pieces of steel together by heating their edges to a molten state so that they fuse together. Additional weld metal is introduced, as part of the process, to build up the weld.

For structural steelwork welding will be by an electric arc formed between the metal being joined and an electrode. A heavy electric current flows from the electrode to the metal, causing a continuous white hot spark to melt the parent metal, and droplets of molten electrode to combine with the parent metal to form the weld.

In manual arc welding the electrode is a rod, held in special tongs, which is coated with a flux to form a gaseous shield around the white hot metal. This provides the right environment for the weld formation.

Most shop welding will be done by machine and the electrode will be a continuous wire, wound on a drum and fed automatically to the arc. This electrode may be bare wire or have a flux coating or core. The area of the weld is enveloped in a cloud of carbon dioxide gas (CO_2 welding).

Another automated process is submerged arc welding. A granular flux is deposited just in front of the wire electrode to 'submerge' the arc. Some is consumed by the process and the remainder is sucked off the completed weld and reclaimed.

Automatic welding is more consistent than manual welding, the size of the arc being determined automatically by the properties of the current being consumed. In all cases the electrode metal must match the parent metal.

Rays given off by the arc are harmful to the skin and particularly the eyes. Protective measures are required for anyone, not just the operator, exposed to them. The fumes given off can also be irritating or even dangerous.

TYPES OF WELDS

The two basic welds are fillet welds and butt welds. Fillet welds are the commonest and designers will sometimes prefer to extend one plate so as to get a fillet weld instead of a butt weld, as is shown in figure 3.9. Butt welds are formed in a variety of shapes, often requiring the butting edges to be specially prepared.

SYMBOLS FOR RIVETS AND BOLTS	
Open holes	
Open holes, countersunk near side	
Open holes, countersunk far side	
Shop rivets	
Shop rivets, countersunk near side	
Shop rivets, countersunk far side	
Shop bolts	
Shop bolts, countersunk near side	
Shop bolts, countersunk far side	
Shop high strength friction grip bolts	
Site high strength friction grip bolts	

Figure 3.8

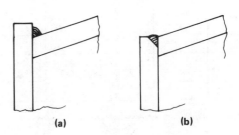

(a)   **(b)**

Figure 3.9 End plate extended beyond end of section to offer fillet weld in place of butt weld: (a) fillet weld, (b) butt weld

Symbols are used to denote the various types of weld and these are illustrated in figure 3.10, extracted from *BS 499: Part 2: Symbols for welding.*

The symbols are used in association with a sloping arrow line, pointing to the location of the weld. Attached to the arrow line is a reference line drawn horizontally. There must be a change of direction between arrow line and reference line, as shown in figure 3.13.

The symbol is attached to the underside of the reference line if the weld is made on the same side as the arrow. It is attached to the top of the reference line if the weld is on the other side to the arrow. A symbol above and below the line denotes a weld on both sides (see figure 3.16).

Where a weld is made around the entire profile of a section, for example where the shaft of a column is welded to the baseplate, a small circle is drawn around the intersection of the reference line and the arrow line, as shown in figure 3.14.

A small black triangular flag in the same position denotes that the weld should be made on site.

Designation	Illustration	Symbol	Designation	Illustration	Symbol
Butt weld between flanged plates (flanges being melted down completely)		ЈL	Single J-butt weld		Ρ
Square butt weld		‖	Backing or sealing run		⌣
Single-bevel butt weld		V	Fillet weld		◺
Single V-butt weld		V	Plug weld (circular or elongated hole, completely filled)		⊓
Single V-butt weld with broad root face		V	Spot weld or projection weld (a) resistance		○
Single-bevel butt weld with broad root face		V	(b) arc		○
Single-U butt weld		Y	Seam weld		⊖

Figure 3.10   Symbols for welding

SIZES OF WELDS

The size of a weld is determined in accordance with figure 3.15. The majority of welds on a job will be one size and this can be

stated as a note close to the title box. Where it is required to state the size of the weld on the drawing, this is done by placing the number representing the size of the weld in millimetres, immediately to the left of the weld symbol, as shown in figure 3.16.

Supplementary symbols

Shape of weld surface	Symbol
(a) flat (usually finished flush)	———
(b) convex	⌢
(c) concave	⌣

Figure 3.11   Supplementary symbols

Examples of application of supplementary symbols

Designation	Illustration	Symbol
Flat (flush) single-V butt weld		▽
Convex double-V butt weld		⋈
Concave fillet weld		◺
Flat (flush) single-V butt weld with flat (flush) backing run		▽

Figure 3.12   Examples of application of supplementary symbols

Sometimes a weld is not continuous, in which case the length of weld and the length of space are indicated by two consecutive numbers to the right of the symbol, the space length being bracketed, as shown in figure 3.17.

The use of these symbols is not obligatory and some companies prefer descriptions, for which the following abbreviations can be used:

FW	fillet weld
SB	square butt weld
SVB	single V butt weld
DVB	double V butt weld
DUB	double U butt weld
SBB	single bevel butt weld
DBB	double bevel butt weld

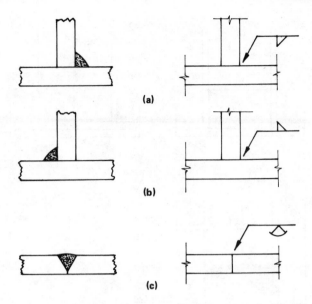

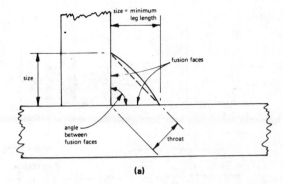

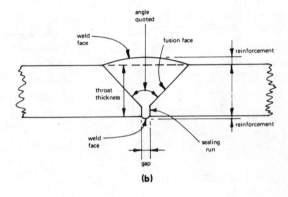

Figure 3.13 Indicating welds using arrow line, reference line and symbol: (a) fillet weld same side (symbol below line), (b) fillet weld other side (symbol above line), (c) V butt weld same side

The portal frame detailed in part II is an example of this method.

Welding can be indicated on the drawing either by a very thick line where it occurs or by short 45° hatching.

Figure 3.15 Weld terminology: (a) fillet weld, (b) butt weld

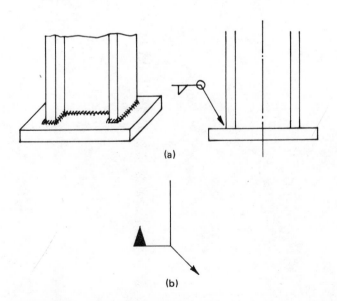

Figure 3.14 Complementary indications: (a) welding all round profile, (b) weld to be made on site

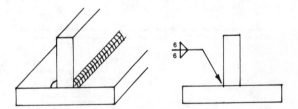

Figure 3.16 Welding both sides

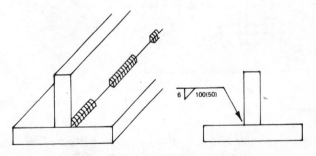

Figure 3.17 Intermittent welding

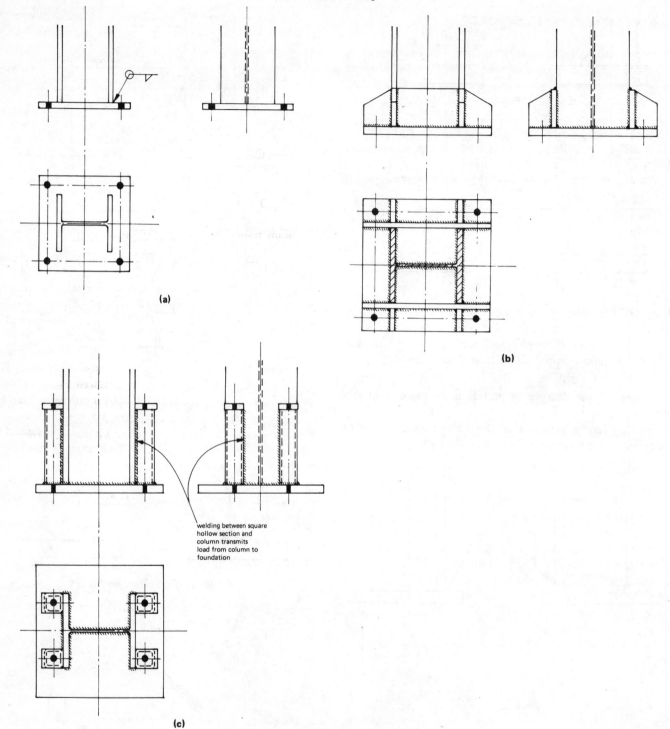

welding between square
hollow section and
column transmits
load from column to
foundation

Figure 3.18 (a) Slab base butt welded to bottom of column. (b) Slab base welded to bottom of column and strengthened to resist bending by means of gussets. (c) Bolt box base to transmit high bending moment to foundation

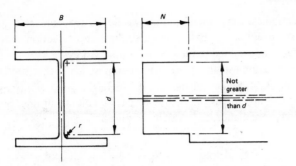

Figure 3.20 *Notching of beam to fit between flanges of universal column*

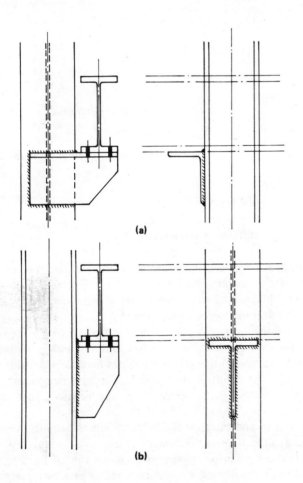

Figure 3.21 *(a) Eccentric connection using angle bracket.*
(b) Eccentric connection using bracket cut out of universal beam

ECCENTRIC CONNECTIONS

Beams frequently join columns other than on the same centre-line. Two examples are shown in figures 3.21(a) and (b), for what could be a beam supporting an overhead crane rail. Although shown here as welded connections, they could equally well be bolted. The structural design implications of eccentric loading are outside the scope of this book.

BEAMS TO BEAMS

There is a resemblance to the connections to columns. In figure 3.22(a) the vertical forces are transmitted by bolts through angle cleats. In figure 3.22(b) they are transmitted by bolts through a flat plate welded to the end of the incoming beam. In figure 3.22(c) the incoming beam rests on a seating cleat fixed to the supporting beam and is provided with stability cleats. Figure 3.22(d) suggests one of many ways of dealing with beam to beam connections where the tops are at different levels.

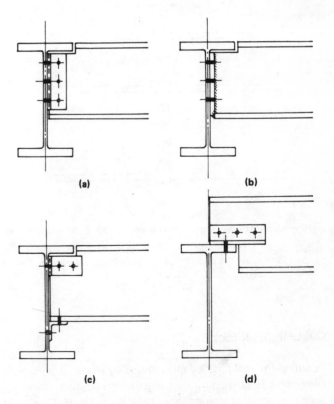

Figure 3.22 *Ways of connecting beams to beams*

In all cases the incoming beam requires notching so that its flanges clear the flanges of the supporting beam. The size of these notches is standard for each section and is given in the appropriate table in part III.

SPLICING BEAMS

Sometimes it is necessary to transport beams in two pieces and join them together at site, with what is called a splice. Figure 3.23 illustrates two ways of doing this, depending upon the nature of the forces that the joint will be expected to withstand. The joint in (a) will transmit bending and shearing forces, but that in (b) will transmit only shearing forces.

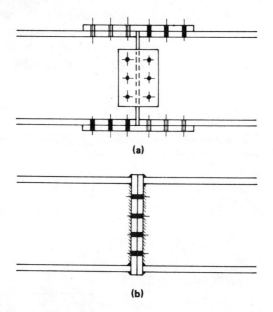

(a)

(b)

Figure 3.23 *Splice joints for beams: (a) joint capable of transmitting bending and shearing forces, (b) joint capable of transmitting shearing forces only*

COLUMN SPLICES

Columns for buildings of more than two storeys are made in convenient lengths and joined together on erection. There are several reasons for doing this: (1) ease of transport, (2) ease of

erection (a very long column would be very unstable when first stood on its base), and (3) the size of section may be smaller as the load reduces in the upper storeys.

The simplest and cheapest column splice is that shown in figure 3.24. While transferring the vertical load, it will transmit no bending forces and only keeps the column in line. Something more elaborate is usually required.

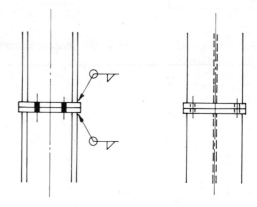

Figure 3.24 *Simplest column splice*

Column splices are needed to join together columns that may be

(1) the same section size
(2) the same serial size but of different section size
(3) different serial sizes.

The first category is illustrated in figure 3.25(a). The ends of the shafts are machined true and butt directly against each other. Flange and web splice plates provide sufficient bolting to transmit the forces through the joint.

The third category is illustrated in figure 3.25(b). The ends of the shaft are machined as before, but now a division plate is inserted between them. Packing plates have to be provided to increase the depth of the upper section to match that of the lower, so that flange splice plates can be used. Four angle cleats connect the webs through the division plate.

The second category can be dealt with in a similar manner, but as all sections of the same serial size have the same distance *between* the flanges, flange splice plates can be fixed to the inside of the flanges, without recourse to packing plates, and the division plate may be omitted. If plated cleats are used to connect the webs, packing plates will be required to make up the thinner web to the thickness of the thicker.

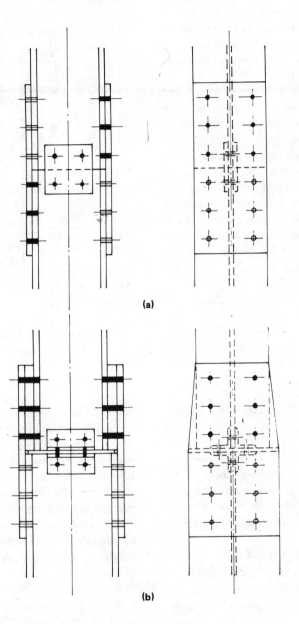

Figure 3.25 Column splices: (a) joining columns of same size, (b) joining columns of different sizes

SIZING OF JOINTS

Once the number and size of bolts have been determined by the structural designer, the next step is to determine the shape and size of the connecting plates and cleats. Consider the beam to column connection in figure 3.19(a).

Assume that the column is a 203 × 203 × 52 kg UC and that the beam is a 356 × 171 × 51 kg UB, that the cleats are 90 × 90 × 10 angles and that the bolts are all 20 mm diameter in 22 mm holes.

First the length of the angle cleats can be calculated. The bolts must be spaced at least 50 mm apart (BS 449 clause 52) and the edge distances not less than 34 mm (BS 449 table 21), making a minimum overall length of 168 mm. However the depth between fillets of a 203 × 203 UC is 312 mm from the tables and the connection would resist rotation better if the bolts were spaced further apart, say 100 mm, giving an overall length of 268 mm — say 270 mm, made up of 35 + 100 + 100 + 35 mm.

The back mark of a 90 × 90 angle is 50 mm (figure 3.4) and, allowing a cleat projection of 3 mm over the end of the beam, means that the holes in the beam must be drilled in a vertical line 50 − 3 = 47 mm from its end face. If the cleat is roughly central in the depth of the beam, the top hole will be drilled 75 mm down from the top of the beam { (356/2) − 100 = 78 mm}.

Finally the horizontal spacing of the holes in the column can be derived from the two back marks, plus the thickness of the beam web (50 + 50 + 7.3 = 107.3 mm). The recommended spacing of holes in this size of section is 140 mm, from figure 3.3, but this could not be accommodated in these cleats. 120 mm would be acceptable and would reduce the edge distance to only 38 mm, which is still adequate. This horizontal spacing of 120 mm should appear on the drawing. Figure 3.26 illustrates the dimensioned joint.

The reader can extend this *modus operandi* to other joints. It is a matter of applying the rules and recommendations in

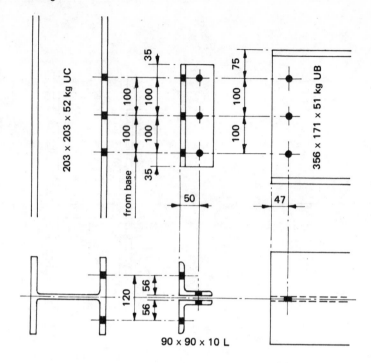

Figure 3.26   Dimensional joint

the best and most economical way, not forgetting that one of the qualities required is adequate strength. The lengthening of the cleats in the calculated example above is one example. A second is to keep the flange splice plate bolts (figure 3.25) as widely spaced horizontally as possible, without reducing the minimum edge distance, thereby providing the maximum strength with the material available.

There are other members to be joined together in structures, but these will be discussed in part II. In chapter 7 joints used in lattice construction, portal frames and plate girders will be dealt with.

4. DETAILING STEELWORK

BEAMS

Some typical beam details are shown on drawing no. 4.1 overleaf.

When detailing a beam from a floor plan, the beam should be viewed looking from the bottom or right-hand side of the plan.

If a beam connects to a seating cleat, the end connections should be dimensioned from the bottom flange upwards.

If a beam connects by other means, the end connections are dimensioned from the top flange downwards.

These rules are illustrated in figures 4.2, 4.3 and 4.4.

In figure 4.2 the incoming beam rests on a seating cleat fixed to the main beam. This cleat is dimensioned downwards from the top of the main beam. Thereafter the holes in the main beam and incoming beams and the notch are all dimensioned from the seating surface upwards. These rules will also apply to beams resting on seating cleats attached to columns.

In figures 4.3 and 4.4 there are no seating cleats and all the holes and notches are dimensioned downwards from the top surfaces of both beams, including the notch in the bottom flange in figure 4.4.

The top beam on drawing no. 4.1 is fixed between the flange of one column and the web of another. It could well be the beam marked B–2A on figure 4.7. Because the flange is too wide to fit between the flanges of the column, the flange is notched. The resulting flange width of 160 mm is derived from the depth between fillets (d = 160.8 mm) for a 203 × 203 × 52 kg UC (see table 2 in part III), which must not be exceeded. The length of the notch is given as 108 mm.

Both ends of the beam rest on seating cleats, so all the stability cleat holes are dimensioned from the bottom flange.

The 2 mm end clearance is to allow the beam to be positioned between the surfaces it joins. It is a fact of life that a 25 mm peg will not fit into a 25 mm hole.

The 3 mm projection of the cleats is needed because the cut ends of the beam may not be perfect, and this ensures the angle cleats bear firmly on the columns.

The exact length of the beam can be calculated as follows.

Column centres		8000
deduct half column depth $\frac{206.1}{2}$ =	103.0	
deduct half web thickness $\frac{8.0}{2}$ =	4.0	
allow 2 mm clearance at each end	4.0	111
Length of beam overall		7889
allow 3 mm projection of cleats		6
Exact length of 610 × 229 × 113 kg UB =		7883 mm

The holes in the middle of the beam are to receive an incoming beam, such as those detailed below it. There are no seating cleats, so the holes are dimensioned from the top surface. The horizontal spacing of 108 mm comes from the back marks of two 90 × 90 angles (50 mm each), plus the web thickness of a 457 × 152 × 60 kg UB (8 mm). The vertical spacing could be as little as 50 mm (according to BS 449 clause 52), but for design reasons it is better to spread the connection between the two beams over a greater depth, hence the 75 mm spacing.

Note that the holes in the bottom flange are positioned 52 mm from the end, a back mark of 55 mm, less 3 mm projection of cleat. The spacing of 140 mm should be the same as the seating cleat. It is the dimension S_1 obtained from figure 3.2.

The length of the 100 × 100 and 100 × 75 angle cleats is determined by adding two edge distances, obtained from BS 449 table 21, of 34 mm each (sheared ends) to the hole centres and rounding up the answer to the nearest 5 mm.

The 100 mm leg dimension is given at the right-hand end to tell the workshop which leg of the 100 × 75 angle is to be bolted to the web. Dimensions of rolled sections are not normally given on drawings.

The middle and lower beams detailed, are examples of bolted-on cleats and welded end plates respectively. Note how the positioning of holes and notches from the ends is taken from the cut ends of the beam and not from the outside of the end plates. This is because holing and notching will be done before the end plates are welded on.

32

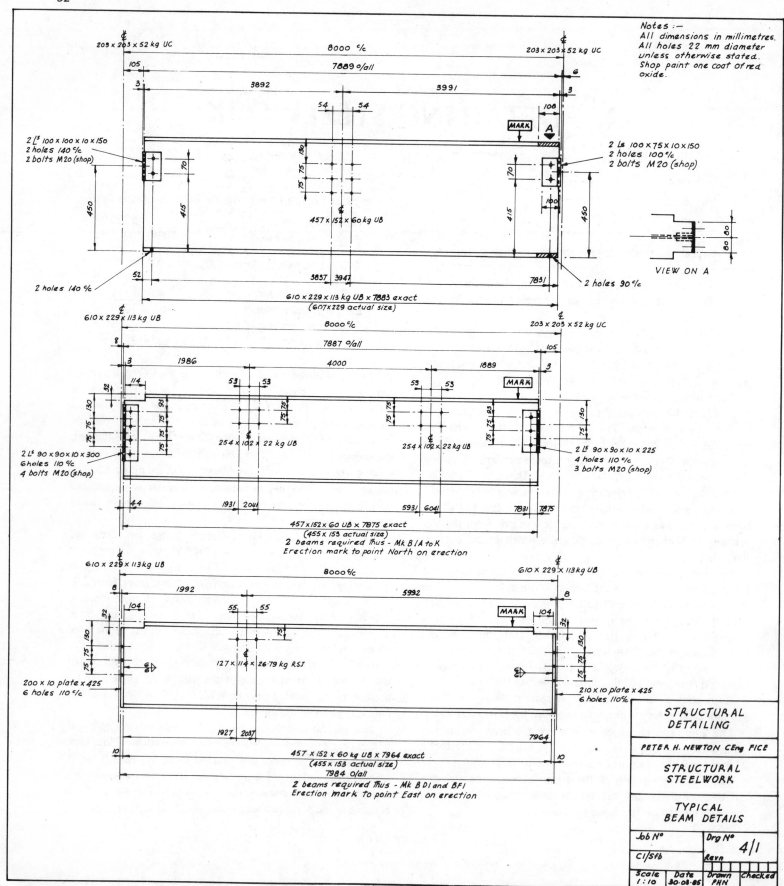

Notes :—
All dimensions in millimetres.
All holes 22 mm diameter
unless otherwise stated.
Shop paint one coat of red
oxide.

203 × 203 × 52 kg UC

8000 c/c

203 × 203 × 52 kg UC

7889 o/all

105

3892

3991

6

3

54   54

108

3

MARK   **A**

2 L's 100 × 100 × 10 × 150
2 holes 140 c/c
2 bolts M20 (shop)

70

70

2 Ls 100 × 75 × 10 × 150
2 holes 100 c/c
2 bolts M20 (shop)

130

450

415

75 75 130

100

415

450

457 × 152 × 60 kg UB

52

2 holes 140 c/c

3857 3947

7831

2 holes 90 c/c

610 × 229 × 113 kg UB × 7883 exact
(607 × 229 actual size)

VIEW ON A

80 80

---

610 × 229 × 113 kg UB

8000 c/c

203 × 203 × 52 kg UC

8

7887 o/all

105

3

1986

4000

1889

3

32

114

53   53

53   53

130

75 75 93

75 75

75 75

75 75 93

130

2 L's 90 × 90 × 10 × 300
6 holes 110 c/c
4 bolts M20 (shop)

254 × 102 × 22 kg UB

254 × 102 × 22 kg UB

2 L's 90 × 90 × 10 × 225
4 holes 110 c/c
3 bolts M20 (shop)

44

1931 2041

5931 6041

7831 7875

457 × 152 × 60 UB × 7875 exact
(455 × 153 actual size)
2 beams required thus - Mk B1A to K
Erection mark to point North on erection

---

610 × 229 × 113 kg UB

8000 c/c

610 × 229 × 113 kg UB

8

1992

5992

8

32

104

55   55

104

32

130

75

130

75 75

127 × 114 × 26·79 kg RSJ

75 75

200 × 10 plate × 425
6 holes 110 c/c

210 × 10 plate × 425
6 holes 110 c/c

10

1927 2037

7964

10

457 × 152 × 60 kg UB × 7964 exact
(455 × 153 actual size)
7984 o/all
2 beams required thus - Mk B D1 and BF1
Erection mark to point East on erection

STRUCTURAL
DETAILING

PETER H. NEWTON CEng FICE

STRUCTURAL
STEELWORK

TYPICAL
BEAM DETAILS

Job Nº		Drg Nº	
			4/1
CI/Sfb		Revn	
Scale 1:10	Date 30·08·85	Drawn PHN	Checked

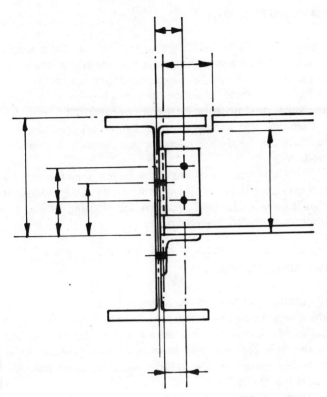

Figure 4.2   *Dimensioning where incoming beam rests on seating cleat*

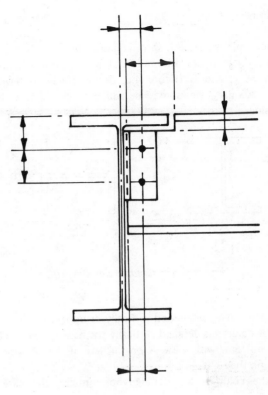

Figure 4.3   *Dimensioning where there is no seating cleat for incoming beam*

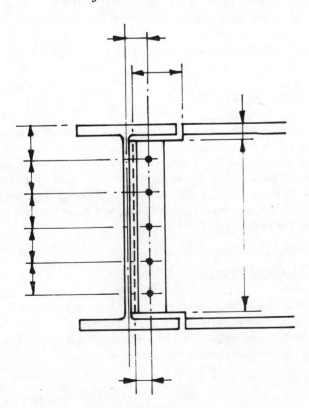

Figure 4.4   *Dimensioning of lower notch from top flange*

COLUMNS

A typical column detail is shown on drawing no 4.5 (facing).

Depending on the orientation of the column in plan, the two views A and B (figure 4.6) should always be given. If needed auxiliary views may be added to give details of the other side.

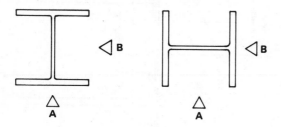

Figure 4.6   Column detailing rules

Columns may be detailed vertically or horizontally.

If the column is detailed vertically the base will naturally be at the bottom, with view A on the left of the drawing and view B on the right.

If the columns are detailed horizontally, the base end should be at the right-hand side of the drawing, with view A at the bottom and view B at the top.

This is third angle projection.

In the example given opposite, auxiliary views are given of the top, at a section just above the first floor seating cleats and of the base, so as to clarify the holing arrangements.

The dimensions for the positioning of seating cleats are taken from the machined end of the column and the positions of the holes are dimensioned from the tops of the cleats. This is because the marking out and the drilling of holes will be done before the baseplate is welded on.

The seating cleats will be attached to the columns in the workshop and in this example are shown welded. With the advent of numerically controlled drilling machines, some fabricators will prefer to drill and bolt.

The standard symbols for welding have been used on this drawing. They imply that 6 mm fillet welds are formed along the full length of each side of the cleat, to which an arrow points. In the case of the base the symbol implies that 6 mm fillet welds are formed around the entire profile of the universal column.

The end of the column shaft is to be machined to ensure that it is in full contact with the baseplate over its entire area. If this does not happen, contact could be made over small areas resulting in overstress of the metal.

MARKING PLANS

Figure 4.7 shows a marking plan for one floor of a simple structure using a grid system. Note that the grid is lettered A to J from left to right, and 1 to 3 from top to bottom.

Figure 4.8 shows a section through a four storey building on which the floors are lettered alphabetically from the bottom up. By combining these two, every member in a structure can be given a reference that uniquely describes its position.

There are several variations of this basic system favoured by different companies — any one of which will be acceptable if it is clearly understood between the drawing office, the fabrication shop and the erector.

THE GRID SYSTEM

The columns are 'marked' according to the grid intersection at which they are to be erected — A1 to J3. If there is more than one lift of columns, then their vertical location can be described by the floor code for their lower end, so that column A1-A starts at ground level and column A1-C continues from the second floor to the roof.

Beams are marked with the line on which they lie, followed by the 'lowest' letter or number at one end. In figure 4.7 the beams across the top are 1A, 1C, 1E and 1G, while the beams along the left-hand end are A1 and A2. The floor number for the beam is indicated by using the floor prefix, thus B-1A will be on the first floor, C-1A on the second floor, and so on.

SEQUENTIAL SYSTEM

In this system the columns are marked in the same way as the grid system described above.

Beams are numbered sequentially — usually starting at the top left-hand corner. These numbers are prefixed by a floor reference, so that beams B1, B2, B3, etc. are on the first floor, C1, C2, C3, etc. on the second floor, and so on. The typical floor plan would look like figure 4.9.

PIECE MARK SYSTEM

Neither of the two systems already described takes account of the fact that many members of a structure are similar. In figure 4.7 member B-1A is the same as member B-3G, member B-A1 the same as member B-J2, and so on.

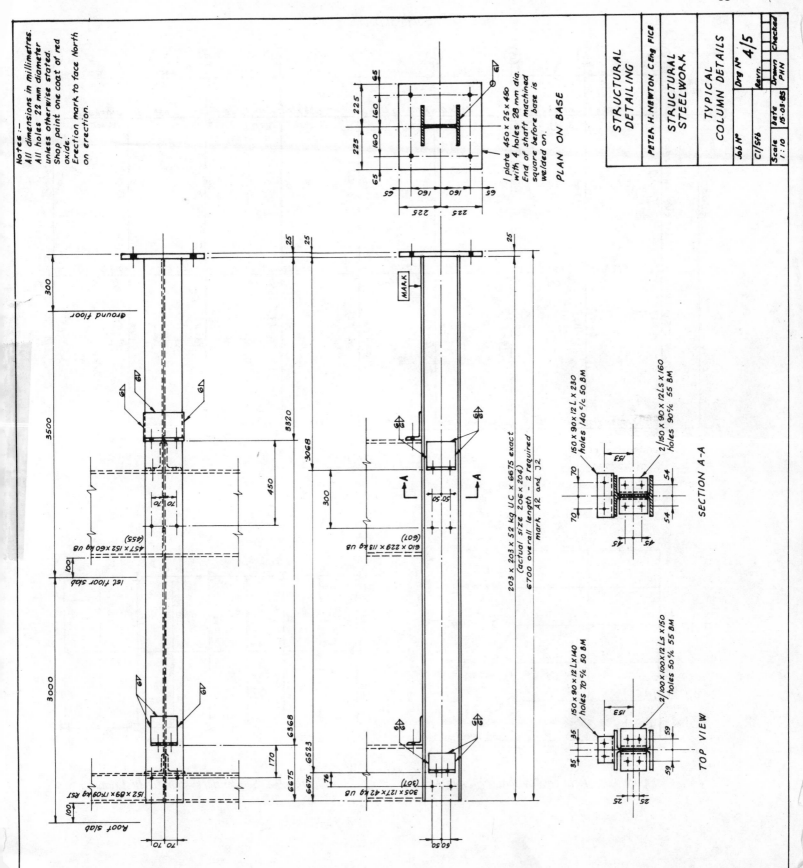

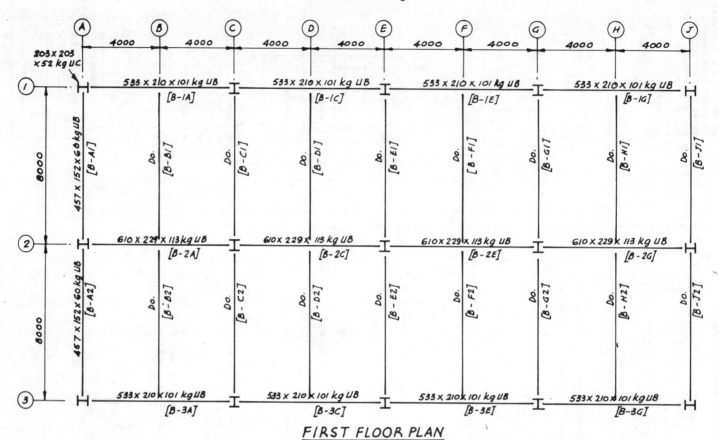

FIRST FLOOR PLAN

Figure 4.7

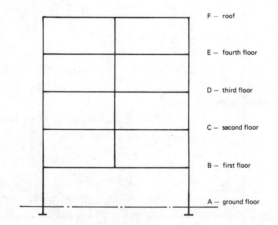

Figure 4.8   Reference system for floors

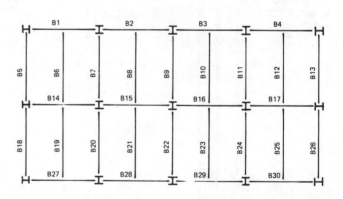

Figure 4.9   Sequential system for first floor

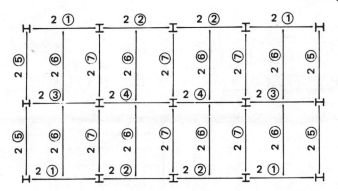

Figure 4.10 Piece mark system

In a piece mark system (figure 4.10) every similar piece is given the same number. This number is prefixed by the detail drawing number, thus 2①️ is piece no. 1 on drawing no. 2, 3⑩ is piece no. 10 on drawing no. 3, and so on. An example of this system will be found on the walkway marking plan in part II, except that, as only samples from several drawings are reproduced, the prefix rule is distorted.

Beams are indicated by their floor number, followed by the drawing number and then the detail number. Hence B-4①️ will identify beams mark 1, detailed on drawing no. 4 and intended for the first floor.

Columns can be indicated in either of two ways: either by the drawing number, followed by the grid reference, or by the drawing number, followed by the piece number. Hence 3–A1 will identify the column at grid reference A1 detailed on drawing no. 3, or 3–S4 will identify column mark 4, detailed on drawing no. 3.

In a variation of the piece mark system used for the portal framed structure illustrated in part II, each piece is given a letter prefix, according to the type of member that it is.

S — column (stanchion)
B — beam
R — rafter
P — purlin
and so on.

There are four different beams used in this structure and they are identified as B1, B2, B3 and B4. This mark number is written against the member, wherever it appears on the drawing, and the total number is shown on the detail drawing.

Whichever system is adopted, the serial size of the section is also written alongside, except that the word 'ditto' is permissible and this can be shortened to 'do'. Obviously it is important

to adopt a single system that is liked by the fabricators, because their requirements are paramount, for it is they who make the profit, not the drawing office.

Whatever the system the following rules must be applied.

1. Each loose piece must have a discrete mark.
2. The use of any suffix such as 'X' for opposite hand, etc. is not recommended. A new mark number should be given.
3. On beams the mark should be painted on the top flange at the North or East end.
4. On columns the mark should be painted on the lower end of the shaft, on the flange facing North or East.
5. On vertical bracings the mark should be painted at the lower end.
6. To indicate on a detail drawing where an erection mark is to painted, the word 'MARK', contained in a rectangle, should be shown on each detail, with an arrow pointing to the position required.
7. If pieces are to be galvanised, the mark should be hard stamped into the metal of the piece.

SCHEDULES

Schedules are lists of materials for ordering and shipping purposes. There are three main types used for structural steelwork:

1. materials lists
2. bolt lists
3. despatch lists.

DRAWING OFFICE MATERIAL LISTS

A typical form is reproduced on page 38. The words 'PRELIMINARY/FINAL' mean that the form can be used at two stages of the process.

The preliminary list is prepared at an early stage, probably before the detail drawings have been completed, following receipt of the designer's layout, on which the sizes of the main structural members have been given.

At this stage only the main members are listed, so that orders can be placed for the bulk of the steelwork. The exact lengths of the pieces will not be known, so the nominal lengths are rounded up to the next 100 mm multiple, less if the section is heavy and the waste would be costly.

Once the details have been drawn, the final materials list is prepared. This will give the exact cutting length and also

Material by .... *BAC* ....
Checked by ....
Weights by ....
Checked by ....

DRAWING OFFICE MATERIAL LIST
PRELIMINARY/~FINAL~
ORDER No. *132   OFFICE BLOCK*

Sheet No. .... *1* ....
Drawing No. *4/7*
Date .... *15 - 03 - 85*

Item No	Location	No Reqd		Description	Size	Length		Note	Pre Sheet Item No.	Total Linear Metres	Kilograms Per Metre	Total weight in Kg					Ordered From	Order Book Folio
		In I	In			m	mm											
1	B ①	4		UB	533 X 210 X 101	7	950											
2	②	4			533 X 210 X 101	8	050											
3	③	2			610 X 229 X 113	7	950											
4	④	2			610 X 229 X 113	8	050											
5	⑤	12			457 X 152 X 60	8	050											
6	⑥	6			457 X 152 X 60	7	850											
7																		
8																		
9																		
10																		
11																		
12																		
13																		
14																		
15																		
16																		
17																		
18																		

MY 73044 D

include the materials required for gussets, baseplates and any other connections. The lists refer to the marks of the pieces and the number of the drawing on which they are detailed. The list reproduced on page 39 could be the final materials list for the beams illustrated in drawing no. 4.1.

BOLT LISTS

Two lists are prepared — one for shop bolts and another for site bolts. The bolts listed on page 40 are the bolts needed to erect the beams illustrated in drawing no. 4.1. The following is an explanation of the sheet.

Columns 1 to 3 refer to quantity. Bolts, washers and nuts can be lost or damaged, so a few spares are included in the despatch. Column 3 lists the actual quantity required and is the only one of these columns filled in at this stage.

Column 4 states the diameter of the bolt in millimetres, preceded by the letter M, which implies they are ISO metric sizes.

Column 5, headed 'Through', lists the plies through which the bolt will pass, in other words the thicknesses of the flange, web, gusset, etc. which it will connect; this is also known as the 'grip'.

Material by ...... **EFD** ......

Checked by ....

Weights by ....

Checked by ....

DRAWING OFFICE MATERIAL LIST

~~PRELIMINARY~~/FINAL

ORDER No. **132 OFFICE BLOCK**

Sheet No. ......**1**......

Drawing No. ....**4/1**....

Date ....**10-04-85**....

Item No	Location	No Reqd In 1	No Reqd In	Description	Size	Length m	Length mm	Note	Pre Sheet Item No.	Total Linear Metres	Kilograms Per Metre	Total weight in Kg				Ordered From	Order Book Folio
1			2	Beams required mkd	4·1①												
2	'	1	2	UB	610 × 229 × 113	7	883		(3)	7·883	113		8	9	1		
3		2	4	ANGLE	100 × 100 × 12		150			0·300	17·8				5		
4		2	4	"	100 × 75 × 12		150			0·300	15·4				5		
5										WT IN ONE			9	0	1		
6										WT IN TWO		1	8	0	2		
7			2	Beams required mkd	4·1②												
8		1	2	UB	610 × 229 × 113	7	982		(4)	7·982	113		9	0	2		
9		4	4	ANGLE	100 × 75 × 12		150			0·600	15·4				9		
10										WT IN ONE			9	1	1		
11										WT IN TWO		1	8	2	2		
12			4	Beams required mkd	4·1⑧												
13		1	4	UB	457 × 152 × 60	7	875		(5)	7·875	60		4	7	3		
14		2	8	ANGLE	90 × 90 × 10		300			0·600	13·4				8		
15		2	8	"	90 × 90 × 10		225			0·450	13·4				6		
16										WT IN ONE			4	8	7		
17										WT IN 4		1	9	4	8		
18										PART TOTAL C/F			5	6	0	8	

MY 73044 D

BRAITHWAITE & COMPANY STRUCTURAL LIMITED.
NEPTUNE WORKS, NEWPORT, GWENT.

SHEET No. *B1*

SITE BOLT LIST

NAME .... OFFICE BLOCK   ORDER No. *132*

Gross	Spare	Nett	Dia.	Through	Length	Head	Scd.	Grade	POSITION IN WORK		R/Wash	T/Wash
MY (1) 56169 D (2)	(3)		(4)	(5)	(6)	(7)	(8)	(9)	(10)		(11)	(12)
DRG Nº		4	M20	12,12	50	XOX		4·6	B - B1	to col.	1	
4/1		8		17,12	55					seating	1	
		6		12,8,12	60				B - B2	to col.	1	
		8		17,12	55					seating	1	
		8		10,8	45				B - B8	to col.	1	
		12		17,10	55					beam	1	
		12		10,16	55				B - B9	to beam (ext)	1	
		6		10,16,10	65					beam (int)	1	

Column 6 lists the length of bolt required, that is the distance from under the head to the end of the bolt for hexagon and cup head bolts, or the length overall for countersunk bolts. The first bolts in the list connect the end cleats of a 610 x 229 x 113 kg UB to the flange of a 203 x 203 x 52 kg UC, and the calculation goes as follows.

Column flange thickness	13	
Cleat leg thickness	12	} 25 = the grip
Allowance for nut and washer*	20 + 6 = 26	
Total length	= 51	
Next longer bolt length	= 55 mm	

* The allowance for black bolts can be taken as d + 6 mm for bolts up to 20 mm diameter and d + 8 mm for larger bolts, where d is the bolt diameter. The allowance for HSFG bolts is given in the table in part III.

Column 7 describes the shape of bolt required:

XOX for hexagon head, round neck and hexagon nut
CupOX for cup head, round neck and hexagon nut
CskOX for countersunk head, round neck and hexagon nut.

Column 9 lists the grade of the bolt in the ISO system. It comprises two numbers separated by a point. The first number represents the ultimate tensile strength of the steel from which the bolt is made, and the second number the ratio of its yield stress to its ultimate stress. This is rather confusing for the beginner and all it is necessary to remember is the higher the number the stronger the steel. The designer will have specified the grade of bolt to be used. (For the record, a grade 4.6 bolt has a minimum ultimate stress of 40 kgf/mm^2 and the yield stress is 60 per cent of that, that is 24 kgf/mm^2.)

The grade in this case is that of a black bolt to BS 4190. Higher strength bolts are available to BS 3692. Both have the letter M on the head of the bolt and the high strength bolt has 8.8 as well, to differentiate between them in the field.

Column 10 is self-explanatory, listing the positions where the bolts are to be used.

Columns 11 and 12 list any washers required. These are normally round, unless they pass through the tapered flanges of a joist or channel, in which case a tapered washer is used to suit the taper of the flange.

The list should specify any special finish required for the bolts. Bolts, nuts and washers can be supplied with various corrosion-resistant finishes:

electroplated with cadmium or zinc to BS 1706
hot-dip galvanised to BS 729
sherardised to BS 4921.

The quantities of bolts are taken off each drawing in turn, the drawing number being written in a prominent position on the list. A summary sheet is then prepared, which collects together all the bolts of the same size and length, to the totals of which is added an allowance for losses (column 2 — Spare) to give the gross quantity to be despatched (column 1 — Gross).

DESPATCH LISTS

These are prepared for shipment of the completed steelwork to site. A typical list is reproduced on page 42. For ease of checking, the order should be that of the erection mark number. The list gives the following information:

package number, if allocated
quantity in the package, including any spares
description of the piece
erection mark of the piece
weight of one piece in kilogrammes
length, depth and breadth of the package
total weight of package
item number, if allocated.

The total weight of the steelwork can now be calculated, together with weight of bolts, nuts and washers. Any paints, brushes and thinners can be listed, if these are to be supplied, to complete the despatch list.

Further examples of schedules can be found in part II.

BRAITHWAITE & CO. STRUCTURAL LIMITED

STRUCTURAL DEPT.

NEWPORT

| B. & Co. | ORDER No. 132 |
| Customers | |

DESPATCH LIST.

List No. *1*
Date *20-04-85*

NAME *OFFICE BLOCK*

Description *COLUMNS AND BEAMS*

G65050 7992R

Package No	No. Inc. Spares	Description	Erection Mark	Weight in One Kilogrammes			Length	Breadth	Depth	Total Weight Kilogrammes				Item No.
	4	COLUMNS	S1		3 6 0		6700	450	450		1 4 4 0			
	6	|	S2		3 6 4		6700	450	450		2 1 8 4			
	2		S3		3 6 6		6700	450	450		7 3 2			
	3	⊥	S4		3 7 0		6700	450	450		1 1 1 0			
	2	BEAMS	B-B1		9 0 1		7883	607	229		1 8 0 2			
	2	|	B-B2		9 1 1		7984	607	229		1 8 2 2			
	4		B-B3		8 1 0		7883	538	210		3 2 4 0			
	4		B-B4		8 1 8		7984	538	210		3 2 7 2			
	4		B-B5		4 9 5		7984	455	153		1 9 8 0			
	8		B-B6		4 9 3		7984	455	153		3 9 4 4			
	6		B-B7		4 8 8		7790	455	153		2 9 2 8			
	2		C-B10		3 5 0		7883	402	142		7 0 0			
	2		C-B11		3 5 9		7984	402	142		7 1 8			
	4		C-B12		3 3 8		7883	307	124		1 3 5 2			
	4		C-B13		3 4 1		7984	307	124		1 3 6 4			
	4		C-B14		1 4 5		7984	153	89		5 8 0			
	8		C-B15		1 4 4		7984	153	89		1 1 5 2			
	6	⊥	C-B16		1 4 1		7790	153	89		8 4 6			
						TOTAL WEIGHT					3 1 1 6 6			

5.   REINFORCED CONCRETE

British Standards codes of practice CP 110, CP 114, CP 115 and CP 116 are no longer valid. They have been replaced by BS 8110 which is now referred to in this book. Not of immediate concern to the detailer, but of greater interest to the designer, is the basis of design used in BS 8110. Known as the limit-state method of design, it will have no meaning to the student who has not studied structural mechanics to a sufficient level. Much computer-aided design (now widely used) tends to be based on BS 8110. It was not well received by a substantial proportion of engineers, who, for the simpler structures, favoured the retention of a permissible stress code, similar to the old CP 114, to operate alongside BS 8110.

A task group of the Institution of Structural Engineers has produced a comprehensive revision of CP 114, extended to incorporate precast and composite construction, excluding that of a specialised character such as water-retaining structures. The author believes this new code will find favour with many designers and has accordingly incorporated it in this book. Currently it has no numerical coding and for convenience it is referred to as the 'new CP 114'.

SIMPLE THEORY

Reinforced concrete is a combination of concrete and steel. Concrete is a hard durable material made of graded aggregate, bound together with a cement and water paste. It is very strong in compression, but relatively weak in tension. Beams or columns made from plain concrete would have to be very large. By placing steel bars in those parts of the concrete subject to tension, acceptable sizes can be obtained. In more advanced work, reinforcement is also used to carry some of the compressive load in the concrete to further reduce the size of members, but this is outside the scope of this chapter.

The reinforced concrete detailer should have an understanding of the behaviour of simple structural members under simple loading conditions. The diagrams in figure 5.1 illustrate how beams and columns may deflect under load and hence the areas that require reinforcement against tensile failure.

Reinforced concrete must have some reinforcement for reasons other than strength. In the case of the beam shown in figure 5.2 longitudinal steel bars, forming the main reinforcement, are placed in the bottom, which is in tension, and transverse steel bars, called stirrups, are placed vertically to counteract shearing forces. But these stirrups will collapse when the concrete is placed, unless they are made into a rigid 'cage'. This is done by adding hanger bars, which complete the cage and hold the stirrups during the concreting operation. The hanger bars can be quite small.

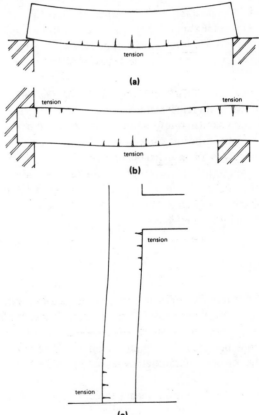

Figure 5.1   Deflection patterns: (a) simply supported beam, (b) continuous beam, (c) column

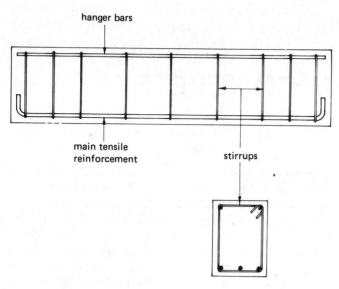

hanger bars

main tensile reinforcement

stirrups

Figure 5.2   Basic beam reinforcement

BS 8110 (paragraph 3.12.5.3) and the 'new CP 114' (paragraphs 314c, 346a and 348a) require there to be a minimum amount of main reinforcement expressed as a percentage of the cross-sectional area of the beam or slab. In the case of columns and slabs (which are just wide beams) they require a minimum of secondary reinforcement, that is bars at right angles to the main reinforcement.

There are similar rules relating to the maximum amount of reinforcement in beams and columns. At this stage the student will probably have insufficient understanding of design to be able to use this information, but, for the sake of completeness, extracts of BS 8110 and the 'new CP 114' are given in part III. In the examples given in this book all such decisions will have been taken by the designer.

CONCRETE

Ordinary structural concrete can be produced in a variety of strengths to meet the needs of the building. These are known as grades of concrete, designated by their characteristic strength in newtons per square millimetre (N/mm^2), determined from test cubes crushed at 28 days, as set out in BS 5328 (see figure 5.3).

The 'new CP 114' recommends three types of mixes:

(a) designed mixes $C(N/mm^2)D$
(b) special prescribed mixes $C(N/mm^2)SP$
(c) ordinary prescribed mixes $C(N/mm^2)P$.

The brackets contain the grade number, that is, the 28-day works cube strength of the concrete. Thus the ordinary prescribed mixes are:

C20P, C25P and C30P

Guidance on specifications and forms for specifying different types of concrete are given in BS 5328.

The size of the coarse aggregate can be varied to suit the size of section and the complexity of reinforcement. The normal maximum size of aggregate used is 20 mm. In smaller more heavily reinforced sections, it may be necessary to reduce this to 14 mm or even 10 mm. However, the smaller the aggregate the more expensive the concrete, so the largest possible size is preferred.

The decision as to the grade and maximum aggregate size will have been taken by the designer.

Mixes can be ordinary prescribed mixes (P), designed mixes (D) or special prescribed mixes (SP), and the difference is indicated by P, D or SP used as a suffix to the grade number, thus C20P, C25D etc.

Grade	Characteristic strength (N/mm^2)	Lowest grade for compliance with appropriate use
C2.5	2.5	
C5	5.0	
C7.5	7.5	Plain concrete
C10	10.0	
C12.5	12.5	
C15	15.0	Reinforced concrete with lightweight aggregate
C20	20.0	Reinforced concrete with dense aggregate
C25	25.0	
C30	30.0	Concrete with post-tensioned tendons
C35	35.0	
C40	40.0	Concrete with pre-tensioned tendons
C45	45.0	
C50	50.0	
C55	55.0	
C60	60.0	

Figure 5.3   Concrete grades according to BS 5328, table 3

REINFORCEMENT

The steel used for reinforcement may be mild steel or high yield steel. The latter will transmit greater forces, size for size, than mild steel. The detailer will need to know which is to be used, because high yield steel cannot be bent as sharply as mild steel.

The various steels for the reinforcement of concrete are covered by the following British Standards.

BS 4449: 1978 Hot rolled steel bars in mild steel and high yield steel
BS 4461: 1978 Cold worked steel bars in high yield steel only
BS 4482: 1969 Hard drawn steel wire in high yield steel only
BS 4483: Steel fabric for the reinforcement of concrete

Hot rolled steel bars can be round or ribbed to improve the bond with the concrete. Cold worked steel bars are typically square in cross-section, twisted in a helix. The steel wire is welded to form a rectangular mesh that is mainly used in slabs.

In order to anchor the ends of the bars in the concrete, bends or hooks are sometimes formed on the ends. The shapes and sizes of these bends and hooks are specified in *BS 4466: 1989 Bending dimensions and scheduling of bars for the reinforcement of concrete*, see figure 5.4. An extract of this standard is included in part III, and the sizes of bars commonly used are also listed. Not all bars are straight and the standard also illustrates the preferred shapes, together with formulae for calculating the length of steel bar required in each case.

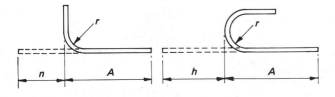

Bar size	Grade 250 bars complying with the requirements of BS 4449 (type and grade R, type and grade S)			Grade 460/425 bars complying with the requirements of BS 4449 or BS 4461 (type and grade S, type and grade T)			Fabric complying with the requirements of BS 4483			
d	r	n	h	r	n	h	d	r	n	h
6*	12	100	100	18	100	100	5	15	100	100
8	16	100	100	24	100	100	6	18	100	100
10	20	100	100	30	100	100	7	21	100	100
12	24	100	100	36	100	100	8	24	100	100
16	32	100	150	48	100	180	9	27	120	135
20	40	100	180	60	110	220	10	30	120	135
25	50	130	230	100	180	350	12	36	130	145
32	64	160	290	128	230	450	–	–	–	–
40	80	200	360	160	280	560	–	–	–	–
50*	100	250	450	200	350	700	–	–	–	–

*Denotes non-preferred size.

Figure 5.4 Minimum former radii, bend and hook allowances

The steel bars are joined to form a rigid cage or mat, using soft iron tying wire or by welding. It is essential that the bars do not move when the concrete is placed around them — an operation that is often done quite roughly. A sufficient number of bars should be provided to ensure that no movement will occur.

The use of hooks for end anchorages is not normally necessary with deformed bars.

CONCRETE COVER

It is essential for the steel bars to be protected by a sufficient layer of concrete, known as 'cover', to protect them from moisture that will rust the steel, and from the heat of any fire that could degrade the steel and lead to a structural collapse.

The amount of cover will depend upon the quality of the concrete and the degree of exposure to the elements in the case of rusting. For fire resistance it will depend upon the length of time that the structure is required to resist a fire, the type of concrete aggregate and whether any additional protective covering is to be provided.

Table 3.4 of BS 8110 specifies the minimum cover to all reinforcement (including links) to meet durability requirements. Durability is regarded today as a most important characteristic of concrete, following the many failures of concrete structures on this account. The reader should note that it is the maximum free water/cement ratio and the minimum cement content of the concrete that matter. The cube crushing strength is only a way of checking the quality of the concrete produced. Table 3.2 defines the terms used for conditions of exposure and table 3.5 (see part III) specifies the nominal cover to all reinforcement (including links) to meet specific periods of fire resistance.

In practice it is very difficult to bend reinforcement to an exact size and this might result in less than the recommended cover. In order to avoid this, further allowances are made to cater for oversized links. These are set out in table 3.26 of BS 8110.

Figure 5.5 illustrates how this table is applied. As well as errors in the cutting and bending of reinforcement, errors can occur in the size of the formwork and the fixing of the reinforcement. A negative tolerance of 5 mm is permitted in the nominal cover, that is the actual cover could be 5 mm less than the nominal cover.

Cover for fire resistance will depend upon the thickness and quality of the concrete surrounding the steel. The reader should refer to section four of BS 8110 or subsection 3K of the 'new CP 114' for particulars of fire resistance.

BS 8110 Table 3.2   Exposure conditions

Environment	Exposure conditions
Mild	Concrete surfaces protected against weather or aggressive conditions
Moderate	Concrete surfaces sheltered from severe rain or freezing whilst wet
	Concrete subject to condensation
	Concrete surfaces continuously under water
	Concrete in contact with non-aggressive soil
Severe	Concrete surfaces exposed to severe rain, alternate wetting and drying or occasional freezing or severe condensation
Very severe	Concrete surfaces exposed to sea water spray, de-icing salts (directly or indirectly), corrosive fumes or severe freezing conditions whilst wet
Extreme	Concrete surfaces exposed to abrasive action, e.g. sea water carrying solids or flowing water with pH $\leq$ 4.5 or machinery or vehicles

BS 8110 Table 3.4 Nominal cover to all reinforcement (including links) to meet durability requirements (Note: this table relates to normal-weight aggregate of 20 mm nominal maximum size)

Conditions of exposure (see 3.3.4)	Nominal cover (mm)				
Mild	25	20	20*	20*	20*
Moderate	–	35	30	25	20
Severe	–	–	40	30	25
Very severe	–	–	50†	40†	30
Extreme	–	–	–	60†	50
Maximum free water/ cement ratio	0.65	0.60	0.55	0.50	0.45
Maximum cement content (kg/m³)	275	300	325	350	400
Lowest grade of concrete	C30	C35	C40	C45	C50

*These covers may be reduced to 15 mm provided that the nominal maximum size of aggregate does not exceed 15 mm.
†Where concrete is subject to normal-weight aggregate of 20 mm nominal size.

The cover is maintained by the use of spacer blocks or stools. These take various forms. At their simplest they are small blocks of concrete of the required thickness, into which has been cast a length of soft iron tying wire for securing them

to the bars. Proprietary alternatives are available, made of plastic materials.

The minimum cover applies to all the reinforcement, including the links and stirrups.

BS 8100 Table 3.26   Bar schedule dimensions: deduction for permissible deviations

Distance between concrete faces (m)	Type of bar	Total deduction (mm)
0–1	Links and other bent bars	10
1–2	Links and other bent bars	15
Over 2	Links and other bent bars	20
Any length	Straight bars	40

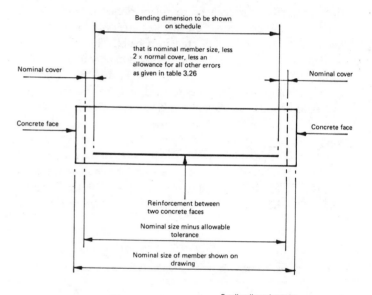

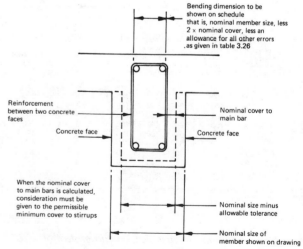

Figure 5.5 Permissible deviations

SPACING OF REINFORCEMENT

If a member is heavily reinforced, with a lot of bars close together, it may not be possible to get the concrete to flow around the bars, with serious implications for strength and durability. To avoid this happening, BS 8110 recommends that the horizontal distance between bars should be 5 mm more than the maximum aggregate size. It further recommends that if there are bars one above the other, the vertical distance between them should not be less than two-thirds of the maximum aggregate size and that the horizontal gaps should be arranged vertically above one another. Where the bar size is larger than h_{agg} + 5 mm, the spacing should be at least as great as the bar size. The full text of 3.12.11.1 of BS 8110 is reproduced in part III. The simple requirements are summed up in figure 5.6. The requirements for spacing in the 'new CP 114' appear in clause 311.

The detailer must also allow the builder to compact the concrete. This is best done by a poker vibrator inserted into the concrete. The top bars in a beam should be so spaced as to leave a gap through which the poker can be inserted without touching the reinforcement. For a 50 mm poker this would mean a 70 mm minimum gap.

DETAILING OF REINFORCEMENT

The standard method of detailing reinforced concrete is described in a report of that name issued by a joint committee of the Concrete Society and the Institution of Structural Engineers. Published by the Concrete Society in 1970, it was reprinted in 1983, with minor amendments to take account of the issue of the 1981 edition of BS 4466.

The purpose of detailing is to convey to the builder the information needed to get each and every bar fixed in its correct position. To draw every bar would be counter-productive, producing a very complicated drawing that would be difficult to read. In the standard method the following rules are recommended.

Beams — all main bars should be drawn in full in elevation and shown in cross-section.

Columns — only one bar of each type need be shown in full in elevation, but all bars should be shown in cross-section.

Slabs — only one bar of each type should be shown in full in plan, but all should be shown in cross-section.

Walls — only one bar of each type should be shown in full in elevation, but all should be shown in cross-section.

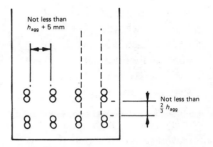

Figure 5.6   Requirements of clause 3.12.11.1 of BS 8110

The exception for both slabs and walls is where bars are staggered or alternate bars are reversed, when a pair of bars should be drawn in full.

For stirrups or links, only one stirrup or set of stirrups in a beam and only one link or set of links in a column need be shown in full. In all cases the spread of each group at the same spacing is indicated by a short line. The method will be discussed further in chapter 6.

Reinforcing bars are shown as single lines, 0.7 mm thick for main bars and 0.5 mm thick for links and stirrups.

Bars are described in a standard way using recognised abbreviations in the following sequence:

    Number of bars required
    Type of steel
    Size of bar
    Identification mark number
    Spacing — centre to centre
    Location
    Comment if any.

A typical bar description might read 24T20–03–200Babr, which would mean twenty-four high yield bars, 20 mm diameter, mark 3, at 200 mm centres in the bottom of the slab with alternate bars reversed. The recognised abbreviations are as follows.

For type of steel: R — grade 250 reinforcement (mild steel)
                    T — grade 460 type 2 reinforcement
                    S — stainless reinforcement
                    W — grade 460 plain reinforcement
                    D — grade 460 type 1 reinforcement
                    X — reinforcement of a type not included in the above list having material properties that are defined in the design or contract specification.

For location: T — top
              B — bottom
              NF — near face

FF   —   far face
EW   —   each way
EF   —   each face
abr   —   alternate bars
           reversed
stgd   —   staggered.

The description is linked to the bar it describes by a dimension line, with an arrowhead at the bar or two arrow heads to denote the spread of a set of bars in a slab or wall. The system is used in the examples in chapter 6, where there is also a variation shown for the description of the links in a column.

Each bar or set of bars must be described once only, usually where it is shown in full in plan or elevation. To do otherwise would risk the bar being scheduled twice, resulting in steel being supplied surplus ro requirements. For clarity the bar mark only should be repeated close to where the bar is shown in section.

If it is necessary to specify the start of a bar that does not run the full length of a member, this should be dimensioned from the outline of the member, which will appear as the face of the formwork to the steelfixer. Dimensions should not be given to centre-lines which are an abstract concept.

It will help the steelfixer if the mark numbers correspond to the order in which the bars will be installed in the formwork. It is usual to number the bars consecutively throughout the job, if it is a small job. On larger jobs it is preferred to start off with mark one on each drawing, for which a separate bar bending schedule will be prepared, so avoiding any confusion.

GENERAL PRINCIPLES FOR DRAWING

Reinforced concrete structures are usually broken down into elements for simplicity. One drawing may contain details of floor slabs, another columns and foundations and so on. Each drawing should give all the information necessary for the construction of that part of the structure, omitting other irrelevant detail.

The various elements are, however, part of an entire structure, with junctions between columns and beams and slabs, which necessitate the intersection of reinforcement. These junctions can be quite complicated, so it is advisable to indicate other reinforcement in broken lines, so that it is not forgotton. There should be cross-referencing between associated drawings.

All instructions given on drawings should be positive and perfectly clear as to their precise meaning. Written descriptions should be as brief as possible, consistent with completeness. Special requirements regarding the sequence of operations,

position and type of construction or movement joints, cambers, etc. should be given on the drawings. Sometimes a separate drawing is prepared to provide this information, together with sizes of members, sizes of holes for services, etc. There is a very real danger that reinforcement may coincide with holes, if they are not shown on the same drawing.

Generally details should be as simple as possible, for this leads to fewer errors and a better understanding of the designer's intentions by the builder.

TYPES OF DRAWINGS USED FOR REINFORCED CONCRETE

There are three main types of drawings prepared:

> General arrangement drawings
> Outline or profile drawings
> Reinforcement drawings.

The general arrangement drawing consists of plans, elevations and sections, drawn to a relatively small scale. It shows the layout of all the concrete work, a reference grid if appropriate (similar to that described for structural steelwork in chapter 3), the sizes of all members and setting-out dimensions.

Outline or profile drawings are optional and are more likely to be produced for larger more complicated structures. They will show to a larger scale the sizes of members, the size and position of holes and recesses, and details of any built-in fixing devices, etc. They are intended primarily for the use of the formwork carpenters.

Reinforcement drawings show the location of reinforcement in relation to the outline and to the relevant holes and fixings. Holes larger than 150 mm square or 250 mm diameter are usually provided with additional reinforcement around them to 'trim' the opening. These drawings are primarily for the use of the steelfixers.

CONSTRUCTION PROCEDURE AND ITS EFFECT ON DETAILING

Reference has already been made, in chapter 1, to the sequence of operations in the construction of a reinforced concrete building. The need to detail each element of the structure separately (base, column, beam, wall and slab) has been shown to meet the requirements of the builder. Similarly the positioning of construction joints permits the concrete to be placed in convenient quantities.

Reference has also been made to the difficulties that may occur where the elements of the structure meet. Two bars cannot occupy the same point in space — they have to be so positioned as to pass by each other. A typical example is where a floor meets a beam. The top steel in the floor slab must pass over or under (usually over) the top steel in the beam. Column and beam junctions can be even more difficult, particularly if they are of the same width, as is quite often the case. The detailer must expect guidance from the designer and, if it is not given, must request it. The arbitrary repositioning of steel could lead to weakness in the completed structure.

Where elements are repeated throughout the structure (many similar beams, many similar floor slabs) the builder likes to prefabricate the cages of reinforcement, if this is possible. It is much easier to do this at ground level and to lift the prefabricated cage or mat into position by crane. It is also quicker than the steelfixer assembling the reinforcement *in situ*, and hence saves on costs. For this reason long bars spanning more than one element are not liked. Instead each cage or mat is limited to the lift of a column, span of a beam or slab, and loose bars are placed where necessary, to link them up.

6. DETAILING REINFORCED CONCRETE

The examples used in this chapter are based upon *Designed and Detailed* by J.B. Higgins and M.R. Hollington, published by the Cement and Concrete Association. Reference to that publication will enable the reader with some knowledge of structural mechanics to discover how the structure was designed using the limit state principles of BS 8110, the code of practice for the structural use of concrete.

The working detailer will start from a knowledge of the areas of steel required at the various points in the structure and the rules governing the conversion of these areas into actual bar sizes and distribution. This is too advanced for many of the readers of this book, so the starting point adopted is where the sizes and spacings have been specified by the designer.

The structure is broken down into identifiable elements for detailing purposes — base, column, beam, floor slab, etc., which are dealt with in this chapter. Other elements are included in chapter 8.

DETAILING COLUMN BASES

Foundations to support columns vary according to the nature of the ground, the disposition of the columns and the magnitude of the loading that they sustain. They may be simple rectangular bases, supporting one or more columns, inverted tee-beams supporting a line of columns, or pile caps, transferring the load to piles previously driven into the ground. Only the simplest type will be dealt with in this chapter, leaving other types to be covered in chapter 8.

Figure 6.1 illustrates a typical base with the tensile reinforcement in the bottom shown in the plan view. A section indicates how the column rises out of the base and the position of the starter bars.

In the plan view, one bar only is shown in full in each direction and short lines are used to indicate the extremes of each group of similar bars. In this example fifteen 25 mm diameter high yield high bond bars (mark 1) are arranged at 200 mm centre to centre in the bottom of the base. They extend over the full width of the base, less twice the concrete cover at the ends. Sometimes the designer will ask for a bend to be formed at the ends to improve the anchorage.

In the elevation one column starter bar is shown in full, standing on the mat of tensile reinforcement. There are six 32 mm diameter high yield high bond bars (mark 2) in this example. The length projecting out of the base will be that required to bond the column bars adequately with the starter bars, in accordance with BS 8110 clause 3.12.8.11 or 'new CP 114' clauses 312h and 312m. This specifies a minimum compression lap of 15 bar diameters or 300 mm, whichever is the greater, to which must be added 75 mm for a kicker, giving a total projection of $15 \times 32 + 75 = 555$ mm. The length of the horizontal leg of the starter bars should be sufficient to rest on a number of bars in the bottom mat, say 300 mm in this case. The steelfixer will need to be able to tie them rigidly together for stability.

Also shown are two column links to stabilise and locate the column bars during concreting. Although they are the same as the column links, they will be scheduled separately, along with the other base reinforcement. In the example there are two 8 mm diameter mild steel bars (mark 3) at 300 mm centre to centre.

All the longitudinal bars in the column starter are indicated as solid blobs in the plan view and all the tension bars spanning at right angles to the paper, are indicated as blobs in the section. The mark numbers (only) are shown alongside a sufficient number of blobs to make it quite clear what they represent.

Note that each group of bars is described in full once only. This assists considerably in scheduling the reinforcement. To repeat the full description could result in double the number of bars being delivered to site.

Note the presence of grid lines, the levels of foundation and ground floor and the information about cover to the reinforcement.

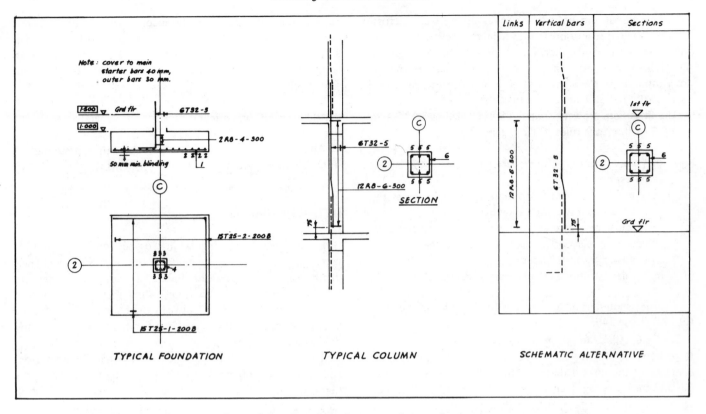

Figure 6.1   *Reinforced concrete base and column*

DETAILING COLUMNS

Columns may be square, rectangular, circular or any of a variety of shapes in cross-section. Theoretically they could get smaller as the loading decreases towards the top of the building. In practice they are usually kept the same size and the quantity of reinforcement is reduced. This is architecturally more acceptable.

Columns are detailed in elevation with sufficient cross-sections to show the arrangement of the longitudinal bars and the shape of the links. A typical column is illustrated in figure 6.1.

The longitudinal bars are shown in elevation by one bar drawn in full and a short line to show the extent of the others. If there is more than one type of bar (a different size or shape) then each type is treated separately. A dimension line is drawn across the set of bars, carrying their description, in this example six 32 mm diameter high yield high bond bars (mark 5).

These bars will stand on the kicker and therefore start 75 mm above the foundation or floor slab. Because they cannot occupy the same space as the starter bars (indicated by a broken line), they have to be cranked as shown. The extent of the crank will be twice the diameter of the bar, rounded up to the next 5 mm multiple. The slope of the crank should not be greater than 1 in 10 (BS 4466 shape code 41).

The alternatives to cranking are to butt the bars using proprietary splices or to butt them and fix splice bars alongside to transfer the load from the upper to the lower bar through the surrounding concrete. The length of such a splice will be 40 diameters plus 300 mm, that is a double splice length.

The longitudinal bars should be made long enough to act as starter bars for the next storey. They should therefore finish 15 x 32 mm x 1.4, plus 75 mm for the kicker, above the next floor level. The factor of 1.4 is used here because bending in the columns may introduce tension into the longitudinal bars and the cover is less than twice the size of the lapped reinforcement (BS 8110, clause 3.12.8.13). The actual laps will be determined by the designer, the rules for which are set out in part III and are too advanced for the reader at this stage.

The shape of the links is shown in the horizontal cross-section. Their distribution is shown in the elevation by one link drawn in full and a short line to indicate the extent of the set of links. A dimension line across the set carries the bar description, in this example sixteen 8 mm diameter mild steel bars (mark 6) at 300 mm centre to centre.

The links here are very simple, BS 8110 clauses 3.12.7.1 to 3.12.7.3 spell out the rules for links generally:

(a)   they must be at least one-quarter the size of the largest compression bar
(b)   they must be spaced at no more than twelve times the size of the smallest compression bar
(c)   there must be a change of direction of the link at each compression bar, of at least 45°, unless there is a re-strained bar within 150 mm
(d)   in circular columns a circular link is adequate.

The reader should compare these with the rules in the 'new CP 114' clause 346.

Figure 6.2 illustrates some of the ways links can be arranged to restrain the longitudinal bars in a column. In figure 6.1 the diameter of the links is derived from 8 mm, being a quarter of 32, and their spacing from 12 × 32 = 384 mm, say 300 mm. With three bars in a face, the middle bar need not have a link

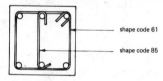

shape code 61

shape code 85

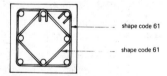

shape code 61

shape code 61

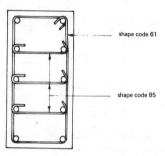

shape code 61

shape code 85

Figure 6.2   Some arrangements of links in columns

passing round it if the clear distance to a corner bar does not exceed 150 mm, and it does not in this case. (With four bars in a face, one of the intermediate bars has to be tied by an additional link, even if the distance to a corner bar is less than 150 mm.)

The structure's grid lines are marked on the section, which should have the same orientation as on the general arrangement drawing.

Also shown in figure 6.1 is an alternative presentation, suitable where there is repetition of elements.

DETAILING BEAMS

Beams are usually rectangular in cross-section. Their width is commonly the same as the columns that support them. Their depth usually includes the floor slab. Sometimes they are fully enclosed within the floor, when they become highly reinforced bands of floor between the columns. This has the advantage of providing a level soffit to the floor, without any downstanding beams.

The simplest beam has tensile reinforcement in the bottom and stirrup reinforcement to resist shearing forces across the depth of beam. Even if not required for strength, two small bars are provided in the top of the beam. Termed 'hanger bars', they are referred to as nominal reinforcement. These enable the stirrups to be supported at their tops and a rigid cage of reinforcement to be formed, which will not collapse when the concrete is placed.

In most construction, beams extend over several spans and are termed continuous beams. In such beams the tensile zone moves to the top over the supports, as is shown in figure 5.1. Accordingly there is an increase in the amount of reinforcement at the top of the beam.

Beams are detailed in elevation, with sufficient cross-sections to illustrate the positions of all the longitudinal bars and the shape of the stirrups. All descriptions of bars are given on the elevation and the bar marks only are repeated in the cross-sections.

Drawing no. 6.3 shows a detail of a typical beam, continuous over two bays. No attempt is made to draw the elevation to scale, as this would produce a long thin view. Instead the depth is exaggerated enough to make the detail clear, without making it look ridiculous. The cross-sections are drawn to a larger scale for the same reason.

The elevation shows the outlines of the supporting columns. The elevation is also a section through the intersecting edge beam and the floor slab. To make the drawing easier to read, the sections of the beam and slab are sometimes shaded. This

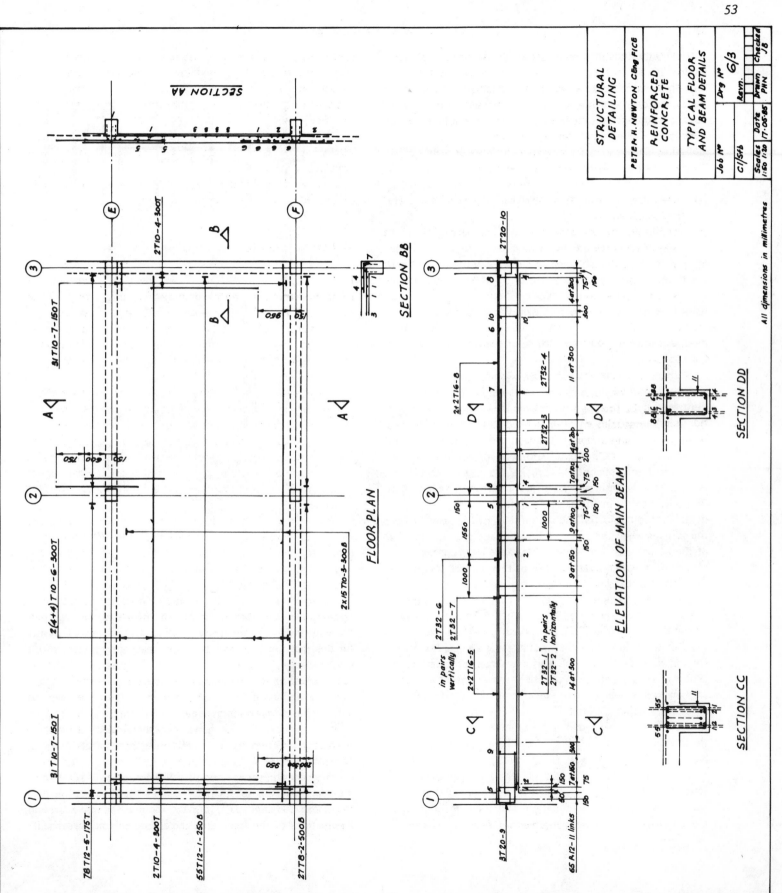

SECTION AA

FLOOR PLAN

ELEVATION OF MAIN BEAM

SECTION BB

SECTION DD

SECTION CC

STRUCTURAL
DETAILING

PETER H. NEWTON CEng FICE

REINFORCED
CONCRETE

TYPICAL FLOOR
AND BEAM DETAILS

Job N°

C1/SfB

Drg N° 6/3

Revn.

Scales   Date   Drawn   Checked
1:50 1:20 17·05·85   PHN   JB

All dimensions in millimetres

53

is commonly done in pencil on the back of the drawing paper or film.

Although there are several bars in the top and bottom of the beam, only one line is drawn to represent them. If a bar does not run the full length, its extremities are indicated by ticks, with the mark number of the beam concerned written alongside. This tick does not mean that the bar is bent.

The positions of the bars are given from the faces of the columns, that is the face of the formwork, rather than from the centre-lines of the columns, which are abstractions. This is easier for the steelfixer.

Over the support there are two layers of bars in the top of the beam, to cater for the high tensile forces in that area. They are placed in two layers so as to leave a gap in the middle of the beam for a poker vibrator to be inserted to compact the concrete. The bars mark 7 may be in contact with the bars mark 6 in this case as a vertical pair. If a vertical gap has to be maintained between two sets of bars, then spacer bars are used, as shown in figure 6.4. These spacer bars must be scheduled.

If there are many bars in a beam, one stirrup may not be enough and multiple stirrups are fixed in sets. Figure 6.5 illustrates how stirrups are commonly arranged in beams. Forms (a) and (b) show normal closed stirrups, (b) being used if the top bars are in compression, to provide lateral restraint to all the top bars. Form (c) shows open stirrups, since the floor slab reinforcement will provide the closing steel. Form (d) is a wide beam in which sufficient stirrups have been used to ensure rigidity of the cage. Form (e) is a deep beam where nominal face reinforcement of the sides of the beam stiffens the stirrups when the concrete is placed and prevents cracking of the beam sides. The use of open-topped stirrups makes the placing of long main bars easier, but then closers are required to complete the cage.

The main bars in the column have been indicated in broken line so that they are not forgotten when positioning the main bars in the beam. Note how bars marked 1, 4, 5 and 8 terminate short of the columns, as they would otherwise clash with the column bars. Continuity of reinforcement is provided by the U-bars marked 9 and 10 at the edge beams and by the straight bars marked 3, 6 and 7 over the central support. The importance of avoiding clashes of bars at intersections cannot be too strongly emphasised. It may be necessary to draw large-scale details of such intersections to investigate exactly what happens there.

Every main reinforcing bar or set of similar bars is described once only in full and their mark numbers only are used to indicate their terminations and their position in the cross-section.

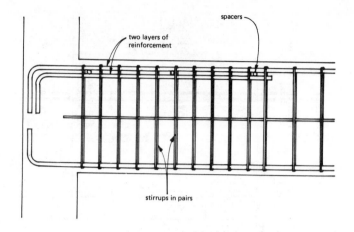

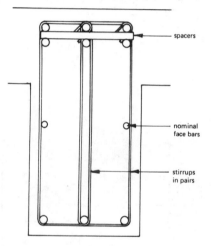

Figure 6.4   Provision of spacer bars

Stirrups are described in full in the elevation and their shape is shown in the sections. The shape and size of the stirrups may be the same, but their spacing may vary to suit the change in magnitude of the shearing forces along the beam. These are greater nearer the supports, so the stirrups are closer together there. The system of notation shown on drawing no. 6.3 is recommended.

Starting from the left-hand end, the first stirrup will be fixed about 25 mm from the ends of the bars marked 1 and 5. The next six are spaced 150 mm apart (remember when calculating quantities that seven bars will occupy only 900 mm of the beam, that is six spaces of 150 mm each). The next fourteen are spaced 300 mm apart, followed by nine 150 mm apart and finally nine 100 mm apart, and the central column is reached.

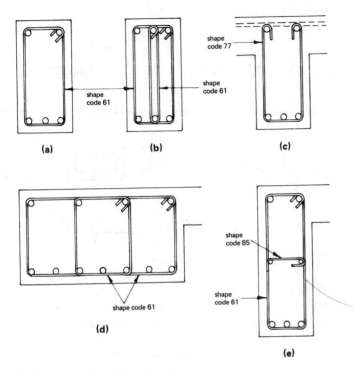

shape
code 77

shape
code 61

shape
code 61

(a)   (b)   (c)

shape
code 85

shape
code 61

shape code 61

(d)

(e)

Figure 6.5   Some arrangements of stirrups in beams

DETAILING FLOOR SLABS

Floor slabs are designed in different ways. The simplest span in one direction, supported by beams or walls along opposite sides. Alternatively they can be made to span in two directions at right angles and supported by beams on all four sides. There is also a type of floor that has no beams, but acts as a plate that is supported on columns alone. In this chapter simple slabs spanning in one direction will be dealt with.

Only in very small structures, such as garages, are slabs simply supported, that is just resting on their supports. In most constructions the floor is rigidly held at the sides or is extended over several supports and continuous, like the beam dealt with earlier. Like the beam, the tensile zone is at the bottom of the slab in the middle of the span and at the top over the supports.

Floor slabs are detailed in plan with sufficient sections to show the positioning of all reinforcement. Descriptions of bars are given in full on the plan view and the bar marks only are repeated in the sections. Dimensions to show the positions of the ends of bars should, if possible, be given in the sections, rather than on the plan.

Sets of similar bars should be indicated by one bar drawn in full and short lines to mark the extreme bars, with a dimension line across the set of bars carrying their description. Where bars are staggered or alternate bars are reversed, it is usual to show a pair of staggered or alternate bars in full on the plan.

No attempt is made to indicate the bent shape of the bars on the plan. This can be done in the sections. In thin slabs care must be taken to ensure that standard hooks and bends can be accommodated without reducing the cover.

Secondary or distribution steel is always provided in slabs. This spreads any point load sideways over the primary reinforcement and also combines with that reinforcement to form a rigid mat, which prevents bars being displaced by the wet concrete. BS 8110 clause 3.12.11.2.7 specifies the minimum amount of secondary reinforcement.

The lower layer of reinforcement is supported on spacers of thickness appropriate to the cover required, but the upper layer requires chairs to support it. Chairs may be formed out of reinforcement to support the upper layer, using code 99 of BS 4466, which requires a dimensional sketch to be drawn over columns A to E of the bending schedule. Proprietary chairs may be used in lieu if they are suitable.

Careful consideration must be given to the chairs as they frequently carry not only the weight of the upper steel, but also the weight of men and equipment. Where slabs are extensive, timber screeds are sometimes fixed to the top steel to determine the top level of the concrete. This may be con-

It is sensible to do a check calculation of the number and spacing of stirrups.

Half column	150 mm
First stirrup (50 + 25)	75
6 spaces at 150	900
15 spaces at 300	4500
9 spaces at 150	1350
8 spaces at 100	800
Last stirrup (50 +25)	75
Half column	150
total	8000 mm — which is the correct distance between the columns

Sometimes the shearing forces in the beam cannot be counteracted by stirrups alone. In this case bent-up bars are used as shown in figure 6.6. Instead of terminating bars no longer required for tensile purposes, they can be bent up (or down) through an angle of about 45°, so that they pass through the area where the shearing forces are at their greatest and help resist them. In very heavily loaded beams there may be more than one set of such bent-up bars.

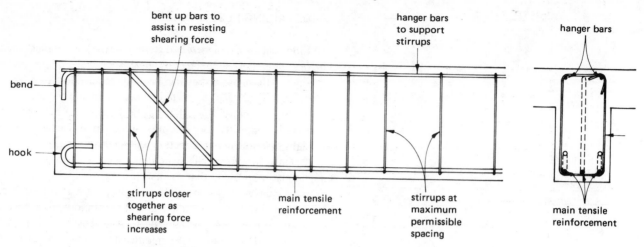

Figure 6.6   Use of bent-up bars to counteract heavy shearing forces

sidered a contractual obligation and the engineer must ensure that the builder provides these screeds. At least if chairs are scheduled, the deplorable practice of pulling the top layer up through the wet concrete as it is placed is avoided, so ensuring that the steel is in its correct place.

Beam reinforcement is shown in broken lines in the section to ensure that due consideration is given to its position relative to the slab steel. The upper reinforcement in the slab usually passes over the beam steel and in so doing may reduce the concrete cover, unless the beam steel is kept low enough.

If the slab is heavily reinforced, leading to a complicated drawing, the upper and lower layers may be shown on separate plan views.

BAR SCHEDULES

Scheduling is the listing of bars required for the reinforcement of concrete, using standard forms, printed in accordance with figure 6.7. This type of scheduling is no longer common commercial practice, but it is retained here so that students may practise preparing bar schedules from the details they draw. A separate schedule is prepared for each structural element, corresponding to the detail drawings, and bars required for multi-storey work are scheduled floor by floor.

Schedules are prepared by the detailer and used by the builder, the reinforcement supplier, the steelfixer, the clerk of works and the quantity surveyor. It is therefore essential that each schedule should be a document complete within itself — reference to other schedules and terms such as 'as before' and 'as first floor' should be avoided.

The term 'bar schedule' is used because the fabricator will probably prepare separate cutting and bending lists for his purposes. While the bar schedule is prepared in the sequence of the structural elements (foundations to roof), the cutting and bending lists are usually sorted into type and size of bar.

The schedules are referenced in their top right-hand corner with a six character reference, comprising the drawing number (001 to 999), followed by the sheet number (10 to 99) and a revision letter (A to Z), which is more than adequate for most jobs.

The schedule is completed as follows.

Column 1 — 'Member' means the structural element for which the bars are scheduled. It is customary to start with the foundations and progress through the building in the order that it is likely to be constructed.

Column 2 — 'Bar mark' means the serial number allocated to the bar on the detail drawing. It is customary to list bars in mark order, which is the order in which they will be assembled in the formwork.

Column 3 — 'Type & size' refers firstly to the type of steel — R, T, S, W, D or X as already instructed on page 47.
Size is the bar size, thus 25R means a 25 mm diameter mild steel bar.

Column 4 — 'No. of mbrs' means the number of similar elements that go to make up the structure.

Column 5 — 'No. of bars in each' means the number of similar bars of this mark in the member.

Column 6 — 'Total no.' means the product of columns 4 and 5.

			METRIC					Rev.

Name of company

METRIC
BAR SCHEDULE ref. ☐☐☐ ☐☐ ☐

Date Prepared by
Checked by

Site

Member	Bar mark	Type & size	No. of mbrs	No. of bars in each	Total no.	Length of each bar* mm	Shape. All dimensions** are in accordance with BS 4466 unless otherwise stated

*Specified to the nearest 25 mm. **Specified to the nearest 5 mm.

Figure 6.7   Bar schedule

Column 7 — 'Length of each bar mm' means what it says and can be calculated only when column 8 has been completed. This length is specified to the nearest 25 mm multiple.

Column 8 — 'Shape' is self-explanatory, but requires the amplification that follows.

HOOKS AND BENDS

The purpose of a hook or bend is to anchor the end of a bar subjected to a tensile force, in a shorter distance than would be required by a straight bar relying entirely on bonding between the steel and the surrounding concrete, to prevent it from slipping.

Standard hooks and bends were illustrated in figure 5.3, together with a table giving hook and bend allowances for bar sizes from 6 to 50 mm. Two sets of allowances are necessary because high yield steel cannot be bent to such a tight radius as mild steel.

THE SHAPE OF REINFORCEMENT

BS 4466 lists eighteen preferred shapes, which account for more than 95 per cent of bars used. By sticking to these preferred shapes, detailers can promote economy in fabrication and fixing, particularly now that most cutting and bending is numerically controlled.

Extracts from BS 4466 of the more common shapes are reproduced in part III. The four columns are self-explanatory. Against each shape code there is a picture of the bent bar, with the crucial dimensions lettered *A, B, C, D* and *E* as required. The dimensions *h* and *n* come from the table in figure 5.4, being the hook allowance and bend allowance respectively, and *r* is the radius of the former around which the bars are bent.

In the third column is the formula to convert these dimensions into the total length of the bar for cutting purposes.

In the fourth column is the line diagram as it should appear on the bar schedule, together with the dimensions that should be given. Note that the word 'straight' is used instead of a straight line for code 20. Note also that hooks and bends are not dimensioned and, where there is more than one dimension, as in the case of codes 37, 38, 41, etc., the last dimension is bracketed. If the total length of the bar has been calculated correctly, the last dimension will be what is left of the bar.

Note that dimension *D* in shape code 41 is taken to the outside faces of the cranked bar.

Note that the dimensions for the stirrup (shape code 61) are external dimensions and that the distances *A* and *B* are written outside the stirrup accordingly.

Where bars are bent in two planes an isometric view of the bar is drawn and the fact noted. Alternatively two orthogonal views can be drawn.

The reader should refer to table 2 of BS 4466 for the dimensions of the other shapes, which include some useful additional stirrup shapes.

COMPUTERISED BAR SCHEDULES

The bar schedule illustrated in figure 6.7 necessitated small dimensioned diagrams to show the shape of the bent bar. But BS 4466 already specifies these shapes and the dimensions *A* to *E* to produce the required size. It is not difficult to write a program to convert the shape code and appropriate dimensions into instructions to a machine. The form illustrated in figure 6.8 comes from BS 4466 and is recommended for this purpose.

COMPLETED BAR SCHEDULES

Figures 6.9 and 6.10 give examples of completed forms, in this case for the beam from drawing no. 6.3. The manuscript notes in the margin are those of the scheduler who has calculated the bar dimensions.

				METRIC								

BAR SCHEDULE ref. ☐☐☐ ☐☐ ☐ Rev.

Date   Prepared by
      Checked by

Site

Member	Bar mark	Type & size	No. of mbrs	No. of bars in each	Total no.	Length of each bar* mm	Shape code	A** mm	B** mm	C** mm	D** mm	E/r** mm

*Specified to the nearest 25 mm.   **Specified to the nearest 5 mm.
This schedule complies with BS 4466.

Figure 6.8   Computer bar schedule

EBRAN CONCRETE CO. LTD

METRIC
BAR SCHEDULE ref. 063 02 Rev.

Date 7/5/85 Prepared by WB
Checked by JS

Site LABORATORY & OFFICE BLOCK

	Member	Bar mark	Type & size	No. of mbrs	No. of bars in each	Total no.	Length of each bar* mm	Shape. All dimensions** are in accordance with BS 4466 unless otherwise stated	
8000 -150 -50 -150 -50	MAIN BEAMS	1	T32	6	2	12	7600	Straight	
8000 -150 -50 -150 -150	(ROWS C–H)	2	T32	6	2	12	6100	Straight	
1000 + 300 + 1000		3	T32	6	2	12	2300	Straight	
		4	T32	6	2	12	5600	Straight	
		5	T16	6	4	24	7600	Straight	
		6	T32	6	2	12	7000	Straight	
		7	T32	6	2	12	4400	Straight	
As 4		8	T16	6	4	24	5600	Straight	
800 -35 +75 + 1060 = 1390 500 -70 -60		9	T20	6	3	18	3075	370, 1400	1400 1400 370 3170 -60 -40
		10	T20	6	3	18	3150	430, 1400	do + 60
500 -70 430		11	R12	6	65	390	1575	430, 230	2[430 + 230] + 20 × 12 = 1560

*Specified to the nearest 25 mm. **Specified to the nearest 5 mm.

Figure 6.9

EBRAN CONCRETE CO. LTD

METRIC
BAR SCHEDULE ref. | 0 | 6 | 3 | | 0 | 2 | Rev. ☐

Date 7/5/85 Prepared by WB
Checked by JS

Site LABORATORY & OFFICE BLOCK

Member	Bar mark	Type & size	No. of mbrs	No. of bars in each	Total no.	Length of each bar* mm	Shape code	A** mm	B** mm	C** mm	D** mm	E/r** mm
MAIN BEAMS	1	T32	6	2	12	7600	20	7600				
(ROWS C-H)	2	T32	6	2	12	6100	20	6100				
	3	T32	6	2	12	2300	20	2300				
	4	T32	6	2	12	5600	20	5600				
	5	T16	6	4	24	7600	20	7600				
	6	T32	6	2	12	7000	20	7000				
	8	T16	6	4	24	5600	20	5600				
	9	T20	6	3	18	3075	38	1400	370			
	10	T20	6	3	18	3150	38	1400	430			
	11	R12	6	65	390	1575	60	430	230			

*Specified to the nearest 25 mm. **Specified to the nearest 5 mm.

Figure 6.10

Part II

This part covers the aims and objectives in B/TEC unit *Structural Detailing III* and is suitable as a second year of study for students of architecture, building and civil engineering

7. FURTHER STRUCTURAL STEELWORK

Chapter 4 provided examples of simple column and beam construction, used in the framework of buildings such as flats, offices and schools. Steel is a very versatile material that has been used to produce some of the most famous structures in the world — the Forth Bridge in Scotland, the Humber Bridge in England, the Howrah Bridge in India, the Eiffel Tower in France, the Hancock Center in the USA, the Sydney Bridge in Australia — the list is endless. It is used for factories, warehouses, hangars, gantries, transmission lines, oil rigs and so on.

This chapter takes the art of detailing a small step forward, to look at lattice construction, portal frames and plate girders.

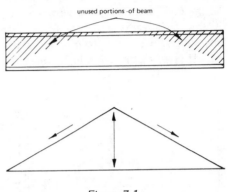

Figure 7.1

LATTICE CONSTRUCTION

A beam supports its load through a combination of compressive forces in the top flange and tensile forces in the bottom flange — known as its moment of resistance. This moment has to be greater than the moment causing the beam to bend. This is greatest at the middle of the span and virtually nil at the supports, so much of the potential strength of the beam is wasted.

Lattice construction is one way of overcoming the problem presented by a roof. Universal beams could be used, but they would be very heavy and relatively costly. Lattice construction means that the beam can be made deeper in the middle of the span and tapered towards the supports. This has the additional advantage of offering a sloping surface to the cladding, which will encourage rain and snow to run off. Figure 7.1 illustrates the point.

Because the depth at the centre can be made quite considerable, much less steel is required to provide an adequate moment of resistance. The lattice roof truss is therefore much lighter and relatively cheaper.

But lattice construction can have parallel top and bottom chords, like a universal beam, if the situation requires it. Later in this chapter a walkway has been used as an example, where the top of the girder is a walking surface and has to be level.

TRIANGULATION

Lattice construction is based on the principle that a three-sided pin-jointed frame is rigid. Figure 7.2 shows how by joining many triangles together large spans can be achieved.

Each member of the trusses illustrated is either a tie in tension or a strut in compression. Because they are pin-jointed, no bending forces are introduced. The calculation of the magnitude and type of force in each member is part of structural mechanics.

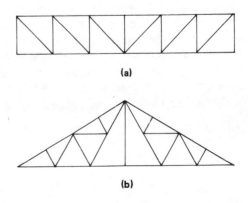

Figure 7.2   Triangulation: (a) N-girder, (b) roof truss

65

To ensure that bending is not introduced, the members must be axially loaded, that is the line of the force must coincide with the centroid of the cross-section of the member.

CENTROID OF CROSS-SECTION

The centroid of a symmetrical section is easily found at the centre of the section — figure 7.3. The sections used in lattice construction tend to be angles and tees, which are asymmetrical sections and the position of the centroid has to be calculated. Fortunately this has already been done for standard sections and the dimensions C, C_x and C_y can be found in the section tables in part III (where the centroid is called the centre of gravity).

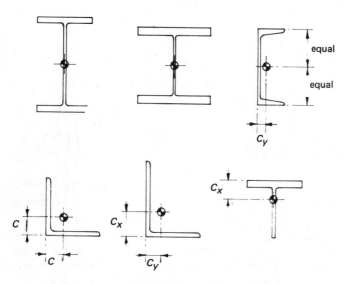

Figure 7.3   Centroid of a rolled steel section

When detailing a truss the members are laid out in such a way that the loci of their centroids lie on the lines of the force diagram, so that they meet at points, known as 'nodes' — figure 7.4. In order to make the drawing compact, yet easy to read, it is common for trusses to be drawn with joints at a larger scale than the truss layout, but correctly located at the nodes. Drawing no. 7.5 illustrates a welded roof truss drawn in this way.

FABRICATION OF TRUSSES

Originally riveting was the commonest way of joining the members of a truss. This was done through flat plates, known as gussets. With the development of welding, the fabrication

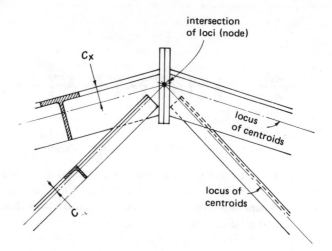

Figure 7.4   Node at the apex of a lattice truss

method illustrated in drawing no. 7.5 superseded riveting. It had several advantages — it dispensed with gussets, presented clean lines and tees were used for the rafters and bottom chords, instead of twin angles. These angles were riveted either side of the gusset plate, so that there was a gap of 8 or 10 millimetres between them. This gap was difficult to paint and keep clean.

The introduction of numerically controlled cropping and hole punching machines has seen a move away from welding to bolting, which in many respects is similar to riveting (the spacing rules in BS 449 are the same for bolting and riveting), with its disadvantages. The advantage is the cost saving of automated methods over the more labour-intensive welding.

A typical bolted roof truss is illustrated in drawing no. 7.6. The centroid rule has been varied in this case and the back mark line has been made to coincide with the force line. This is done simply for convenience and to reduce the possibility of error in the fabrication shop, owing to the presence of too many lines. The 80 × 60 × 6 angle has a C_x value of 24.7 mm and a back mark of 45 mm, so there is a 20 mm discrepancy. This is acceptable for the small truss illustrated, but for large, heavily loaded trusses the C_x value should be used to avoid eccentric loading.

Another dispensation concerns some of the gussets. Consider the gusset at the middle of the rafter. Theoretically it should look like (a) in figure 7.7, but this would result in rather a large gusset plate — even bigger if the centroid rule had been observed. The alternative, known as 'nesting', shown in (b) is acceptable if the designer allows for it in his calculations.

Note that the twin angles are bolted together between the joints to prevent the two angles spreading apart under their axial compressive force.

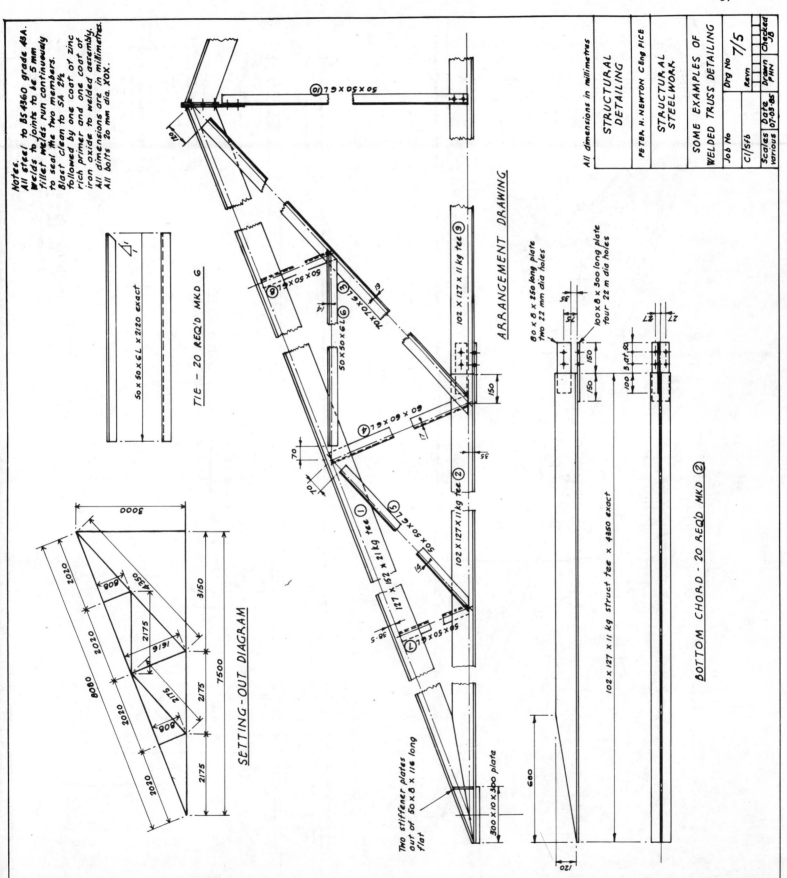

67

Notes.
All steel to BS 4360 grade 43A.
Welds to joints to be 5 mm
fillet welds run continuously
to seal the two members.
Blast clean to SA 2½
followed by one coat of zinc
rich primer and one coat of
iron oxide to welded assembly.
All dimensions are in millimetres.
All bolts 20 mm dia. XOX.

TIE – 20 REQ'D MKD 6

50 x 50 x 6L x 2120 exact

SETTING-OUT DIAGRAM

ARRANGEMENT DRAWING

Two stiffener plates
out of 50 x 8 x 116 long
flat

300 x 10 x 300 plate

80 x 8 x 250 long plate
two 22 mm dia holes

100 x 8 x 300 long plate
four 22 mm dia holes

102 x 127 x 11 kg struct tee x 4350 exact

BOTTOM CHORD – 20 REQ'D MKD 2

All dimensions in millimetres

STRUCTURAL
DETAILING

PETER H. NEWTON CEng FICE

STRUCTURAL
STEELWORK

SOME EXAMPLES OF
WELDED TRUSS DETAILING

Job No	Drg No	7/5
CI/Sfb	Revn	
Scales various	Date 07·03·85	Drawn PHN
		Checked JB

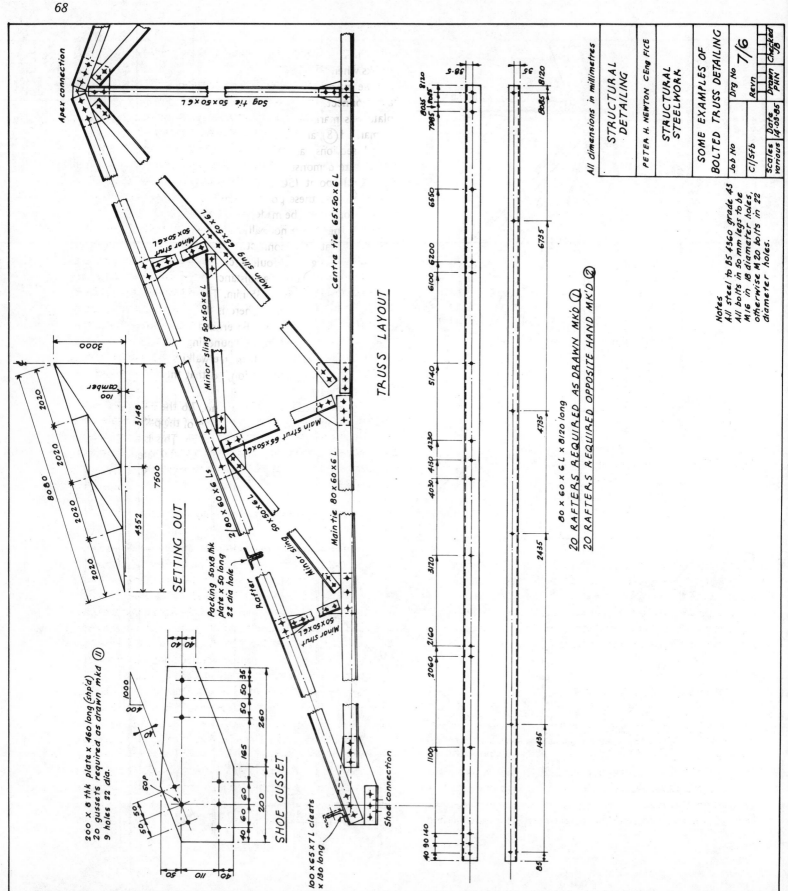

SETTING OUT

TRUSS LAYOUT

SHOE GUSSET

Apex connection

Sag tie 50×50×6 L

Minor sling 65×50×6 L

Minor strut 50×50×6 L

Main sling 50×50×6 L

Centre tie 65×50×6 L

Main strut 65×50×6 L

2/80×60×6 L

Minor strut 50×50×6 L

Minor sling 50×50×6 L

Main tie 80×60×6 L

Rafter

Packing 50×8 thk plate × 50 long 22 dia hole

Shoe connection

100×65×7 L cleats × 130 long

200 × 8 thk plate × 460 long (shp'd)
20 gussets required as drawn mkd (11)
9 holes 22 dia.

3000
100 camber
8080   2020   2020   2020   2020
2020
3148
7500
4552
1000
400
40 40
50 50 35
50 50
260
165
200
40 60 60
40 60 60
50P   50P
50
110
40

80 × 60 × 6 L × 8120 long
20 RAFTERS REQUIRED AS DRAWN MK'D (1)
20 RAFTERS REQUIRED OPPOSITE HAND MK'D (2)

38·5
8120
8035   8085
7985   8035
6650
6200   6100
5140
4230
4030   4130   4130
4735
3720
6735
2160
2060   2060
2435
1100
1435
40 90 140

35
8120
8085
85

All dimensions in millimetres

STRUCTURAL DETAILING

PETER H. NEWTON CEng FICE

STRUCTURAL STEELWORK

SOME EXAMPLES OF BOLTED TRUSS DETAILING

Job No
C1/5fb

Drg No 7/6

Revn

Drawn PHN   Checked JB

Scales various   Date 14·03·85

Notes
All steel to BS 4360 grade 43
All bolts in 50 mm legs to be
M16 in 18 diameter holes,
otherwise M20 bolts in 22
diameter holes.

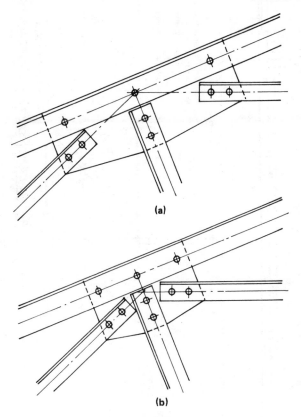

(a)

(b)

*Figure 7.7   Treatment of large gusset to reduce it in size:
(a) loci of back mark lines meeting at node,
(b) internal members nested*

Trusses are quite large when assembled and can be delivered to site completely knocked down or in two halves. Even in the welded truss the apex joint is partly bolted and the centre tie and sag tie are loose pieces. The sag tie is to prevent the centre tie sagging, as its name implies. In either case the truss is assembled on the ground before erection.

DETAILING OF LATTICE FRAMES

The individual pieces of the frame have to be detailed separately for fabrication. The walkway, partly illustrated in drawing no. 7.8, consists of a box section, triangulated to give it strength in both horizontal and vertical planes. The four main corner members are 120 x 120 x 8 angles and one length is detailed on drawing no. 7.9. Angle purlins, rails, bracings, etc. should, whenever possible, be detailed with the outstanding

legs on the far side. This method helps considerably in the works when marking off.

The main members are braced together with smaller angles and connected with gussets. Sometimes these are plain flat plates, as marked ⑦, sometimes they are welded assemblies, as marked ⑧, and sometimes they are formed out of standard rolled sections, as marked ⑲. The principles of detailing gussets are demonstrated by these typical examples. Note the setting-out point (SOP) in each and the way all dimensions relate back to these points, including the angles at which the connections are to be made.

Gusset plates are normally kept back from the edges of the members that they connect. This is to avoid any danger of their projecting and fouling connecting assemblies. In the gusset marked ⑦ the edge distance of the holes, connecting to the angle marked ⑤, is 35 mm. The back mark for a 120 x 120 x 8 angle is 45 mm. There is therefore a nominal margin of 10 mm, but this could be eroded by hole clearances and inaccuracies in guillotining and punching.

The durbar plates that form the walking surface are 10 mm narrower than the box section, so that they do not foul the handrail standards.

In the bolted truss in drawing no. 7.6 the rafter angles are detailed. To save time only one angle of the pair is drawn and the other is said to be of opposite hand. This is acceptable to the fabrication shop, but each must be allocated a separate mark number, so as to avoid mistakes in assembly.

PORTAL FRAMED CONSTRUCTION

Portal frames consist of two uprights, rigidly connected at the top by a third member, which may be horizontal, sloping or curved. The pitched portal frame provides an alternative to the lattice roof truss, over which it has several advantages.

Drawing no. 7.10 illustrates a typical pitched portal frame, consisting of universal beam rafters supported on universal beam columns. The junctions at the ridge and the eaves are strongly connected so as to transmit bending moments and their depth is increased accordingly at these points.

Unlike the lattice truss, the roof space can be fully used and there are no ties to limit the use of fork lift trucks. The surface area of the beams is less than that of the angles and tees of the lattice truss. The structure is easier to keep clean and to paint, thus resulting in lower maintenance costs.

Drawings nos 7.11 and 7.12 illustrate the detailing of the columns and rafters for this frame, and also a valley beam to support alternate rafters and so reduce the obstruction caused by columns. These drawings are based on an actual structure

SIDE ELEVATION
(VIEWED ON AA)

TYPICAL CROSS-SECTION

Handrail standards 60 × 60 × 8 L.
Handrailing 20 mm bore tube.
Kick plate 100 × 10 flat.

SECTION DD

2/M20 × 320 long H D bolts and nuts with 1/100 × 10 thk anchor flat to each bolt

110 wide × 12 thick rubber bearing pad

PLAN ON LH END
(SHEWING FOUNDATION BOLTS SET OUT)

PART OF DRAWING OF WALKWAY

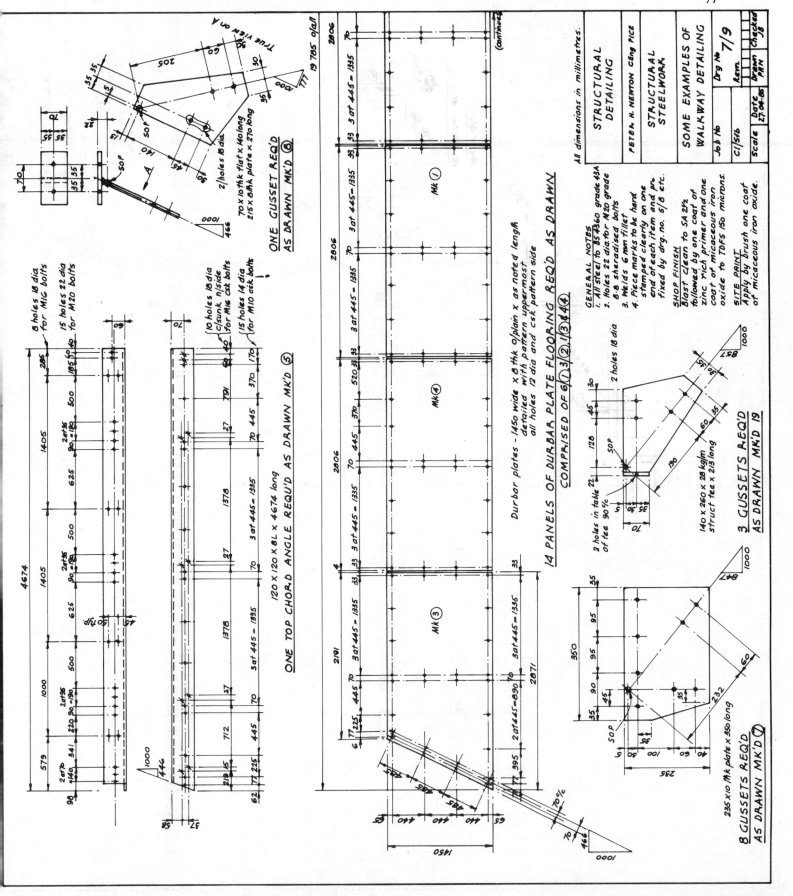

ONE GUSSET REQ'D
AS DRAWN MK'D ⑥

ONE TOP CHORD ANGLE REQU'D AS DRAWN MK'D ⑤

14 PANELS OF DURBAR PLATE FLOORING REQ'D AS DRAWN
COMPRISED OF 6①3②①③&④

Durbar plates - 1450 wide x 8 thk o/plain x as noted length
detailed with pattern uppermost
all holes 12 dia and csk pattern side

3 GUSSETS REQ'D
AS DRAWN MK'D 19

8 GUSSETS REQ'D
AS DRAWN MK'D ①

All dimensions in millimetres.

STRUCTURAL
DETAILING

PETER H. NEWTON CEng FICE

STRUCTURAL
STEELWORK

SOME EXAMPLES OF
WALKWAY DETAILING

Job No
Cl/Sfb
Scale | Date
27.04.85

Drg No 7/9
Rev.
Drawn PHN | Checked JB

GENERAL NOTES
1. All steel to BS 4360 grade 43A
2. Holes 22 dia for M20 grade
   8.8 sheradised bolts
3. Welds 6 mm fillet
4. Piece marks to be hard
   stamped clearly on one
   end of each item and pro-
   fixed by drg. no. 5/8 etc.

SHOP FINISH
Blast clean to SA 2½
followed by one coat of
zinc rich primer and one
coat of micaceous iron
oxide to TDFS 150 microns.

SITE PAINT
Apply by brush one coat
of micaceous iron oxide.

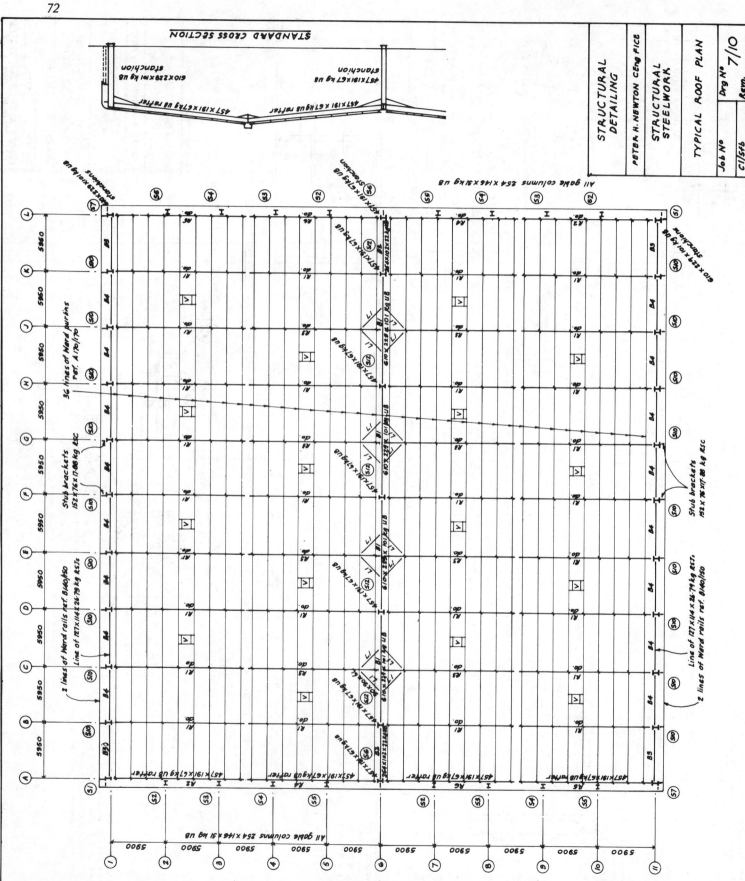

STANDARD CROSS SECTION

STRUCTURAL DETAILING

PETER H. NEWTON CEng FICE

STRUCTURAL STEELWORK

TYPICAL ROOF PLAN

Job N°	Drg N° 7/10
C1/Stb	Rev.
	Scale	Date	Drawn	Checked

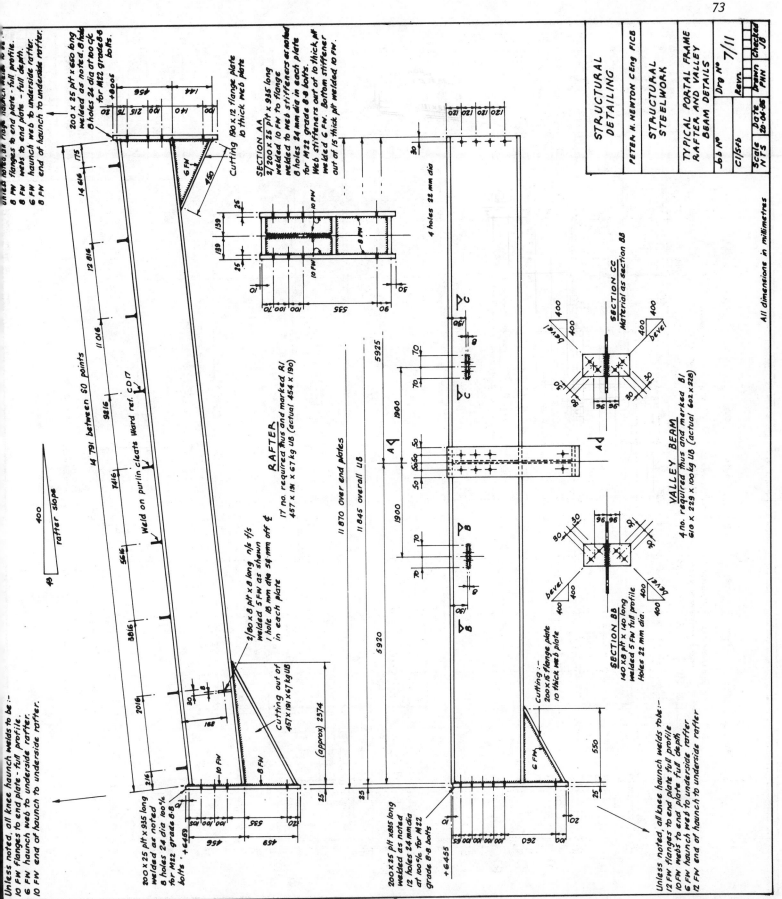

All dimensions in millimetres

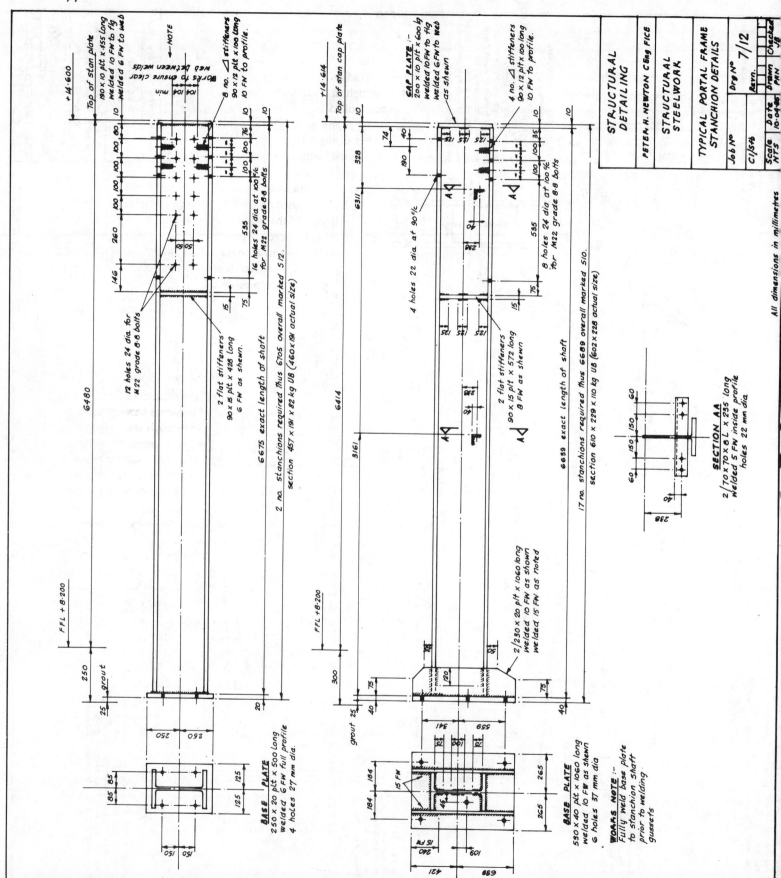

All dimensions in millimetres

STRUCTURAL
DETAILING

PETER H. NEWTON CEng FICE

STRUCTURAL
STEELWORK

TYPICAL PORTAL FRAME
STANCHION DETAILS

Job N°   Drg N°   7/12

CI/SfB   Revn.

Scale   Date   Drawn   Checked
NTS   10 Oct 85   PHN   HB

BASE PLATE
250 x 20 plt x 500 long
welded 6 FW full profile
4 holes 27 mm dia.

BASE PLATE :-
550 x 40 plt x 1060 long
welded 10 FW as shown
6 holes 37 mm dia

WORKS NOTE :-
Fully weld base plate
to stanchion shaft
prior to welding
gussets

SECTION AA
2/70x70x6 L x 255 long
welded 5 FW inside profile
holes 22 mm dia.

Top of stan plate

190 x 10 plt x 455 long
welded 10 FW to flg
welded 6 FW to web

8 no. △ stiffeners
90 x 12 plt x 100 long
10 FW to profile.

△ stiffeners
WORKS to ensure clear
web between welds
NOTE

12 holes 24 dia for
M22 grade 8.8 bolts

16 holes 24 dia at 100 %
for M22 grade 8.8 bolts

2 flat stiffeners
90 x 15 plt x 428 long
6 FW as shewn

6675 exact length of short

2 no. stanchions required thus 6705 overall marked S12.
Section 457 x 191 x 82 kg UB (460x191 actual size)

2/230 x 20 plt x 1060 long
welded 10 FW as shown
welded 15 FW as noted

CAP PLATE :-
200 x 10 plt x 600 lg
welded 10 FW to flg
welded 6 FW to web
as shewn

Top of stan cap plate

4 no. △ stiffeners
90 x 12 plt x 100 long
10 FW to profile.

4 holes 22 dia at 90 %

8 holes 24 dia at 100 %
for M22 grade 8.8 bolts

2 flat stiffeners
90 x 15 plt x 572 long
8 FW as shewn

6689 exact length of shaft

17 no. stanchions required thus 6689 overall marked S10.
section 610 x 229 x 110 kg UB (602 x 228 actual size)

15 FW

and the method of detailing is that used by the manufacturer. The system of symbols for welding, described in BS 499, could equally well have been used.

At 30 metres this is quite a large span for this type of construction. For smaller spans simpler joints can be used. Figure 7.13 illustrates typical eaves and ridge connections, suitable for 10 to 15 metre spans. Even smaller frames can have the ridge joint completed in the fabrication shop, and the two rafters sent to site in one piece.

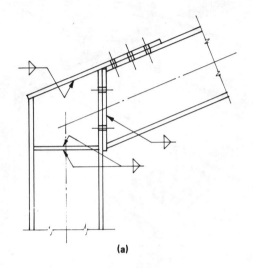

(a)

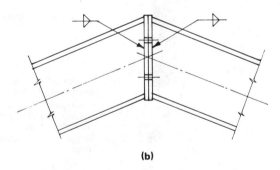

(b)

Figure 7.13 Connections for small pitched portal frames: (a) eaves connection, (b) ridge connection

THE CLADDING OF STEEL STRUCTURES

The roof is usually covered with corrugated sheeting made of steel, aluminium or fibre cement. The walls can follow suit or be made of solid materials, such as brick or concrete block. If corrugated materials are to be used there has to be a means of fixing them to the steel framework, usually purlins and hook bolts.

Traditionally purlins have been hot rolled angles, bolted through angle cleats to the tops of the rafters. More recently cold rolled sections have been developed to provide an economical and efficient alternative. Cold rolled sections have a higher strength to weight ratio, can be accurately formed and are supplied with a galvanised finish. A typical system is shown in figures 7.14 and 7.15.

These illustrations are from the catalogue of the proprietary system that was used on the portal framed building in drawing no. 7.10. Tables of the sections used in this system and the zed purlins are reproduced in part III with the permission of the suppliers. Their systems are extensive and in no way represented by these tables. The reader is recommended to write to the companies to obtain copies of their manuals for commercial use.

WELDED PLATE GIRDERS

The largest section rolled is a 914 x 419 x 388 kg universal beam. If a larger beam is required then castellated beams are available. These consist of standard universal beams that have been cut in two along a zig-zag line through their webs. The two halves are then rejoined by welding together the crests of the zig-zag, as shown in figure 7.16. The resulting beam is then 50 per cent deeper and approximately 50 per cent stronger than the original beam. The same is done to produce castellated columns.

If an even stronger beam is required, then it has to be made. Originally this was done by joining flat plates, forming the flanges, to a flat plate, forming the web, by means of continuous riveted angle cleats. The *Structural Steel Handbook* still carries tables of the section properties of the flange plates, web plate and sets of angles for the design of riveted plate girders. Many examples of these can be found in bridges built during the first half of the century.

Nowadays plate girders are welded in the factory in lengths as long as can be conveniently transported to site, where they are either bolted or welded together. Because of the expertise that has to be provided, site welding is avoided, unless there is enough to make it worth employing the necessary plant and welders. Bolted connections use HSFG bolts, as shown in figure 7.18.

Drawing no. 7.17 illustrates a typical plate girder. Note how the flange plates reduce in thickness as the bending moment reduces towards the supports. If the change in thickness were too abrupt, an increase in stress concentration could occur, so

Double Span Purlins

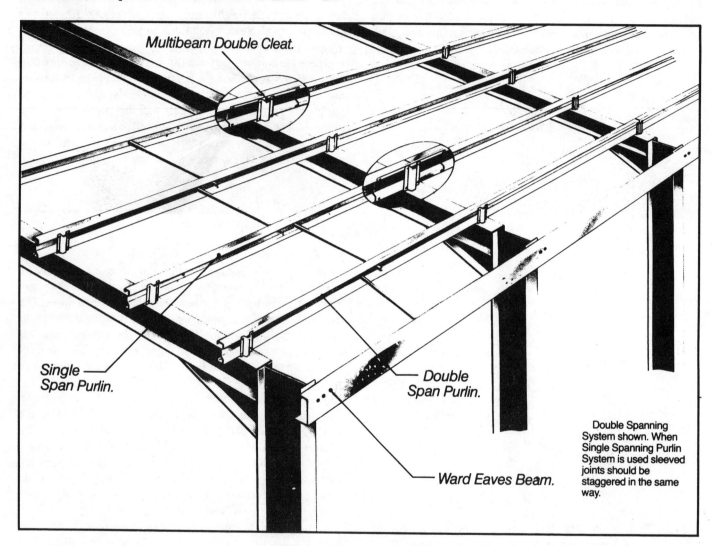

Multibeam Double Cleat.

Single
Span Purlin.

Double
Span Purlin.

Ward Eaves Beam.

Double Spanning
System shown. When
Single Spanning Purlin
System is used sleeved
joints should be
staggered in the same
way.

Figure 7.14   Proprietary cold rolled purlin system

Weld on Cleat

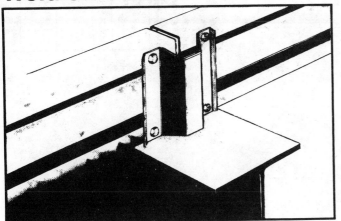

Bolt on Cleat

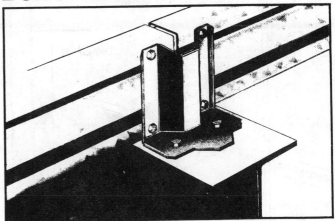

Figure 7.15   Proprietary purlin cleats

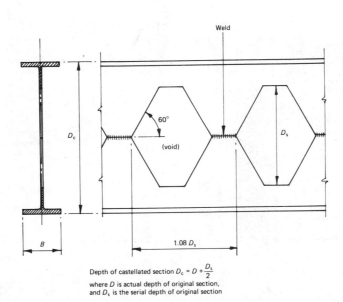

Depth of castellated section $D_c = D + \dfrac{D_s}{2}$
where D is actual depth of original section,
and D_s is the serial depth of original section

Figure 7.16   Castellated universal beam

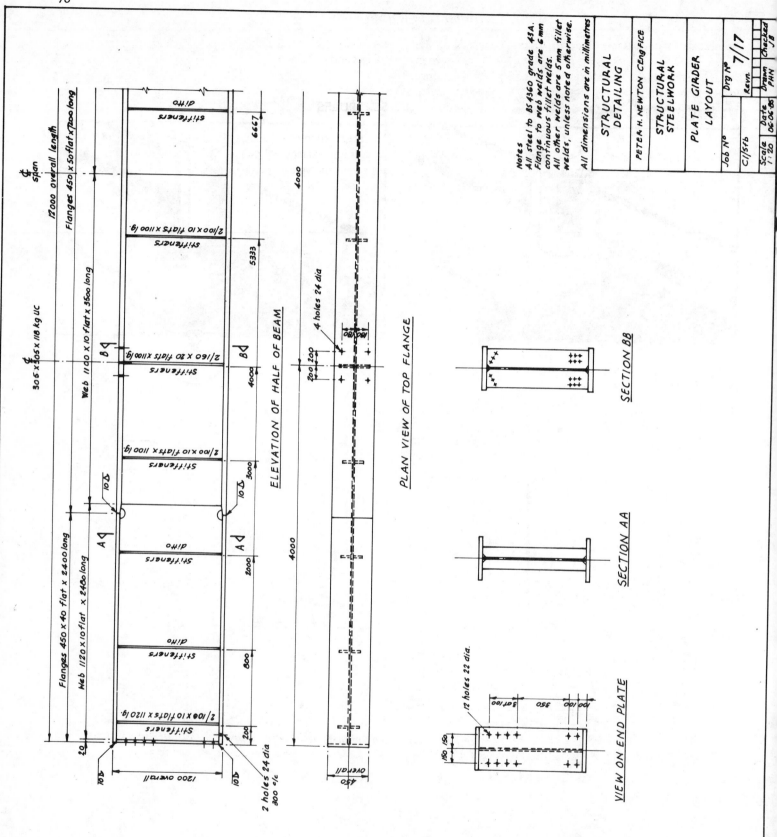

the thicker plate is tapered down to the thickness of the thinner plate, with a slope not steeper than 1 in 4, as shown in figure 7.19. Note the cope holes in the web where the flange welds occur. The figure also illustrates a bottom flange prepared for downhand welding, that is from above. If the girder is joined by welding on site, then it is easier and quicker to do it in this way.

Because the web is so slender, it could easily buckle under load. To prevent this happening, stiffeners are welded between the top and bottom flanges. Note how the inside corners of these stiffeners are cropped off to clear the welds between flanges and web.

SCHEDULES

The preparation of schedules was dealt with in chapter 4 and very simple examples were given. On pages 80, 81, 82 and 83 are copies of typical schedules for the walkway illustrated on drawing no. 7.8.

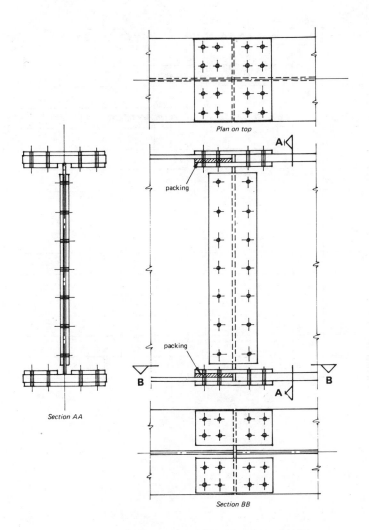

Figure 7.18   Typical bolted splice in a plate girder

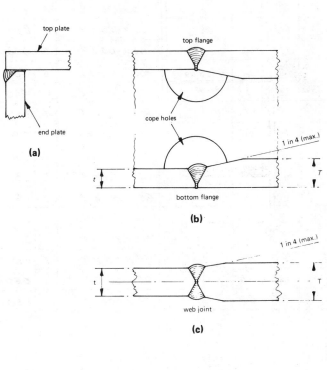

Figure 7.19   Plate girder joints: (a) end plate to flanges, (b) flange to flange — bottom flange arranged for downhand welding, (c) web to web

Material by A J CHAPEL
Checked by
Weights by
Checked by

DRAWING OFFICE MATERIAL LIST

PRELIMINARY/~~FINAL~~
ORDER No. S319 ~ WALKWAY

Sheet No. 1A
Drawing No.
Date 15/9/84

Item No	Location	No Regd		Description	Size	Length		Note	Pre Sheet Item No.	Total Linear Metres	Kilograms Per Metre	Total weight in Kg	Ordered From	Order Book Folio
		In I	In			m	mm							
1	(1)	4		ANGLE	120 x 120 x 8	~~9~~	~~000~~	9200	O.K.	CONFIRMED WITH K. MANSTED			16/9/84	
2	(2)	6			120 x 120 x 8	5	400							
3	(3)	1			120 x 120 x 8	5	450							
4	(4)	1			120 x 120 x 8	4	800							
5	(5)	4			100 x 100 x 8	~~9~~	~~000~~	9200	O.K.	CONFIRMED WITH K. MANSTED			16/9/84	
6	(6)	6			100 x 100 x 8	5	400							
7	(7)	1			100 x 100 x 8	5	450							
8	(8)	1			100 x 100 x 8	4	800							
9	(9)	58			100 x 65 x 8	1	250							
10	(10)	2			100 x 65 x 8	1	500							
11	(11)	28			65 x 50 x 8	2	000							
12	(12)	12			65 x 50 x 8	1	260							
13	(13)	3			100 x 100 x 8	1	260							
14	(14)	1			100 x 100 x 8	1	500							
15	(15)	16			65 x 50 x 8	1	850							
16	(16)	60			65 x 50 x 8	1	060							
17	(17)	56			65 x 50 x 8	1	850							
18														

MY 73044 D

Material by .... *T.N. HARDY* ....

Checked by ....

Weights by ....

Checked by ....

DRAWING OFFICE MATERIAL LIST

~~PRELIMINARY~~/FINAL

ORDER No. *5319 – WALKWAY*

Sheet No. ..... *1* .....

Drawing No. ..... *5319/1* .....

Date ..... *12-10-84* .....

ItemNo	Location	No Reqd In I	No Reqd In	Description	Size	Length m	Length mm	Note	Pre Sheet ItemNo.	Total Linear Metres	Kilograms Per Metre	Total weight in Kg			Ordered From	Order Book Folio
1		,	3	TOP CHORD ANGLES REQ'D MKD ①												
2		/	3	ANGLE	120 X 120 X 8L	5	287		(2)	5·287	14·7		7	8		
3										WT IN 3		2	3	4		
4			4	TOP CHORD ANGLES REQ'D MKD ②												
5		/	4	ANGLE	120 X 120 X 8L	9	200		(1)	9·200	14·7		1	3	5	
6										WT IN 4		5	4	0		
7			3	TOP CHORD ANGLES REQ'D MKD ③												
8		/	3	ANGLE	120 X 120 X 8L	5	287		(2)	5·287	14·7		7	8		
9										WT IN 3		2	3	4		
10				ONE TOP CHORD ANGLE REQ'D MKD ④												
11		/	/	ANGLE	120 X 120 X 8L	5	298		(3)	5·298	14·7		7	8		
12										TOTAL WT			7	8		
13				ONE TOP CHORD ANGLE REQ'D MKD ⑤												
14		/	/	ANGLE	120 X 120 X 8L	4	674		(4)	4·674	14·7		6	9		
15										TOTAL WT			6	9		
16																
17					TOTAL DRAWING WEIGHT							1	1	5	5	
18																MY 73044 D

BRAITHWAITE & COMPANY STRUCTURAL LIMITED.
NEPTUNE WORKS, NEWPORT, GWENT.

SITE BOLT LIST

SHEET No. B1

NAME WALKWAY   ORDER No. 5319

MY (1) 56169 D   ✱ ALL BOLTS NUTS & WASHERS SHERADISED

Gross	Spare	Nett	Dia.	Through	Length	Head	Scd.	Grade	POSITION IN WORK	R/Wash	T/Wash
DRG	Nº	24	M20	8,10	45	XOX		8.8	GUSSETS TO TOP CHORDS 1/1 &3 3/1	1	
5319/3		18		8,10	45				GUSSETS TO BOTTOM CHORDS 2/1,2,4&5 3/2	1	
		16		8,10	45				GUSSETS TO TOP CHORDS 1/1,3,4&5 3/3	1	
		16		8,10,11	55				GUSSETS TO TOP CHORDS 1/1,3,4&5 & TEE 5/7 3/3	1	
		16		8,10	45				GUSSETS TO BOTTOM CHORDS 2/1,2,4,5,6&7 3/4	1	
		16		8,10,11	55				GUSSETS TO BOTTOM CHORDS 2/1,2,4,5 & TEE 3/21 22 6&7 3/4	1	
		16		8,10	45				GUSSETS TO TOP CHORDS 1/1,3,4&5 3/5	1	
		16		8,10,11	55				GUSSETS TO TOP CHORDS 1/1,3,4&5 & TEE 3/19 5/7 3/5	1	
		32		8,10	45				GUSSET TO BOTTOM CHORDS 2/1,3,4,5,6&7 3/6	1	
		16		8,10	45				GUSSET TO TOP CHORDS 1/1,3,4&5 3/7	1	
		16		8,10,11	55				GUSSET TO TOP CHORD 1/1,3,4&5 & TEE 5/7 3/7	1	
		16		8,10	45				GUSSET TO BOTTOM CHORD 2/3 3/8	1	
		16		8,10,11	55				GUSSET TO BOTTOM CHORD 2/3 & TEE 3/21 3/22 3/8	1	
		16		8,10	45				GUSSET TO TOP CHORD 1/2 3/9	1	
		16		8,10,11	55				GUSSET TO TOP CHORD 1/2 & TEE 3/19 5/7 3/9	1	
		32		8,10	45				GUSSET TO BOTTOM CHORD 2/3 3/10	1	
		16		8,10	45				GUSSET TO TOP CHORD 1/3 3/11	1	
		16		8,10,11	55				GUSSET TO TOP CHORD 1/3 & TEE 5/7 3/11	1	
		16		8,10	45				GUSSET TO BOTTOM CHORD 2/3 3/12	1	
		16		8,10,11	55				GUSSET TO BOTTOM CHORD 2/3 & TEE 3/21 3/22 3/12	1	
		16		8,10	45				GUSSET TO TOP CHORD 1/3 3/13	1	
		16		8,10,11	55				GUSSET TO TOP CHORD 1/3 & TEE 3/19 5/7 3/13	1	
		20		8,10	45				GUSSET TO BOTTOM CHORD 2/3 3/14	1	
		8		8,10	45				GUSSET TO BOTTOM CHORDS 2/1,2,4,5,6&7 3/15	1	
		8		8,10,11	55				GUSSETS TO BOTTOM CHORDS 2/1,2 & TEE 3/18 5&7 5/10 3/15&15A	1	
		8		8,10	45				GUSSETS TO TOP CHORDS 1/3 3/16	1	
		8		8,10	45	CSK-OX			GUSSETS TO BOTTOM CHORDS 2/4&5 & ANGLE 2/4 3/17	1	

BRAITHWAITE & CO. STRUCTURAL LIMITED
NEWPORT

STRUCTURAL DEPT.
List No. _1_
Date _12-10-84_

ORDER No.			DESPATCH LIST.
B. & Co.	S 319	NAME	WALKWAY
CUSTOMERS		Description	BRIDGE ANGLES

G65050 7992R

Package No	No. Inc. Spares	Description	Erection Mark	Weight in One Kilogrammes	Length	Breadth	Depth	Total Weight Kilogrammes	Item No.
	3	TOP CHORD ANGLES	1/①	78	5287	120	120	234	
	4		1/②	135	9200	120	120	540	
	3		1/③	78	5287	120	120	234	
	1		1/④		5298	120	120	78	
	1		1/⑤		4674	120	120	69	
	2	BTM CHORD ANGLES	2/①	73	5287	310	135	146	
	2		2/②	73	5287	310	135	146	
	4		2/③	112	9200	100	100	448	
	1		2/④		5287	100	100	65	
	1		2/⑤		5287	100	100	65	
	1		2/⑥		5298	100	100	65	
	1		2/⑦		4665	100	100	57	
	24	TOP DIAGONALS	2/⑧	18	1858	65	58	432	
	3		2/⑨	17	1846	65	58	51	
	1		2/⑩		1513	65	58	14	
	55	SIDE DIAGONALS	2/⑪	10	1488	65	50	550	
	1		2/⑬		1138	65	50	8	
	1	BTM ANGLE	2/⑭		1230	100	100	15	
	2		2/⑮	15	1230	100	100	30	
	12		2/⑯	8	1210	65	50	96	
	60	SIDE ANGLES	2/⑰	7	1025	65	50	420	
	58	TOP ANGLES	2/⑱	12	1204	100	65	696	
	15	DIAG BRACINGS	2/⑲	11	1624	65	50	165	
	1	BTM ANGLE	2/⑳		1427	100	100	17	
	2	TOP ANGLES	2/㉑	13	1355	100	65	26	
	1	DIAG BRACING	2/22		1721	65	50	12	
				TOTAL WEIGHT C/F				4679	

PRE-PRINTED DETAIL SHEETS

Some fabricators use pre-printed drawing sheets for detailing straightforward items such as purlins. Typical sheets are shown in figures 7.20 and 7.21, for beams, channels, angles and zed purlins. Examples of the use of these sheets are given in figures 7.22 and 7.23.

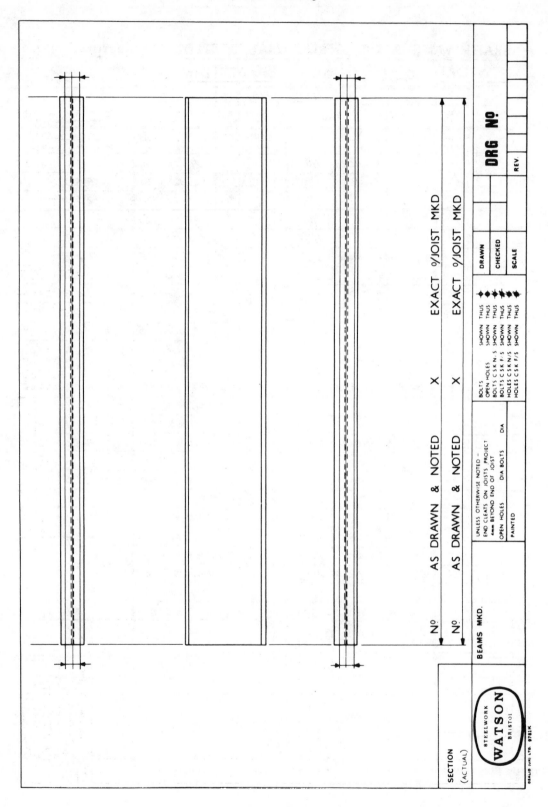

Figure 7.20

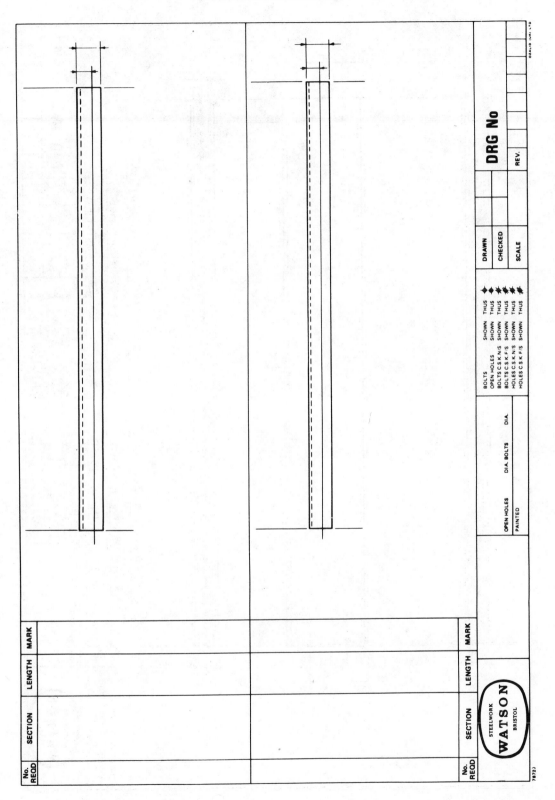

Figure 7.21

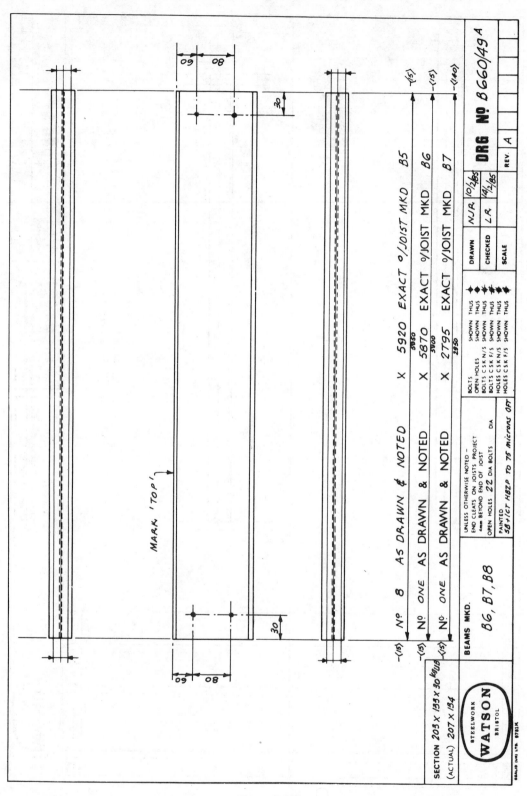

Figure 7.22

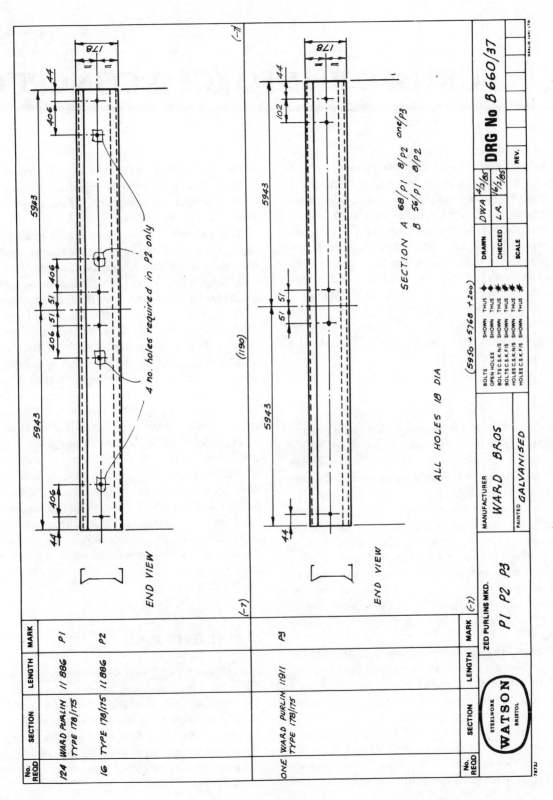

Figure 7.23

8. FURTHER REINFORCED CONCRETE

Chapter 6 provided examples of simple column, beam and slab construction. Like steel, reinforced concrete is an extremely versatile material that has been used for many and varied structures. It is particularly suitable for multi-storey work, such as flats, offices, car parks, hospitals and schools; for bridges, particularly the hundreds associated with motorways; water retaining structures and even cathedrals. There have been troubles with materials and with bad detailing, particularly with precast concrete structures. These are outside the scope of this book.

The purpose of this chapter is to consider the detailing of slightly more elaborate foundations, cantilevers, walls, staircases and retaining walls, still using reinforced concrete in a traditional way.

FOUNDATIONS

Foundations can vary so much, according to the nature of the ground and the magnitude of the load, that it would be impossible to cover all types in a book like this. The foundation illustrated in drawing no. 8.1 is for a water treatment works constructed in the Middle East. It is a spread foundation consisting of a raft of concrete 500 mm thick, over the entire area of the building. On this stands a grid of beams to brace the raft and to carry the floor of the works. The reinforcement of these beams is shown in broken line, where they connect with the slab reinforcement. In this case the bar mark is made up of the drawing number (7) followed by the bar number (00 upwards). Notice how the distribution of the total number of bars in each group is given by the numbers close to the arrow heads.

Chairs will be required to support the top layer of reinforcement, which can be proprietary chairs or specially bent 'saddles' like inverted Us. These chairs should be capable of carrying the weight of the reinforcement and the weight of workmen walking on it during concreting.

The size and frequency of chairs will depend upon the size of slab and the weight of reinforcement. *Technical Report No.2* recommends that mild steel bars at least 10 mm diameter are used and that the chairs are positioned not more than 1250 mm apart in directions at right angles. A sufficient number of chairs should be scheduled to give the steelfixer some flexibility in installation. These chairs have not been shown on drawing no. 8.1.

The ground conditions may require piles to be driven to support the structure. To make the connection between these piles and the columns, pile caps are formed. There may be one, two, three, four or even more piles connected into one pile cap. However many, they have the following in common.

If the piles are precast, the top metre (approximately) of concrete is broken off the driven pile to reveal enough reinforcement to link into the pile cap. If they are cast *in situ* piles, sufficient reinforcement is left projecting for this purpose. The top of the concrete in the pile is taken down to about 75 mm above the intended bottom of the pile cap. Once the ground is excavated the bottom is covered with 70 to 80 mm of blinding concrete and the side shutters are fixed.

Typical pile cap layouts are shown in figure 8.2. Except for the single pile, the pile cap will act as a beam or slab spanning across the tops of the piles, spreading the load from column to piles. It will therefore require tensile reinforcement in the bottom and the column starter bars will stand on this. The thickness of the pile cap must be sufficent to provide adequate bond for both the projecting pile reinforcement and the column starters, and it must prevent the column 'punching' through the cap (figure 8.3). A plan and an elevation of a typical pile cap are shown in figure 8.4.

CANTILEVERED SLABS

The failure of a cantilever slab is usually a tensile failure in the top of the slab, close to the support, as illustrated in figure 8.5. The designer will endeavour to provide reinforcement to prevent this happening, but his intentions may be frustrated by the builder, who fails to ensure that the reinforcement stays in the tensile zone when the concrete is placed. The detailer can help by providing reinforcement that is so shaped as to stay where it is required.

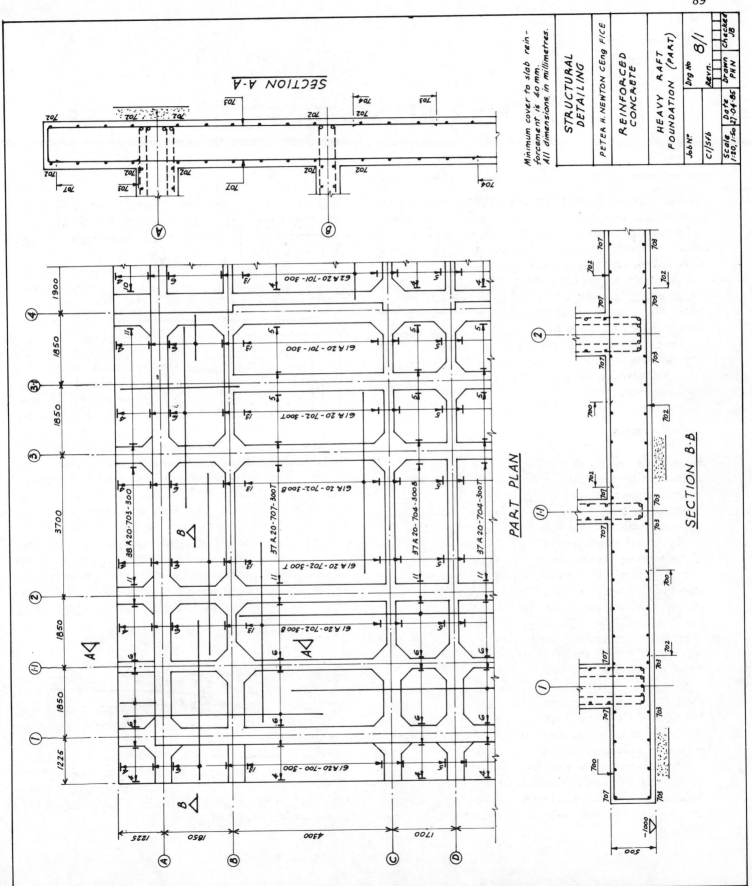

SECTION A-A

PART PLAN

SECTION B·B

Minimum cover to slab reinforcement is 40 mm.
All dimensions, in millimetres.

STRUCTURAL DETAILING		
PETER H. NEWTON CEng FICE		
REINFORCED CONCRETE		
HEAVY RAFT FOUNDATION (PART)		
Job No.	Drg No	8/1
CI/SfB	Revn.	
Scale 1:20, 1:50	Date 27·04·85	Drawn PHN / Checked JB

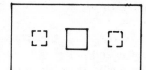

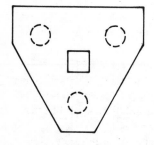

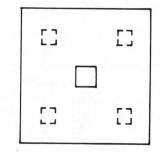

Figure 8.2   Pile cap layouts featuring one to four piles

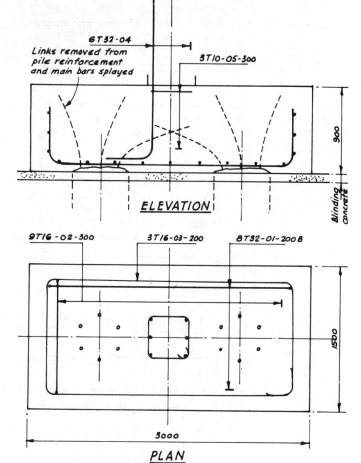

Figure 8.4   Typical pile cap detail

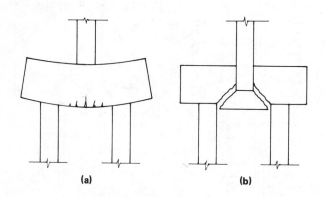

Figure 8.3   Pile cap failure patterns: (a) bending failure,
(b) shearing failure

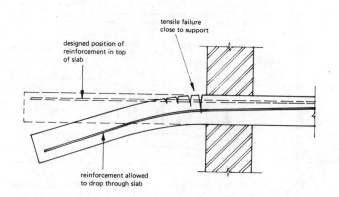

Figure 8.5   Failure of a cantilever due to reinforcement
being displaced

Figure 8.6 illustrates how the main tensile reinforcement in the top of the slab can be returned round at the free end. By providing distribution steel, as shown, a rigid cage is formed, which, if supported by spacers off the soffit shutter, will support the main reinforcement. The inner end is already supported on the beam reinforcement.

If there is no beam, as in the lower section, *Technical Report No.2* recommends placing concrete blocks of an appropriate thickness about 250 mm from the wall and at 1200 to 1500 mm spacing along the slab, with a bar spanning over them to support the main tensile reinforcement.

Where cantilever slabs are thicker and there is reinforcement in the bottom as well, steel chairs can be provided to space the top and bottom bars correctly, the bottom bars being provided with concrete spacers off the soffit shutter.

WALLS

Reinforced concrete walls are frequently used to provide additional stability to a structure that might collapse sideways, like a house of cards, if it consisted entirely of slabs and columns. This is the way buildings often collapse in earthquakes, ending up with the floors stacked one upon the other. Normally it is wind forces that reinforced concrete walls are designed to resist, for which purpose they are known as shear walls.

A reinforced concrete wall will be tied into the structure above and below, just like a column, which in many ways it resembles. The main difference is that a wall has long straight horizontal bars instead of links. There may still be links in a wall, however, if the designer is treating part of it as a column.

Drawing no. 8.7 details a typical shear wall and illustrates its important features. Note the starter bars from the foundation and the provision at the top for starter bars for the next storey. Kickers may be used to locate the lower ends of the wall formwork, hence the 75 mm dimension.

In order to maintain the correct position of the reinforcement in the two faces, U-type spacers should be provided. The number and location of these spacers will depend upon the size of the wall, but at least one horizontal line should be provided and these spacers should be scheduled.

The decision as to which bars should be on the outside will depend upon whether the wall spans (structurally) vertically or horizontally. If this is not a consideration, then it makes concreting easier if the vertical bars are on the outside. In this case the designer has placed the horizontal bars on the outside to provide the maximum restraint against thermal and shrinkage cracking over the longer length.

Very light walls, less than 120 mm thick, may have only one layer of horizontal bars and one layer of vertical bars placed in the middle of the wall.

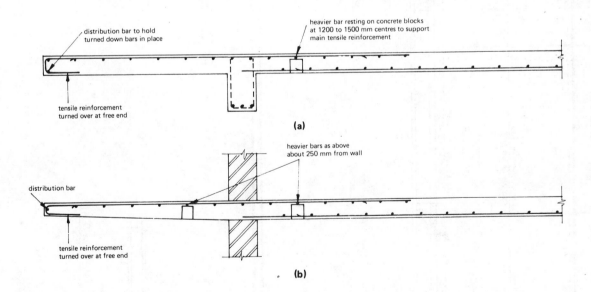

Figure 8.6   Treatment of cantilevered slabs to ensure tensile reinforcement stays in tensile zone: (a) cantilever over structural beam, (b) cantilever through brick/block wall

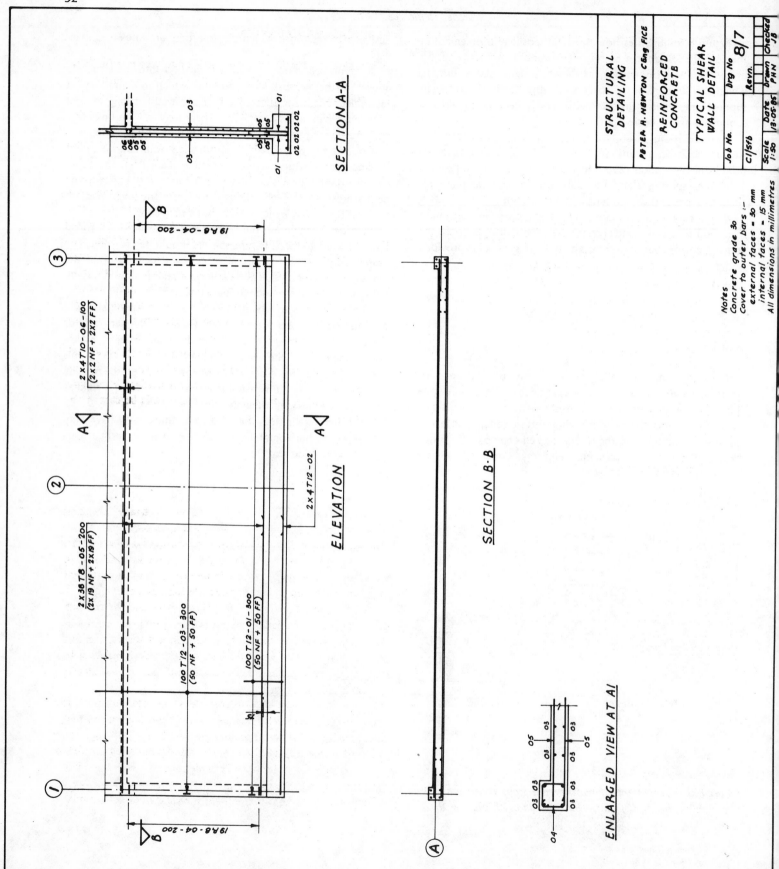

SECTION A-A

ELEVATION

SECTION B-B

ENLARGED VIEW AT A1

2 x 4 T10 - 06 - 100
(2x2 NF + 2x2 FF)

2 x 36 T8 - 05 - 200
(2x19 NF + 2x19 FF)

100 T12 - 03 - 300
(50 NF + 50 FF)

100 T12 - 01 - 300
(50 NF + 50 FF)

2 x 4 T12 - 02

19 R8 - 04 - 200

19 R8 - 04 - 200

STRUCTURAL
DETAILING

PETER H. NEWTON CEng FICE

REINFORCED
CONCRETE

TYPICAL SHEAR.
WALL DETAIL

Job No.

Drg No. 8/7

Revn.

Cl/Sfb

Scale 1:50

Date 13-05-85

Drawn PHN

Checked JB

Notes
Concrete grade 30
Cover to outer bars :-
   external faces = 30 mm
   internal faces = 15 mm
All dimensions in millimetres

Where a wall ends without a column, as shown in figure 8.8, the reinforcement should be closed at the ends to prevent cracking. The U-bars serve this purpose.

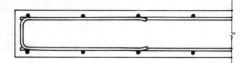

Figure 8.8   Closure of reinforcement at the end of a wall

Where a wall turns through 90°, as shown in figure 8.9, it is necessary to tie together the reinforcement in the two legs. Wall reinforcement lends itself to prefabrication into flat panels on the ground for lifting into position by crane — a considerable saving in time and money. It further eases fixing if the panels are discrete, that is without interlocking bars. The junction is then formed by short linking bars and three recommended arrangements are illustrated in figure 8.9. In (a) the linking bars are L-shaped and in (b) they are horizontal U-bars — both of which are satisfactory in normal circumstances.

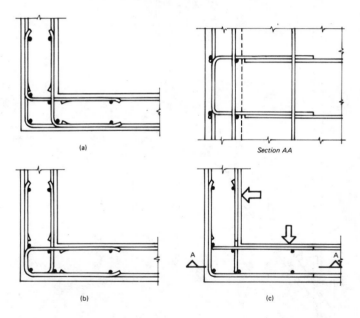

Figure 8.9   Treatment of junctions between two walls

There are times when the corner tends to open up, as indicated by the arrows, and then the vertical U-bars shown in (c) are recommended.

STAIRCASES AND LANDINGS

A staircase is virtually a sloping slab upon which treads have been cast. Staircases do not lend themselves to construction (in multi-storey work) at the same time as the floors that support them, so starter bars are left projecting from the slabs at the top and bottom, for the flight to be built later.

Staircases are usually built with a half landing to prevent people falling too far. The landing is built as part of the staircase (drawing no. 8.10) and the flight, with landings at each end, spans as a slab from the wall on line Ⓐ to the beam on line Ⓑ. Note that the main reinforcement is in the tensile zone in the bottom of the flight slab, but rises into the top in the landings at each end. The U-bars mark 07 tie into the reinforcement in the shear wall (drawing no. 8.7). The staircase has a rise of 175 mm and a going of 250 mm, but the tread depth is increased to 300 mm by raking the riser back 50 mm.

In practice the construction of staircases is a slow business and it is a good idea to precast the flights, which can rest on the floors and half landings. The flights can be cast upside down or on their sides, which makes manufacture easier and the finished product better. Figure 8.11 illustrates a typical precast flight (that could replace the *in situ* flight in drawing no. 8.10), resting on the landings, that would be cast at the same time as the floors.

RETAINING WALLS

Reinforced concrete retaining walls are virtually L-shaped slabs, which act as cantilevers to retain a vertical bank of soil. The wall can face either way, but the reinforcement will differ.

Figure 8.12 shows how the walls retain the soil and also, in heavy line, those parts that are in tension. It is these parts that have to be reinforced, each leg being treated as a cantilever.

As the wall gets higher the forces trying to rend the two legs apart increase considerably and it is often preferred to provide 'brackets', known as counterforts, to connect the vertical and horizontal legs. The wall and base are then designed as slabs spanning between the counterforts and not as cantilevers (figure 8.13).

Drawing no. 8.14 shows a typical small retaining wall. It employs light fabric reinforcement in the front face to counteract cracking. This fabric comes in flat sheets (rolls are too difficult to handle) 2400 mm wide and 4800 mm long. Allowing a lap of 300 mm between adjoining sheets means there will be a sheet every 4500 mm. It is convenient to base the drawing of the wall on a 4500 mm length, the quantities being multi-

Notes
Nominal cover to reinforcement – 15 mm.
Concrete grade 30.
All dimensions in millimetres

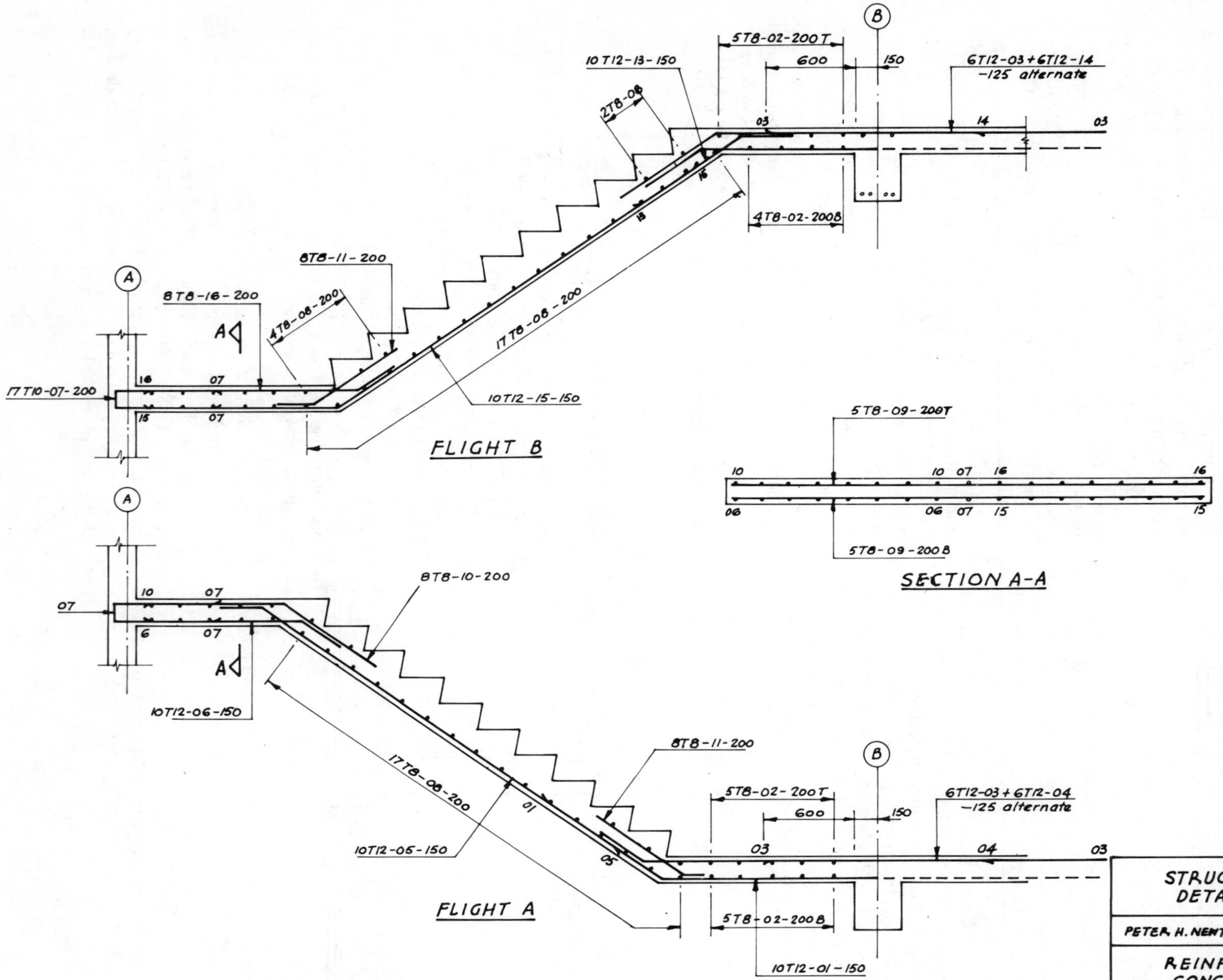

5T8-02-200T
600
150
10T12-13-150
2T8-06
6T12-03+6T12-14
-125 alternate
03
14
03
15
13
4T8-02-200B
B
8T8-11-200
A
8T8-16-200
4T8-08-200
17T8-08-200
16
07
17T10-07-200
15
07
10T12-15-150
FLIGHT B
5T8-09-200T
10
10 07
16
16
06
06 07
15
15
5T8-09-200B
SECTION A-A
A
8T8-10-200
10
07
07
6
07
10T12-06-150
17T8-08-200
01
10T12-05-150
05
8T8-11-200
B
5T8-02-200T
600
150
6T12-03+6T12-04
-125 alternate
03
04
03
5T8-02-200B
10T12-01-150
FLIGHT A

STRUCTURAL DETAILING	
PETER H. NEWTON C Eng FICE	
REINFORCED CONCRETE	
STAIRCASE WITH HALF LANDING	
Job No. C1/5f6	Drg No 8/10 Revn
Scale 1:20 · Date 04·05·85	Drawn PHN · Checked JB

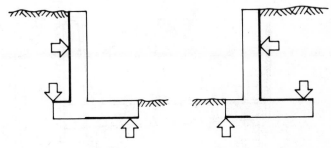

Figure 8.12   Forces on cantilever retaining wall

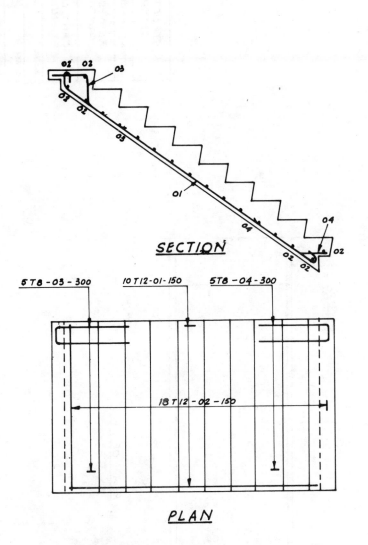

5 T8 - 03 - 300   10 T12 - 01 - 150   5 T8 - 04 - 300

18 T 12 - 02 - 150

SECTION

PLAN

Figure 8.11   An example of a precast flight of stairs

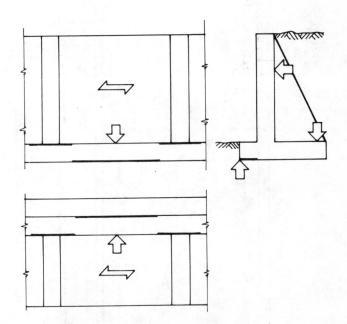

Figure 8.13   Retaining wall with counterforts

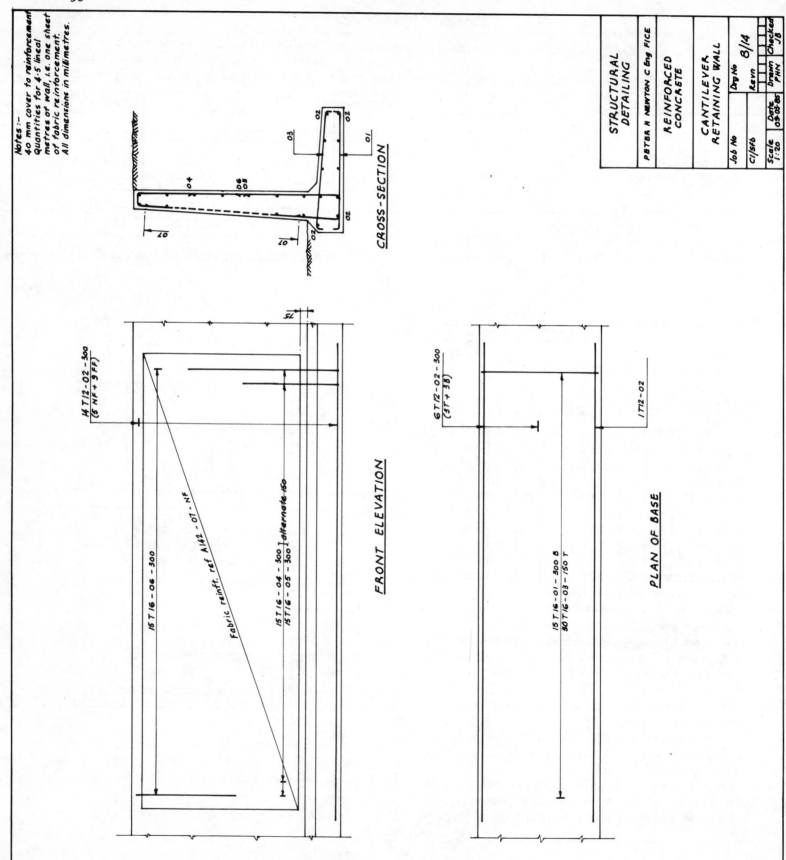

plied up to suit the actual length, which will probably be determined by construction joints.

The crucial tensile faces are the back of the wall and the top surface of the base, so these are more heavily reinforced. As the bending moment in the wall decreases towards the top, only 50 per cent of the vertical bars are taken to the full height. The U-bars mark 06 tie the front and back steel across the top to avoid cracking here.

The base will probably be cast first with the bars mark 04 and 05 acting as starters for the wall. The fabric is shown resting on a 75 mm kicker. The overlap between the bars mark 04 and 06 will need to be at least the minimum tension lap but, by arranging for this lap, any variation in the height of the wall (quite common) can be catered for without scheduling successively shorter bars, just by varying the lap.

FABRIC REINFORCEMENT

Fabric reinforcement is made by welding steel wire into a rectangular mesh. The wire is of hard drawn steel to BS 4461, with a high tensile strength of 460 N/mm^2. It can be plain round, indented or otherwise deformed and be welded or interwoven.

Fabric is used in floors and walls and (very extensively) in pavements. It is more efficiently employed where whole sheets can be used, without bending or complicated cutting around openings. The sheets used in the retaining wall will have to be reduced in width and the waste utilised elsewhere.

Each sheet is shown on the drawing as a rectangle with a diagonal drawn to indicate its extent, figure 8.15. The direction of the diagonal can be used to indicate whether the fabric is at the top or bottom, front or back of the slab or wall. If this is too complicated then a separate drawing can be made of each layer. The abbreviations B and T, NF and FF can also be used.

An extract from BS 4483 is printed in part III, from which it will be seen that sheets in the B and C series have more steel in their longitudinal direction than in their transverse direction. To make sure it is placed the correct way, a double-headed arrow should be drawn in the rectangle, to indicate the direction of the main bars.

Double strength fabric can be achieved by nesting the sheets as shown in figure 8.16.

Fabric is shown in section by heavy broken lines, using long dashes to indicate the main bars and short dashes to indicate the transverse bars — if these are different.

Fabric should be scheduled separately from bars, using the form shown in part III. The fabric should be grouped together according to weight per square metre and size of sheet. A simple manual schedule is illustrated on the next page for students to practise scheduling fabric reinforcement. The reader should refer to BS 4466 for detailed guidance on scheduling fabric.

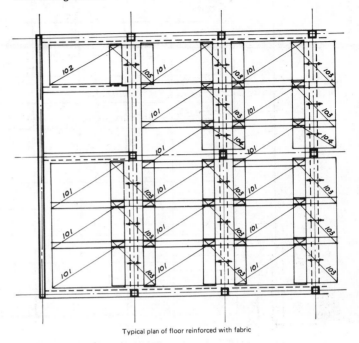

Typical plan of floor reinforced with fabric

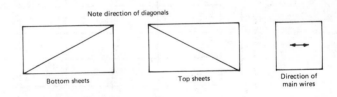

Note direction of diagonals

Bottom sheets   Top sheets   Direction of main wires

Figure 8.15   Detailing steel fabric reinforcement

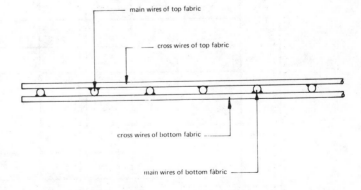

main wires of top fabric

cross wires of top fabric

cross wires of bottom fabric

main wires of bottom fabric

Figure 8.16   Nesting two layers of fabric

Name of company					METRIC		
					BAR SCHEDULE ref. ☐☐☐ ☐☐ ☐		Rev. ☐
					Date		

Site

Location	Fabric mark	Type	No. of sheets	Length (main wires) mm	Width mm	Bend or cut

XY and partners
Site ref:

Fabric schedule ref: ☐☐☐ ☐☐ ☐   Rev. letter

Date prepared: Date revised:
Prepared by: Checked by:

Fabric mark	BS reference or sheet details						Sheet length 'L'† m	Sheet width 'B'† m	No. of sheets	Special details and/or bending dimensions						
	No. of wires	Type and size of wires mm	Pitch † mm	Length † mm	Overhangs O₁ O₃ mm	O₂ O₄ mm				Shape code	Bending instruction	A* mm	B* mm	C* mm	D* mm	E/r* mm

This schedule complies with BS 4466
*Specified in multiples of 5 mm   †Specified in multiples of 25 mm

9. STRUCTURAL TIMBER

Timber has been used structurally longer than any other material. It still forms the floors and roofs of the majority of domestic buildings, except where fire safety requires the use of less flammable materials. In recent years it has become popular as the prefabricated carcase of houses — a popularity that has waned for a variety of reasons, although not the fault of the wood itself.

Unlike steel and concrete, the joining of timber members to give economical high strength connections has always been a problem. Timber as a structural material has an excellent strength to weight ratio and is very easy to use on site. Timber structures cannot always achieve the full potential of the material, because of the relative weakness of the joints.

Historically joints in hardwoods, such as oak, were formed by tongues in mortices, secured with dowels. Many of our fine old buildings, still standing today, reveal the most skilful jointing techniques. But softwoods have entirely replaced hardwoods and clever joints, such as tusk-tenons, are labour-intensive and thus too costly, so alternatives have had to be found.

NAILS

Nails have been in use for centuries. Once they were square in cross-section and were known as cut nails and rose-head nails. Today most nails are formed from wire and are round or oval in cross-section.

The trouble with plain wire nails is that their resistance to withdrawal is low and joints have to be designed to load the nails in shear. To overcome this weakness improved nails have been developed. These may be square twisted or annular ring-shanked, which names describe their appearance. The code of practice for the structural use of timber (BS 5268) accepts that improved nails are $1\frac{1}{2}$ times as strong as plain nails in their resistance to withdrawal.

Nails are often used in association with pre-drilled metal nail plates or with plywood gussets. These techniques are suitable for small production runs, using ordinary carpentry tools.

SCREWS

Screws for structural purposes are made of steel. Holes have to be drilled in the timber to suit the diameter and length of the screws, and they have to be rotated in order to instal them. They make an excellent job, but are expensive and so rarely used.

Coach screws are large screws, with square heads that are turned with a spanner. They are commonly available only as 12 mm diameter, 150 mm long, and again are rarely used today.

BOLTS

Ordinary mild steel bolts, with hexagon heads and nuts, are now the type of bolt most commonly used, although coach bolts are also available. These latter have a cup/square head and either a square or hexagonal nut. The square under the head is drawn into the timber as the nut is tightened, and so stops the bolt from rotating.

The disadvantage of bolts is that they are too strong for the timber that they are joining. The material around the bolt will be overstressed, causing it to crush the grain perpendicularly or shear the grain longitudinally, long before the bolt reaches its full potential.

TIMBER CONNECTORS

The purpose of a connector is to spread the load over a greater area of timber and thus reduce the stress concentrations. Connectors take three basic forms

(1)   toothed plate connectors (figure 9.1(a))

(2)   split ring connectors (figure 9.1(b))
(3)   shear plate connectors (figure 9.1(c)).

Toothed plate connectors are flat metal plates, round or square, with a hole through the middle for the bolt. The perimeter consists of triangular teeth, which are turned through 90° in alternate directions (double-sided connectors) or in the same direction — alternate teeth being removed (single-sided connectors). The plates are sandwiched between the two members to be joined and the teeth are embedded in the timber by the tightening of the bolt.

Split ring connectors consist of a band of steel, between 50 and 100 mm diameter and about 25 mm wide. They are split with a tongue and groove joint, to make the bedding of the ring in the timber more effective. In cross-section the ring can be straight or bevelled. Annular grooves have to be formed in the timber at the joints to take the rings. The whole is held together by a bolt at the centre of the ring. They work in a similar way to toothed plate connectors.

Shear plate connectors consist of a shallow cup of pressed steel, whose rim fits into an annular groove, as above, but in the timber on one side of the joint only. The flat base of the cup transfers the load to the hole through its centre. Like the single-sided toothed plate connector, it is used where a timber member is connected to steelwork, or where two are used back-to-back in demountable timber structures, when each connector is secured by screws through the two holes provided.

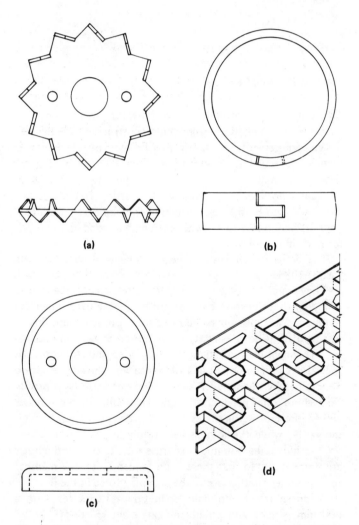

METAL PLATE FASTENERS

There are three basic forms of metal plate connectors:

(1)   punched metal plates (figure 9.1(d))
(2)   hand-nail-plates   -
(3)   framing anchors (figure 9.2(a)).

Punched metal plates are suitable for installation only in a factory with special machinery, employed under controlled conditions by fabricators who normally hold manufacturers' licences for the use of a particular make of plate. The plate manufacturer usually carries the design responsibility for the structures in which they are installed.

The advantages lie in the formation of a joint of members all in the same plane and in rapid assembly line production of the components.

Hand-nail-plates are not subject to the same proprietary restrictions as punched metal plates and are intended for use out of the factory, needing only a hammer or mechanical hand-nail gun to fabricate components, which need not be dissimilar to those employing punched metal plates. The design work may be undertaken by the engineer in the field, in accordance with BS 5268: Part 3 *Trussed rafters for roofs of dwellings*.

Framing anchors are shaped metal brackets used for secondary connections in timber framing — purlin cleats, studding, joist trimming, etc. — hardly structural! BS 5268 does not give any guidance on the use of framing anchors, but sections referring to the use of nails through steel sheet can be applied.

Figure 9.1   Types of timber connectors: (a) toothed plate connector, (b) split ring connector, (c) shear plate connector, (d) punched metal plates

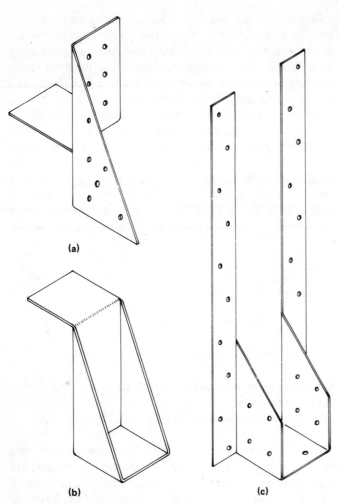

(a)

(b)   **(c)**

Figure 9.2   Types of joist hangers: (a) framing anchor, (b) joist hanger to wall, (c) joist hanger to another beam

JOIST HANGERS

Joist hangers are being used in rapidly increasing numbers. Many varieties are used. They may be thin pressed and/or folded sheet metal or thicker welded steel plate, and always galvanised. Some are holed for nails or screws and some are plain (see figure 9.2(b) and (c)). The use of plain hangers must ensure that they are well wedged in position by the joists they are supporting and have adequate bearing within the wall.

FRAMED CONSTRUCTION IN THE 1990s

A textbook should not only inform the reader about the various ways in which timber can be formed into structures, but it should also give guidance as to which of these ways is most commonly used. It would be a waste of the reader's time to burden him with outdated or rarely used technologies.

The use of punched metal plate connectors is widespread for all the more normal buildings, with which this book is concerned. The remainder of this chapter will deal exclusively with this method, although it will be possible for the reader to see how the methods of detailing may be extended to nailed plywood gussets and to TRADA-type roof trusses.

TRUSSED RAFTERS

The term 'trussed rafter' here covers prefabricated timber roof trusses, beams and other components, constructed to individual design requirements, by fabricators licensed by the punched plate manufacturers. These plates are made in a wide range of sizes, which have integral rows of teeth punched in 20, 18 or 14 gauge hot-dipped galvanised steel strip. The plates are impressed into both sides of the timber members to produce a rigid distortion-free joint, with a strength as good as any other form of timber jointing.

The design of trusses and beams is covered by BS 5268: Part 3: 1985.

They are manufactured from stress-graded softwood timber with a moisture content not exceeding 22 per cent. If required, the timber may be protected against rot and insect attack, after it has been cut, by immersion or vacuum processing. The members are tightly butt joined and assembled in special jigging equipment in accordance with the configuration determined by the designer, so ensuring a uniformity of profile throughout the production run. Hydraulic platen presses embed the connector plates on both sides of the joint simultaneously, while the joint is held firmly in position. Drawing no. 9.3 illustrates a simple fink truss and shows how the butts are double cut, so that there is no tendency for one member to slide under another under the clamping force in the jig.

Standard trusses normally span up to 12 metres, with a 600 mm spacing and pitches ranging from $15°$ to $50°$ in $2\frac{1}{2}°$ increments. Special trusses can span up to 35 metres, spaced up to 5 metres and be of any pitch.

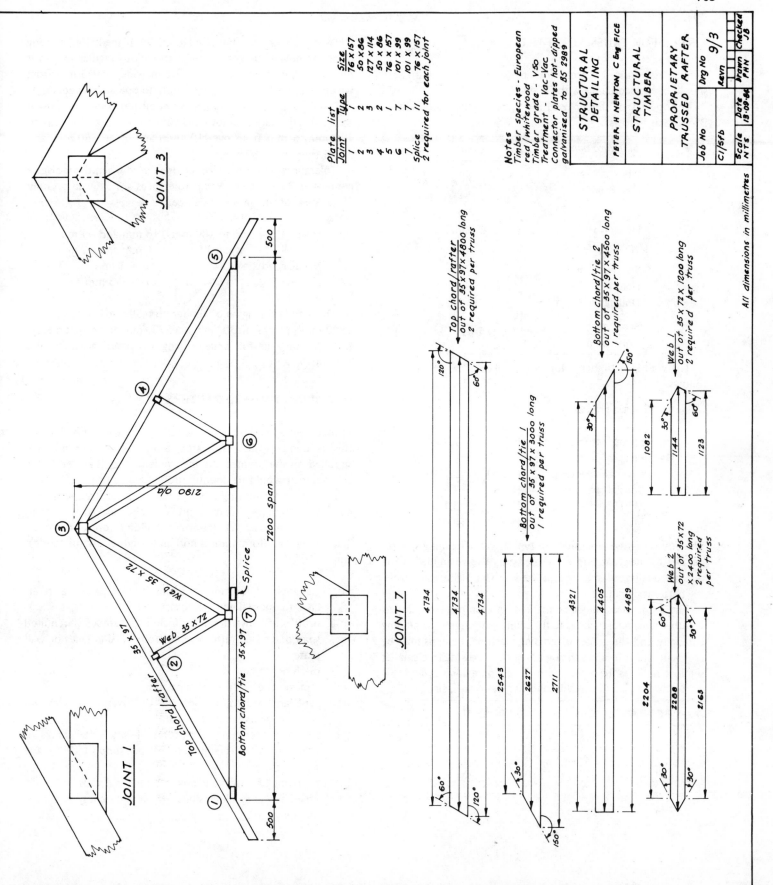

JOINT 3

JOINT 1

JOINT 7

7200 span

2190 o/o

500

500

Top chord/rafter 35 × 97

Web 35 × 72

Web 35 × 72

Bottom chord/tie 35 × 97

Splice

① ② ③ ④ ⑤ ⑥ ⑦

Plate list

Joint	Type	Size
1	1	76 × 157
2	2	50 × 86
3	3	127 × 114
4	2	50 × 86
5	1	76 × 157
6	7	101 × 99
7	7	101 × 99
Splice	11	76 × 157

2 required for each joint

Notes
Timber species - European
red/whitewood
Timber grade - V50
Treatment - Vac-Vac
Connector plates hot-dipped
galvanised to BS 2989

Top chord/rafter
out of 35 × 97 × 4800 long
2 required per truss

120°
60°
4734
4734
4734
60°
120°
150°

Bottom chord/tie 1
out of 35 × 97 × 3000 long
1 required per truss

2543
2627
2711
30°

Bottom chord/tie 2
out of 35 × 97 × 4500 long
1 required per truss

150°
30°
4321
4405
4489

Web 1
out of 35 × 72 × 1200 long
2 required per truss

30°
60°
1082
1144
1123

Web 2
out of 35 × 72 × 2400 long
2 required per truss

60°
30°
30°
30°
2204
2208
2163

STRUCTURAL
DETAILING

PETER H NEWTON C Eng FICE

STRUCTURAL
TIMBER

PROPRIETARY
TRUSSED RAFTER

Job No		Drg No	9/3
C1/5Fb		Revn	
Scale NTS	Date 13·09·84	Drawn PHN	Checked JB

All dimensions in millimetres

TIMBER FOR TRUSSED RAFTERS

Timber for trussed rafters (or any other designed trusses) should be in accordance with BS 4978.

The species of timber used for trussed rafters are listed in BS 5268 as follows.

Standard name	Origin
Whitewood Redwood	Europe
Hem-fir Douglas fir-larch Spruce-pine-fir	Canada
Southern pine Hem-fir Douglas fir-larch	USA
Scots pine Corsican pine	Britain

The grades of timber commonly available, are described as follows.

Visual stress graded:
General structural	(GS)	5.1 N/mm^2
Special structural	(SS)	7.3

Machine graded:
General structural	(MGS)	5.1
Special structural	(MSS)	7.3
M50	(M50)	6.1
M75	(M75)	10.0

The stresses listed alongside are typical grade bending stresses parallel to the grain, and are quoted only to give an idea of the relative quality of the various grades. The higher the stress, the better the grade.

The grade stress must be marked on each piece of timber, together with references as to the country of origin, the grading company and the grader or grading machine. Lengths may be cross-cut and still retain their grading, but resawing into smaller sections nullifies the grading, which has to be done again.

Timber is available in the following basic sawn sizes.

Thickness (mm)	Width (mm)						
	75	100	125	150	175	200	225
38	X	X	X	X	X	X	X
47	X	X	X	X	X	X	X
50	X	X	X	X	X	X	X
63			X	X	X	X	
75			X	X	X	X	

Sawn timber may be 'regularised' or planed. Regularising means removing timber to make the width regular. 3 mm is removed from timber up to 150 mm wide, and 5 mm from wider sections. Regularising can apply to one or both edges.

Planing must remove timber from all four sides. It is usual to plane all round, removing 3 mm from dimensions up to 100 mm, 5 mm from over 100 mm and up to 150 mm, and 6 mm from over 150 mm.

Tolerances on timber sizes are measured when the moisture content is 20 per cent. Minus tolerances are allowed on only 10 per cent of the pieces in a parcel.

Sawn	up to 100 mm	: +3 mm and −1 mm
	over 100 mm	: +6 mm and −2 mm
Regularised		: + or −1 mm
Planed		: + or −0.5 mm

The standard lengths of timber normally produced go from 1800 mm in steps of 300 mm, to 5700 mm and sometimes up to 6300 mm. The tolerance on length is customarily size plus 50 mm.

DETAILING TRUSSED RAFTERS

In practice there is no point in detailing trussed rafters, because this is done by the fabricator, using a computer program supplied by the licensee. As the whole factory is geared to the computer, it would be counter-productive to provide detailed calculations and drawings, as this would make it a special and consequently more expensive process. The local authority will accept the computer calculations for building-control purposes. The following information is normally required by the fabricator:

(a) geographical location of building, with particular reference to unusual wind exposure

(b) profile of trussed rafter, including camber if required

(c) span of trussed rafter overall from outside faces of wall plates

(d) pitch or pitches

(e) method and position of supports

(f) type and weight of roof tile or covering, sarking, insulation, ceiling materials, etc.

(g) size and approximate position of any water tanks or other ancillary equipment to be supported by the trussed rafters

(h) overhang of rafters and any other eaves details

(i) positions and dimensions of any hatches, openings, chimneys, etc.

(j)   whether preservative treatment is required

(k)   spacing of trussed rafters and/or timber sizes where these may be required to match existing construction.

COMPUTER EXAMPLE

On pages 106 to 111 is an example of a computer printout for a simple fink truss, spanning 7.2 metres. The section of each timber member is calculated and also the precise shape for sawing it into the components for the truss. Note that every member is based upon its centre line. The cutting sheet used by the sawyer appears on page 109. Drawing no. 9.3 explains the cutting sheet and illustrates a manual detailing of the truss members.

Page 108 provides the jig set-up points, so that the components can be correctly laid out on the beds of the hydraulic platen presses. All points are set out, on a rectangular coordinate system, with the mid-point of the bottom chord as the origin. Negative X dimensions are to the left of the centre of the truss.

MANUFACTURE OF TRUSSED RAFTERS

A timber requisition is produced by the computer, for the stockyard to assemble the material required. Timber is purchased already prepared in three common sizes: 35 × 72, 35 × 97 and 35 × 122 mm. Preparation is necessary because sawn timber cannot be reliably thicknessed and any variation could affect the strength of the joints. Other sizes can be provided to special order. If a stronger truss is required, then it is more economical to place two, or even three, trusses together, rather than order specials.

The timber assembled for the order is then sent to the machine shop, where the sawyer cuts it to the right length and profile, using a multiple bladed machine, that can make up to four cuts simultaneously, two at each end.

At this stage any preservative treatment can be applied, so that the cut ends are treated after sawing. An organic solvent system is preferred, but if a water-based system is used, it is important for the timber to dry out to a moisture content of 22 per cent or less, before it passes to the next stage.

The shaped timber goes to the fabrication shop, where large tables are provided, upon which the trusses are set out, using the setting-out data provided by the computer. This table is equipped with special clamps that enable the joints to be brought tightly together and held while the metal plates are installed. The lower plates are held magnetically or by temporary adhesive taping. The timbers are then laid out on top and clamped together. The upper metal plates are positioned on top of the timbers and tapped with a hammer to start the 'nails' enough to hold them in place. The travelling hydraulic platen press then moves across the table, pressing vertically on the joints of the truss, so that both plates are simultaneously embedded in the timber.

The trusses are then turned into a vertical plane, similar to that which they will assume in the roof. During all subsequent handling, delivery to site and erection, it is best if this attitude is maintained. The trusses are very weak in a transverse direction and any faulty handling could damage them.

WORK ON SITE

Once the trusses are erected, they are provided with stability bracing as follows.

(1)   Longitudinal bracing out of 38 × 75 or 25 × 100 mm timbers running continuously through the trusses at key positions, such as near the apex and at the third points of the bottom chord.

(2)   Rafter diagonal bracing out of 25 × 100 mm timbers fixed diagonally across the undersides of the rafters.

(3)   Web longitudinal bracing out of 25 × 100 mm timber fixed (when called for) longitudinally across the webs.

(4)   Web diagonal bracing out of 25 × 100 mm timber fixed to the webs of trusses spanning in excess of 8 metres and up to 11 metres.

(5)   Tiling battens fixed after the trusses are completely plumb and straight, and after all the other bracing has been installed. They laterally brace the top chords (rafters) of the trusses.

The suppliers and fabricators produce illustrated manuals covering all aspects of truss manufacture and installation, including provision for water tank supports, chimney openings, hatch openings, etc., and the reader is recommended to write for a copy of these.

Trussed rafters must not be drilled or cut at any time. Bracings are nailed with two 10 gauge × 63 mm galvanised wire nails at each truss. The trusses may be skew nailed to the wall plates using two 7 gauge × 100 mm galvanised wire nails at each end, driven in from each side. Alternatively, purpose-made framing anchors or wall plate straps may be used.

```
*-*-*-*-*-*-*-*-*-*-*-*-*-*-*-*-*-*-*-*-*-*-*-*-*-*-*-*-*-*-*-*-*-*-*-*-*-*-*-*-*-*-*-*-*-*-*-*-*-*-*
* GANG-NAIL  CONCEPT 2000 *          HUNTER TIMBER ENGINEERING LIMITED          * GANG-NAIL  CONCEPT 2000 *
*-*-*-*-*-*-*-*-*-*-*-*-*-*-*-*-*-*-*-*-*-*-*-*-*-*-*-*-*-*-*-*-*-*-*-*-*-*-*-*-*-*-*-*-*-*-*-*-*-*-*
```

Filename   : MEN1   Truss   Concept 2000 Version 6.00

Job Reference   : P.H.MENTON   Date: 2 Apr 90 14:44

Truss Type   : Fink   Tested Truss

Span overall S.O.P's	7200mm	Bottom Chord Grade	M75ERW
Left Top Chord Pitch	30.00deg	Web Grade	M75ERW
Right Top Chord Pitch	30.00deg	Plate File	GN20
No of Trusses	1	Plating Tolerance	5mm
Truss Centres	600mm	Left Heel Joint	Standard
Truss Thickness	35mm	Right Heel Joint	Standard
Top Chord Live Load	750N/m2	Left Overhang	450mm
Top Chord Dead Load	685N/m2	Right Overhang	450mm
Btm Chord Live Load	250N/m2	Left Overhang Cut	Plumb
Btm Chord Dead Load	250N/m2	Right Overhang Cut	Plumb
Tank Load per Truss	900N	Timber Treatment	Vac-Vac
Top Chord Restraint	360mm	Nominal Bearing	100mm
Top Chord Grade	M75ERW	Design Code	UK LMS

Top chord   35 * 72
Btm chord   35 * 97

Web Ref   H   I   J   K
Depth+Braces   60+0   60+0   60+0   60+0

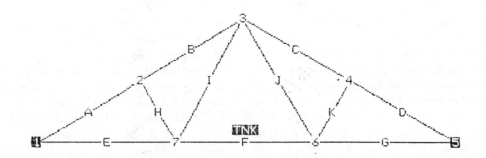

```
*-*-*-*-*-*-*-*-*-*-*-*-*-*-*-*-*-*-*-*-*-*-*-*-*-*-*-*-*-*-*-*-*-*-*-*-*-*-*-*-*-*-*-*-*-*-*-*
* GANG-NAIL  CONCEPT 2000 *           HUNTER TIMBER ENGINEERING LIMITED          * GANG-NAIL  CONCEPT 2000 *
*-*-*-*-*-*-*-*-*-*-*-*-*-*-*-*-*-*-*-*-*-*-*-*-*-*-*-*-*-*-*-*-*-*-*-*-*-*-*-*-*-*-*-*-*-*-*-*
```

Filename   : MEN1   Truss   Concept 2000 Version 6.00

Job Reference : P.H.MENTON   Date: 2 Apr 90 14:44

Truss Type   : Fink   Tested Truss

Design in accordance with : BS 6399 Part 1 (1984)
                          : BS 5268 Part 2 (1988) & Part 3 (1985)

Load Sharing Factor   : 1.1

			Bend	Tens	Comp Para	Comp Perp	Shear	Emean
TIMBER GRADES & STRESSES (N/mm2)			Bend	Tens	Comp Para	Comp Perp	Shear	Emean
Top Chord	M75	European Red/Whitewood	10.0	6.0	8.7	2.80	1.32	11000
Btm Chord	M75	European Red/Whitewood	10.0	6.0	8.7	2.80	1.32	11000
Web	M75	European Red/Whitewood	10.0	6.0	8.7	2.80	1.32	11000

TESTED TRUSSES

The size of the chord members are taken from the full scale test data given in
the appropriate code of practice.

Top Chord : 35 * 72
Btm Chord : 35 * 97

APPLIED STRESSES & FORCES				Long Term		Medium Term		Short Term		
Web	Depth	Length	Br	Axial	CSI	Axial	CSI	Axial	CSI	L/R
Member	mm	mm		N		N		N		
Web H	60	1143	0	−740	.101	−1441	.183	−1441	.174	101Y
Web I	60	2287	0	2091	.129	2792	.138	3572	.147	

DEFLECTION AT JOINT 7   Medium Term   5mm   Perm 22mm

REACTIONS	------- Load Duration -------			Minimum
Location	Long	Medium	Short	Bearing
Joint 1	3239N	4859N	5534N	75mm
Joint 5	3239N	4859N	5534N	75mm

Contact : MR.D.J.HILL TEL:BRIDGWATER (0278) 445222
          HUNTER TIMBER ENGINEERING LIMITED
          THE LEGGAR,BRIDGWATER,SOMERSET. TA6 4AF.

```
*-*-*-*-*-*-*-*-*-*-*-*-*-*-*-*-*-*-*-*-*-*-*-*-*-*-*-*-*-*-*-*-*-*-*-*-*-*-*-*-*-*-*-*-*-*-*-*-*-*-*-*-*
* GANG-NAIL  CONCEPT 2000 *        HUNTER TIMBER ENGINEERING LIMITED        * GANG-NAIL  CONCEPT 2000 *
*-*-*-*-*-*-*-*-*-*-*-*-*-*-*-*-*-*-*-*-*-*-*-*-*-*-*-*-*-*-*-*-*-*-*-*-*-*-*-*-*-*-*-*-*-*-*-*-*-*-*-*-*
```

Filename   : MEN1   Truss   Concept 2000 Version 6.00

Job Reference   : P.H.MENTON   Date: 2 Apr 90 14:45

Pitch   : 30.0

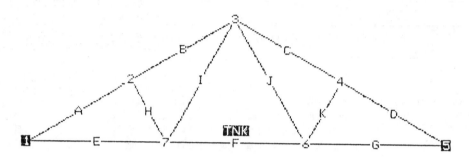

JIG SET-UP POINTS

X,Z & H DIMENSIONS FROM JOINT 3

JT	X	Y	Z	H	O/H
1	-3600	0	-3963	-3432	520
2	-1716	1088	-1981		
3	0	2078			
4	1716	1088	1981		
5	3600	0	3963	3432	520
6	1144	97			
7	-1144	97			

SPLICE MEMBER	SPLICE POSITION	JT NO	DISTANCE FROM JOINT			TOLERANCE	
			ACT	MIN	MAX	<--	-->
6/ 7	.249	6	569	350	572	3	219

	SET-UP	PRODUCTION	TOTAL
EQUIVALENT FINKS :	17.54	1.00	18.54

	INCLUDING OVERHANGS	EXCLUDING OVERHANGS
OVERALL SPAN :	8100	7200
OVERALL HEIGHT :	2421	2162

```
*-*-*-*-*-*-*-*-*-*-*-*-*-*-*-*-*-*-*-*-*-*-*-*-*-*-*-*-*-*-*-*-*-*-*-*-*-*-*-*-*-*-*-*-*-*-*-*-*-*-*-*-*
* GANG-NAIL  CONCEPT 2000 *        HUNTER TIMBER ENGINEERING LIMITED        * GANG-NAIL  CONCEPT 2000 *
*-*-*-*-*-*-*-*-*-*-*-*-*-*-*-*-*-*-*-*-*-*-*-*-*-*-*-*-*-*-*-*-*-*-*-*-*-*-*-*-*-*-*-*-*-*-*-*-*-*-*-*-*
```

```
*-*-*-*-*-*-*-*-*-*-*-*-*-*-*-*-*-*-*-*-*-*-*-*-*-*-*-*-*-*-*-*-*-*-*-*-*-*-*-*-*-*-*-*-*-*-*-*-*-*-*
* GANG-NAIL  CONCEPT 2000 *           HUNTER TIMBER ENGINEERING LIMITED           * GANG-NAIL  CONCEPT 2000 *
*-*-*-*-*-*-*-*-*-*-*-*-*-*-*-*-*-*-*-*-*-*-*-*-*-*-*-*-*-*-*-*-*-*-*-*-*-*-*-*-*-*-*-*-*-*-*-*-*-*-*
```

Filename   : MEN1   Truss   Concept 2000 Version 6.00

Job Reference : P.H.MENTON   Date: 2 Apr 90 14:45

Top Chord : M75 European Red/Whitewood   Internal Cutting Angles
Btm Chord : M75 European Red/Whitewood   Minimum Cutting Angle : 15.0 deg
Webs   : M75 European Red/Whitewood   Maximum Web Cut Length: 250mm
Treatment : Vac-Vac   Vertical Web Tolerance: 10.0 deg

ANGLE	SHAPE	ANGLE	PART	LENGTH O/A	EX	TIMBER SECTION	GRADE	NO OFF
60.0	*****************	120.0	4677					
36	* TC (1- 3) *	36	4677	4718	4800	35 x 72	M75 ERW	2
120.0	*****************	60.0	4677					
90.0	****************	30.0	4007					
49	* BC (1- S) *	48	4091	4175	4200	35 x 97	M75 ERW	1
90.0	*****************	150.0	4175					
90.0	***************	30.0	2857					
49	* BC (S- 5) *	48	2941	3025	3300	35 x 97	M75 ERW	1
90.0	*****************	150.0	3025					
30.0	***************	90.0	1092					
30	* WEB (2- 7) *	30	1144	1144	1200	35 x 60	M75 ERW	2
60.0	***************	90.0	1127					
30.0	**************	30.0	2184					
30	* WEB (7- 3) *	30	2288	2288	2400	35 x 60	M75 ERW	2
60.0	**************	30.0	2219					

```
*-*-*-*-*-*-*-*-*-*-*-*-*-*-*-*-*-*-*-*-*-*-*-*-*-*-*-*-*-*-*-*-*-*-*-*-*-*-*-*-*-*-*-*-*-*-*-*-*-*-*
* GANG-NAIL  CONCEPT 2000 *           HUNTER TIMBER ENGINEERING LIMITED           * GANG-NAIL  CONCEPT 2000 *
*-*-*-*-*-*-*-*-*-*-*-*-*-*-*-*-*-*-*-*-*-*-*-*-*-*-*-*-*-*-*-*-*-*-*-*-*-*-*-*-*-*-*-*-*-*-*-*-*-*-*
```

```
*-*-*-*-*-*-*-*-*-*-*-*-*-*-*-*-*-*-*-*-*-*-*-*-*-*-*-*-*-*-*-*-*-*-*-*-*-*-*-*-*-*-*-*-*-*-*-*-*
* GANG-NAIL  CONCEPT 2000 *           HUNTER TIMBER ENGINEERING LIMITED           * GANG-NAIL  CONCEPT 2000 *
*-*-*-*-*-*-*-*-*-*-*-*-*-*-*-*-*-*-*-*-*-*-*-*-*-*-*-*-*-*-*-*-*-*-*-*-*-*-*-*-*-*-*-*-*-*-*-*-*
```

Filename   : MEN1   Truss   Concept 2000 Version 6.00

Job Reference   : P.H.MENTON   Date: 2 Apr 90 14:45

Profile Truss   : Fink

Timber Requisition for 1 Truss

Top Chord   : M75 European Red/Whitewood   Treatment : Vac-Vac
Btm Chord   : M75 European Red/Whitewood
Webs   : M75 European Red/Whitewood

Timber Section	Grade	Ex Length	Cubic Metres	Linear Metres	No Off	
38 * 63	M75 ERW	1200	.006	2.4	2	....
38 * 63	M75 ERW	2400	.011	4.8	2	....
38 * 75	M75 ERW	4800	.027	9.6	2	....
38 * 100	M75 ERW	3300	.013	3.3	1	....
38 * 100	M75 ERW	4200	.016	4.2	1	....
			******	*******		
			.073	24.3		
			******	*******		

GROSS CUBE PER TRUSS   .073 CU.M.
NETT CUBE PER TRUSS   .063 CU.M.

-
* GANG-NAIL   CONCEPT 2000 *   HUNTER TIMBER ENGINEERING LIMITED   * GANG-NAIL   CONCEPT 2000 *
-

Filename   : MEN1   Truss   Concept 2000 Version 6.00
Job Reference : P.H.MENTON   Date: 2 Apr 90 14:46
Scale   1 : 42

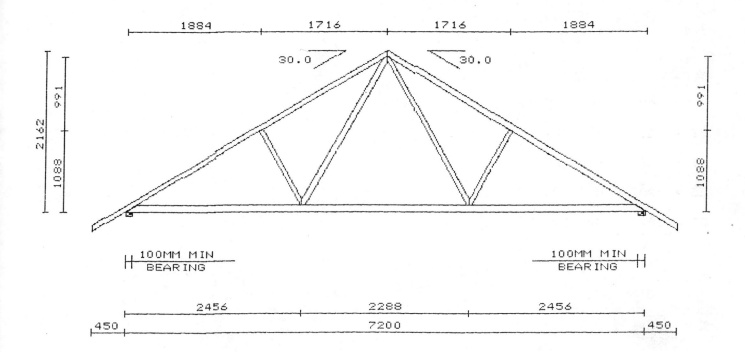

MR.D.J.HILL TEL:BRIDGWATER (0278) 445222
HUNTER TIMBER ENGINEERING LIMITED
THE LEGGAR,BRIDGWATER,SOMERSET. TA6 4AF.

Part III

Reference material

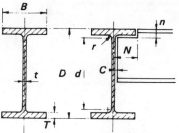

Table 1. Universal beams — dimensions for detailing

Serial size (mm)	Mass per metre (kg)	Depth of section D (mm)	Root radius r (mm)	Flange Width B (mm)	Flange Thickness T (mm)	Web Thickness t (mm)	Web Depth d (mm)	End clearance C (mm)	Notch N (mm)	Notch n (mm)
914 × 419	388	920.5	24.1	420.5	36.6	21.5	799.0	13	210	62
	343	911.4	24.1	418.5	32.0	19.4	799.0	12	210	58
914 × 305	289	926.6	19.1	307.8	32.0	19.6	824.4	12	156	52
	253	918.5	19.1	305.5	27.9	17.3	824.4	11	156	48
	224	910.3	19.1	304.1	23.9	15.9	824.4	10	156	44
	201	903.0	19.1	303.4	20.2	15.2	824.4	10	156	40
838 × 292	226	850.9	17.8	293.8	26.8	16.1	761.7	10	150	46
	194	840.7	17.8	292.4	21.7	14.7	761.7	9	150	40
	176	834.9	17.8	291.6	18.8	14.0	761.7	9	150	38
762 × 267	197	769.6	16.5	268.0	25.4	15.6	685.8	10	138	42
	173	762.0	16.5	266.7	21.6	14.3	685.8	9	138	40
	147	753.9	16.5	265.3	17.5	12.9	685.8	8	138	36
686 × 254	170	692.9	15.2	255.8	23.7	14.5	615.0	9	132	40
	152	687.6	15.2	254.5	21.0	13.2	615.0	9	132	38
	140	683.5	15.2	253.7	19.0	12.4	615.0	8	132	36
	125	677.9	15.2	253.0	16.2	11.7	615.0	8	132	32
610 × 305	238	633.0	16.5	311.5	31.4	18.6	537.2	11	158	48
	179	617.5	16.5	307.0	23.6	14.1	537.2	9	158	42
	149	609.6	16.5	304.8	19.7	11.9	537.2	8	158	38
610 × 229	140	617.0	12.7	230.1	22.1	13.1	547.2	9	120	36
	125	611.9	12.7	229.0	19.6	11.9	547.2	8	120	34
	113	607.3	12.7	228.2	17.3	11.2	547.2	8	120	32
	101	602.2	12.7	227.6	14.8	10.6	547.2	7	120	28
533 × 210	122	544.6	12.7	211.9	21.3	12.8	476.5	8	110	36
	109	539.5	12.7	210.7	18.8	11.6	476.5	8	110	32
	101	536.7	12.7	210.1	17.4	10.9	476.5	7	110	32
	92	533.1	12.7	209.3	15.6	10.2	476.5	7	110	30
	82	528.3	12.7	208.7	13.2	9.6	476.5	7	110	26
457 × 191	98	467.4	10.2	192.8	19.6	11.4	407.9	8	102	30
	89	463.6	10.2	192.0	17.7	10.6	407.9	7	102	28
	82	460.2	10.2	191.3	16.0	9.9	407.9	7	102	28
	74	457.2	10.2	190.5	14.5	9.1	407.9	7	102	26
	67	453.6	10.2	189.9	12.7	8.5	407.9	6	102	24

The dimension N is based upon the outstand from web face to flange edge + 10 mm to nearest 2 mm above, and makes due allowance for rolling tolerance.
The dimension $n = [(D - d)/2]$ to the nearest 2 mm above.
The dimension $C = (t/2) + 2$ mm to the nearest mm.

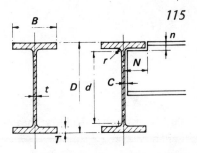

Table 1 (continued). Universal beams — dimensions for detailing

Serial size (mm)	Mass per metre (kg)	Depth of section D (mm)	Root radius r (mm)	Flange		Web		End clearance C (mm)	Notch	
				Width B (mm)	Thickness T (mm)	Thickness t (mm)	Depth d (mm)		N (mm)	n (mm)
457 × 152	82	465.1	10.2	153.5	18.9	10.7	406.9	7	82	30
	74	461.3	10.2	152.7	17.0	9.9	406.9	7	82	28
	67	457.2	10.2	151.9	15.0	9.1	406.9	7	82	26
	60	454.7	10.2	152.9	13.3	8.0	407.7	6	82	24
	52	449.8	10.2	152.4	10.9	7.6	407.7	6	82	22
406 × 178	74	412.8	10.2	179.7	16.0	9.7	360.5	7	96	28
	67	409.4	10.2	178.8	14.3	8.8	360.5	6	96	26
	60	406.4	10.2	177.8	12.8	7.8	360.5	6	96	24
	54	402.6	10.2	177.6	10.9	7.6	360.5	6	96	22
406 × 140	46	402.3	10.2	142.4	11.2	6.9	359.6	5	78	22
	39	397.3	10.2	141.8	8.6	6.3	359.6	5	78	20
356 × 171	67	364.0	10.2	173.2	15.7	9.1	312.2	7	94	26
	57	358.6	10.2	172.1	13.0	8.0	312.2	6	94	24
	51	355.6	10.2	171.5	11.5	7.3	312.2	6	94	22
	45	352.0	10.2	171.0	9.7	6.9	312.2	5	94	20
356 × 127	39	352.8	10.2	126.0	10.7	6.5	311.1	5	70	22
	33	348.5	10.2	125.4	8.5	5.9	311.1	5	70	20
305 × 165	54	310.9	8.9	166.8	13.7	7.7	265.6	6	90	24
	46	307.1	8.9	165.7	11.8	6.7	265.6	5	90	22
	40	303.8	8.9	165.1	10.2	6.1	265.6	5	90	20
305 × 127	48	310.4	8.9	125.2	14.0	8.9	264.6	6	70	24
	42	306.6	8.9	124.3	12.1	8.0	264.6	6	70	22
	37	303.8	8.9	123.5	10.7	7.2	264.6	6	70	20
305 × 102	33	312.7	7.6	102.4	10.8	6.6	275.8	5	58	20
	28	308.9	7.6	101.9	8.9	6.1	275.8	5	58	18
	25	304.8	7.6	101.6	6.8	5.8	275.8	5	58	16
254 × 146	43	259.6	7.6	147.3	12.7	7.3	218.9	6	80	22
	37	256.0	7.6	146.4	10.9	6.4	218.9	5	80	20
	31	251.5	7.6	146.1	8.6	6.1	218.9	5	80	18
254 × 102	28	260.4	7.6	102.1	10.0	6.4	225.0	5	58	18
	25	257.0	7.6	101.9	8.4	6.1	225.0	5	58	16
	22	254.0	7.6	101.6	6.8	5.8	225.0	5	58	16
203 × 133	30	206.8	7.6	133.8	9.6	6.3	172.3	5	74	18
	25	203.2	7.6	133.4	7.8	5.8	172.3	5	74	16

The dimension N is based upon the outstand from web face to flange edge + 10 mm to nearest 2 mm above, and makes due allowance for rolling tolerance.
The dimension $n = [(D - d)/2]$ to the nearest 2 mm above.
The dimension $C = (t/2) + 2$ mm to the nearest mm.

Table 1 (continued).   Universal beams – dimensions for detailing

Serial size (mm)	Mass per metre (kg)	Depth of section D (mm)	Root radius r (mm)	Flange		Web		End clearance C (mm)	Notch	
				Width B (mm)	Thickness T (mm)	Thickness t (mm)	Depth d (mm)		N (mm)	n (mm)
203 x 102	23	203.2	7.6	101.6	9.3	5.2	169.4	5	58	18
178 x 102	19	177.8	7.6	101.6	7.9	4.7	146.8	5	58	18
152 x 89	16	152.4	7.6	88.9	7.7	4.6	121.8	4	52	16
127 x 76	13	127.0	7.6	76.2	7.6	4.2	96.6	4	52	16

The dimension N is based upon the outstand from web face to flange edge + 10 mm to nearest 2 mm above, and makes due allowance for rolling tolerance.
The dimension $n = [(D - d)/2]$ to the nearest 2 mm above.
The dimension $C = (t/2) + 2$ mm to the nearest mm.

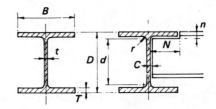

Table 2. Universal columns — dimensions for detailing

Serial size (mm)	Mass per metre (kg)	Depth of section D (mm)	Root radius r (mm)	Flange Width B (mm)	Flange Thickness T (mm)	Web Thickness t (mm)	Web Depth d (mm)	End clearance C (mm)	Notch N (mm)	Notch n (mm)
356 × 406	634	474.7	15.2	424.1	77.0	47.6	290.1	26	200	94
	551	455.7	15.2	418.5	67.5	42.0	290.1	23	200	84
	467	436.6	15.2	412.4	58.0	35.9	290.1	20	200	74
	393	419.1	15.2	407.0	49.2	30.6	290.1	17	200	66
	340	406.4	15.2	403.0	42.9	26.5	290.1	15	200	60
	287	393.7	15.2	399.0	36.5	22.6	290.1	13	200	52
	235	381.0	15.2	395.0	30.2	18.5	290.1	11	200	46
Column core	477	427.0	15.2	424.4	53.2	48.0	290.1	26	200	70
356 × 368	202	374.7	15.2	374.4	27.0	16.8	290.1	10	190	44
	177	368.3	15.2	372.1	23.8	14.5	290.1	9	190	40
	153	362.0	15.2	370.2	20.7	12.6	290.1	8	190	36
	129	355.6	15.2	368.3	17.5	10.7	290.1	7	190	34
305 × 305	283	365.3	15.2	321.8	44.1	26.9	246.5	15	158	60
	240	352.6	15.2	317.9	37.7	23.0	246.5	13	158	54
	198	339.9	15.2	314.1	31.4	19.2	246.5	12	158	48
	158	327.2	15.2	310.6	25.0	15.7	246.5	10	158	42
	137	320.5	15.2	308.7	21.7	13.8	246.5	9	158	38
	118	314.5	15.2	306.8	18.7	11.9	246.5	8	158	34
	97	307.8	15.2	304.8	15.4	9.9	246.5	7	158	32
254 × 254	167	289.1	12.7	264.5	31.7	19.2	200.2	12	134	46
	132	276.4	12.7	261.0	25.3	15.6	200.2	10	134	40
	107	266.7	12.7	258.3	20.5	13.0	200.2	9	134	34
	89	260.4	12.7	255.9	17.3	10.5	200.2	7	134	32
	73	254.0	12.7	254.0	14.2	8.6	200.2	6	134	28
203 × 203	86	222.3	10.2	208.8	20.5	13.0	160.8	8	108	32
	71	215.9	10.2	206.2	17.3	10.3	160.8	7	108	28
	60	209.6	10.2	205.2	14.2	9.3	160.8	7	108	26
	52	206.2	10.2	203.9	12.5	8.0	160.8	6	108	24
	46	203.2	10.2	203.2	11.0	7.3	160.8	6	108	22
152 × 152	37	161.8	7.6	154.4	11.5	8.1	123.4	6	84	20
	30	157.5	7.6	152.9	9.4	6.6	123.4	5	84	18
	23	152.4	7.6	152.4	6.8	6.1	123.4	5	84	16

The dimension N is based upon the outstand from web face to flange edge + 10 mm to nearest 2 mm above, and makes due allowance for rolling tolerance.
The dimension $n = [(D - d)/2]$ to the nearest 2 mm above.
The dimension $C = (t/2) + 2$ mm to the nearest mm.

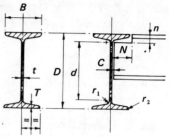

Table 3. Joists — dimensions for detailing

Serial size (mm)	Mass per metre (kg)	Depth of section D (mm)	Root radius r_1 (mm)	Toe radius r_2 (mm)	Flange Width B (mm)	Flange Thickness T (mm)	Web Thickness t (mm)	Web Depth d (mm)	End clearance C (mm)	Notch N (mm)	Notch n (mm)
254 × 203	81.85	254.0	19.6	9.7	203.2	19.9	10.2	166.6	7	102	44
254 × 114	37.20	254.0	12.4	6.1	114.3	12.8	7.6	199.2	6	60	28
203 × 152	52.09	203.2	15.5	7.6	152.4	16.5	8.9	133.2	7	78	36
152 × 127	37.20	152.4	13.5	6.6	127.0	13.2	10.4	94.3	7	64	30
127 × 114	29.76	127.0	9.9	4.8	114.3	11.5	10.2	79.4	7	58	24
127 × 114	26.79	127.0	9.9	5.0	114.3	11.4	7.4	79.5	6	60	24
127 × 76	16.37	127.0	9.4	4.6	76.2	9.6	5.6	86.5	5	42	22
114 × 114	26.79	114.3	14.2	3.2	114.3	10.7	9.5	60.8	7	58	28
102 × 102	23.07	101.6	11.1	3.2	101.6	10.3	9.5	55.1	7	52	24
102 × 44	7.44	101.6	6.9	3.3	44.4	6.1	4.3	74.7	4	26	14
89 × 89	19.35	88.9	11.1	3.2	88.9	9.9	9.5	44.1	7	46	24
76 × 76	14.67	76.2	9.4	4.6	80.0	8.4	8.9	38.0	7	42	20
76 × 76	12.65	76.2	9.4	4.6	76.2	8.4	5.1	37.9	5	42	20

Availability should be checked with BS Sections Product Unit.
Flanges of BS 4 joists have a taper at 8°.

The dimension N is equal to the outstand from web face to flange edge + 6 mm to nearest 2 mm above.
The dimension $n = [(D - d)/2]$ to the nearest 2 mm above.
The dimension $C = (t/2) + 2$ mm to the nearest mm.

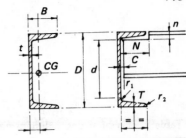

Table 4. Channels — dimensions for detailing

Serial size (mm)	Mass per metre (kg)	Depth of section D (mm)	Root radius r_1 (mm)	Toe radius r_2 (mm)	Flange Width B (mm)	Flange Thickness T (mm)	Web Thickness t (mm)	Web Depth d (mm)	End clearance C (mm)	Notch N (mm)	Notch n (mm)
432 × 102	65.54	431.8	15.2	4.8	101.6	16.8	12.2	362.5	14	96	36
381 × 102	55.10	381.0	15.2	4.8	101.6	16.3	10.4	312.4	12	98	36
305 × 102	46.18	304.8	15.2	4.8	101.6	14.8	10.2	239.3	12	98	34
305 × 89	41.69	304.8	13.7	3.2	88.9	13.7	10.2	245.4	12	86	30
254 × 89	35.74	254.0	13.7	3.2	88.9	13.6	9.1	194.8	11	86	30
254 × 76	28.29	254.0	12.2	3.2	76.2	10.9	8.1	203.7	10	76	26
229 × 89	32.76	228.6	13.7	3.2	88.9	13.3	8.6	169.9	11	88	30
229 × 76	26.06	228.6	12.2	3.2	76.2	11.2	7.6	178.1	10	76	26
203 × 89	29.78	203.2	13.7	3.2	88.9	12.9	8.1	145.3	10	88	30
203 × 76	23.82	203.2	12.2	3.2	76.2	11.2	7.1	152.4	9	76	26
178 × 89	26.81	177.8	13.7	3.2	88.9	12.3	7.6	120.9	10	88	30
178 × 76	20.84	177.8	12.2	3.2	76.2	10.3	6.6	128.8	9	76	26
152 × 89	23.84	152.4	13.7	3.2	88.9	11.6	7.1	97.0	9	88	28
152 × 76	17.88	152.4	12.2	2.4	76.2	9.0	6.4	105.9	8	76	24
127 × 64	14.90	127.0	10.7	2.4	63.5	9.2	6.4	84.1	8	64	22
102 × 51	10.42	101.6	9.1	2.4	50.8	7.6	6.1	65.8	8	52	18
76 × 38	6.70	76.2	7.6	2.4	38.1	6.8	5.1	45.7	7	40	16

All channels are rolled with a 5° slope to inside flanges.
The dimension N is equal to the outstand from web face to flange edge + 6 mm to nearest 2 mm above.
The dimension $n = [(D − d)/2]$ to the nearest 2 mm above.
The dimension C for channels = $t + 2$ to the nearest mm.

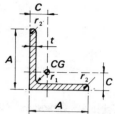

Table 5. Equal angles — dimensions for detailing

Designation		Leg length A (mm)	Thickness t (mm)	Mass per metre (kg)	Radius		Area of section (cm²)	Distance of centre of gravity C (cm)
Size (mm)	Thickness (mm)				Root r₁ (mm)	Toe r₂ (mm)		
200 × 200	24		24	71.1			90.6	5.84
	20		20	59.9			76.3	5.68
	18	200	18	54.2	18	4.8	69.1	5.60
	16		16	48.5			61.8	5.52
150 × 150	18		18	40.1			51.0	4.37
	15		15	33.8			43.0	4.25
	12	150	12	27.3	16	4.8	34.8	4.12
	10		10	23.0			29.3	4.03
120 × 120	15		15	26.6			33.9	3.51
	12		12	21.6			27.5	3.40
	10	120	10	18.2	13	4.8	23.2	3.31
	8		8	14.7			18.7	3.23
100 × 100	15		15	21.9			27.9	3.02
	12	100	12	17.8	12	4.8	22.7	2.90
	8		8	12.2			15.5	2.74
90 × 90	12		12	15.9			20.3	2.66
	10		10	13.4			17.1	2.58
	8	90	8	10.9	11	4.8	13.9	2.50
	6		6	8.30			10.6	2.41
80 × 80	10		10	11.9			15.1	2.34
	8	80	8	9.63	10	4.8	12.3	2.26
	6		6	7.34			9.35	2.17

Some of the thicknesses given in this table are obtained by raising the rolls. (Practice in this respect is not uniform throughout the industry). In such cases the legs will be slightly longer and the backs of the toes will be slightly rounded.

100 × 100 × 10 mm angle is also frequently rolled; as an ISO size its properties are given in Appendix A (Table A1) to BS 4848: Part 4. Other non-standard sections, particularly other thicknesses of the standard range, may also be available. Enquiries should be made to BS Sections Product Unit.

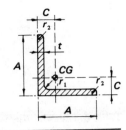

Table 5 (continued). Equal angles — dimensions for detailing

Designation		Leg length A (mm)	Thickness t (mm)	Mass per metre (kg)	Radius		Area of section (cm²)	Distance of centre of gravity C (cm)
Size (mm)	Thickness (mm)				Root r_1 (mm)	Toe r_2 (mm)		
70 × 70	10	70	10	10.3	9	2.4	13.1	2.09
	8		8	8.36			10.6	2.01
	6		6	6.38			8.13	1.93
60 × 60	10	60	10	8.69	8	2.4	11.1	1.85
	8		8	7.09			9.03	1.77
	6		6	5.42			6.91	1.69
	5		5	4.57			5.82	1.64
50 × 50	8	50	8	5.82	7	2.4	7.41	1.52
	6		6	4.47			5.59	1.45
	5		5	3.77			4.80	1.40
45 × 45	6	45	6	4.00	7	2.4	5.09	1.32
	5		5	3.38			4.30	1.28
	4		4	2.74			3.49	1.23
40 × 40	6	40	6	3.52	6	2.4	4.48	1.20
	5		5	2.97			3.79	1.16
	4		4	2.42			3.08	1.12
25 × 25	5	25	5	1.77	3.5	2.4	2.26	0.80
	4		4	1.45			1.85	0.76
	3		3	1.11			1.42	0.72

Some of the thicknesses given in this table are obtained by raising the rolls. (Practice in this respect is not uniform throughout the industry). In such cases the legs will be slightly longer and the backs of the toes will be slightly rounded.

100 × 100 × 10 mm angle is also frequently rolled; as an ISO size its properties are given in Appendix A (Table A1) to BS 4848: Part 4. Other non-standard sections, particularly other thicknesses of the standard range, may also be available. Enquiries should be made to BS Sections Product Unit.

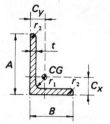

Table 6. Unequal angles — dimensions for detailing

| Designation | | Leg lengths | | Thickness t (mm) | Mass per metre (kg) | Radius | | Area of section (cm²) | Distance of centre of gravity | |
Size (mm)	Thickness (mm)	A (mm)	B (mm)			Root r_1 (mm)	Toe r_2 (mm)		C_x (cm)	C_y (cm)
200 × 150	18			18	47.1			60.0	6.33	3.85
	15	200	150	15	39.6	15	4.8	50.5	6.21	3.73
	12			12	32.0			40.8	6.08	3.61
200 × 100	15			15	33.7			43.0	7.16	2.22
	12	200	100	12	27.3	15	4.8	34.8	7.03	2.10
	10			10	23.0			29.2	6.93	2.01
150 × 90	15			15	26.6			33.9	5.21	2.23
	12	150	90	12	21.6	12	4.8	27.5	5.08	2.12
	10			10	18.2			23.2	5.00	2.04
150 × 75	15			15	24.8			31.6	5.53	1.81
	12	150	75	12	20.2	11	4.8	25.7	5.41	1.69
	10			10	17.0			21.6	5.32	1.61
125 × 75	12			12	17.8			22.7	4.31	1.84
	10	125	75	10	15.0	11	4.8	19.1	4.23	1.76
	8			8	12.2			15.5	4.14	1.68
100 × 75	12			12	15.4			19.7	3.27	2.03
	10	100	75	10	13.0	10	4.8	16.6	3.19	1.95
	8			8	10.6			13.5	3.10	1.87

Some of the thicknesses given in this table are obtained by raising the rolls. (Practice in this respect is not uniform throughout the industry.) In such cases the legs will be slightly longer and the backs of the toes will be slightly rounded.

Additional non-standard sizes may be available, especially other thicknesses of the standard range and certain sizes in the old Imperial range, namely 125 × 75 × 6.5 and 137 × 102 × 9.5, 7.9 and 6.4 (purlin angles) and 100 × 75 × 6.5. Enquiries should be made to BS Sections Product Unit.

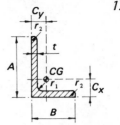

Table 6 (continued).   Unequal angles — dimensions for detailing

Designation		Leg lengths		Thickness t (mm)	Mass per metre (kg)	Radius		Area of section (cm²)	Distance of centre of gravity	
Size (mm)	Thickness (mm)	A (mm)	B (mm)			Root r_1 (mm)	Toe r_2 (mm)		C_x (cm)	C_y (cm)
100 × 65	10			10	12.3			15.6	3.36	1.63
	8	100	65	8	9.94	10	4.8	12.7	3.27	1.55
	7			7	8.77			11.2	3.23	1.51
80 × 60	8			8	8.34			10.6	2.55	1.56
	7	80	60	7	7.36	8	4.8	9.38	2.51	1.52
	6			6	6.37			8.11	2.47	1.48
75 × 50	8	75	50	8	7.39	7	2.4	9.41	2.52	1.29
	6			6	5.65			7.19	2.44	1.21
65 × 50	8			8	6.75			8.60	2.11	1.37
	6	65	50	6	5.16	6	2.4	6.58	2.04	1.29
	5			5	4.35			5.54	1.99	1.25

Some of the thicknesses given in this table are obtained by raising the rolls. (Practice in this respect is not uniform throughout the industry.) In such cases the legs will be slightly longer and the backs of the toes will be slightly rounded.

Additional non-standard sizes may be available, especially other thicknesses of the standard range and certain sizes in the old Imperial range, namely 125 × 75 × 6.5 and 137 × 102 × 9.5, 7.9 and 6.4 (purlin angles) and 100 × 75 × 6.5. Enquiries should be made to BS Sections Product Unit.

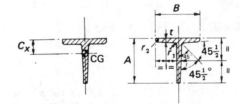

Table 7.   Rolled tees — dimensions for detailing

Designation					Radius			Centre of gravity
Size (mm)	Mass per metre (kg)	Width B (mm)	Depth A (mm)	Thickness t (mm)	r_1 (mm)	r_2 (mm)	Area (cm²)	C_x (cm)
51 × 51	6.92	50.8	50.8	9.5	6.1	4.3	8.82	1.60
	4.76	50.8	50.8	6.4	6.1	4.3	6.06	1.47
44 × 44	4.11	44.4	44.4	6.4	5.8	3.8	5.24	1.32
	3.14	44.4	44.4	4.8	5.8	3.8	4.00	1.24
38 × 38	3.49	38.1	38.1	6.4	5.3	3.8	4.45	1.17
	2.66	38.1	38.1	4.8	5.3	3.8	3.39	1.09

Size 44 × 44 is a non-standard. Enquiries should be made to BS Sections Product Unit for availability.

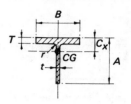

Table 8. Structural tees cut from universal beams — dimensions for detailing

Serial size (mm)	Mass per metre (kg)	Cut from universal beam		Width of section B (mm)	Depth of section A (mm)	Thickness		Root radius r (mm)	Area of section (cm²)	Dimension C_x (cm)
		Serial size (mm)	Mass (kg/m)			Web t (mm)	Flange T (mm)			
305 × 457	127	914 × 305	253	305.5	459.2	17.3	27.9	19.1	161.4	12.0
	112		224	304.1	455.2	15.9	23.9	19.1	142.6	12.1
	101		201	303.4	451.5	15.2	20.2	19.1	128.2	12.5
292 × 419	113	838 × 292	226	293.8	425.5	16.1	26.8	17.8	144.4	10.8
	97		194	292.4	420.4	14.7	21.7	17.8	123.6	11.1
	88		176	291.6	417.4	14.0	18.8	17.8	112.1	11.4
267 × 381	99	762 × 267	197	268.0	384.8	15.6	25.4	16.5	125.4	9.90
	87		173	266.7	381.0	14.3	21.6	16.5	110.2	9.99
	74		147	265.3	376.9	12.9	17.5	16.5	94.0	10.20
254 × 343	85	686 × 254	170	255.8	346.5	14.5	23.7	15.2	108.3	8.67
	76		152	254.5	343.8	13.2	21.0	15.2	96.9	8.6
	70		140	253.7	341.8	12.4	19.0	15.2	89.3	8.65
	63		125	253.0	339.0	11.7	16.2	15.2	79.8	8.87
305 × 305	119	610 × 305	238	311.5	316.5	18.6	31.4	16.5	151.9	7.11
	90		179	307.0	308.7	14.1	23.6	16.5	114.0	6.65
	75		149	304.8	304.8	11.9	19.7	16.5	95.1	6.43
229 × 305	70	610 × 229	140	230.1	308.5	13.1	22.1	12.7	89.2	7.61
	63		125	229.0	305.9	11.9	19.6	12.7	79.8	7.55
	57		113	228.2	303.7	11.2	17.3	12.7	72.2	7.60
	51		101	227.6	301.1	10.6	14.8	12.7	64.6	7.80
210 × 267	61	533 × 210	122	211.9	272.3	12.8	21.3	12.7	77.9	6.67
	55		109	210.7	269.7	11.6	18.8	12.7	69.3	6.60
	51		101	210.1	268.4	10.9	17.4	12.7	64.6	6.57
	46		92	209.3	266.6	10.2	15.6	12.7	58.9	6.56
	41		82	208.7	264.2	9.6	13.2	12.7	52.2	6.73
191 × 229	49	457 × 191	98	192.8	233.7	11.4	19.6	10.2	62.6	5.55
	45		89	192.0	231.8	10.6	17.7	10.2	57.0	5.49
	41		82	191.3	230.1	9.9	16.0	10.2	52.3	5.48
	37		74	190.5	228.6	9.1	14.5	10.2	47.5	5.42
	34		67	189.9	226.8	8.5	12.7	10.2	42.7	5.47

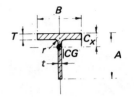

Table 8 (continued). Structural tees cut from universal beams — dimensions for detailing

| Serial size (mm) | Mass per metre (kg) | Cut from universal beam | | Width of section B (mm) | Depth of section A (mm) | Thickness | | Root radius r (mm) | Area of section (cm²) | Dimension C_x (cm) |
		Serial size (mm)	Mass (kg/m)			Web t (mm)	Flange T (mm)			
152 × 229	41	457 × 152	82	153.5	232.5	10.7	18.9	10.2	52.2	6.03
	37		74	152.7	230.6	9.9	17.0	10.2	47.5	5.98
	34		67	151.9	228.6	9.1	15.0	10.2	42.7	5.99
	30		60	152.9	227.3	8.0	13.3	10.2	38.0	5.82
	26		52	152.4	224.9	7.6	10.9	10.2	33.2	6.03
178 × 203	37	406 × 178	74	179.7	206.4	9.7	16.0	10.2	47.5	4.80
	34		67	178.8	204.7	8.8	14.3	10.2	42.7	4.73
	30		60	177.8	203.2	7.8	12.8	10.2	38.0	4.62
	27		54	177.6	201.3	7.6	10.9	10.2	34.2	4.81
140 × 203	23	406 × 140	46	142.4	201.2	6.9	11.2	10.2	29.5	5.05
	20		39	141.8	198.6	6.3	8.6	10.2	24.7	5.27
171 × 178	34	356 × 171	67	173.2	182.0	9.1	15.7	10.2	42.7	4.01
	29		57	172.1	179.3	8.0	13.0	10.2	36.1	3.95
	26		51	171.5	177.8	7.3	11.5	10.2	32.3	3.92
	23		45	171.0	176.0	6.9	9.7	10.2	28.5	4.02
127 × 178	20	356 × 127	39	126.0	176.4	6.5	10.7	10.2	24.7	4.41
	17		33	125.4	174.2	5.9	8.5	10.2	20.9	4.52
165 × 152	27	305 × 165	54	166.8	155.4	7.7	13.7	8.9	34.2	3.19
	23		46	165.7	153.5	6.7	11.8	8.9	29.5	3.09
	20		40	165.1	151.9	6.1	10.2	8.9	25.8	3.07
127 × 152	24	305 × 127	48	125.2	155.2	8.9	14.0	8.9	30.4	3.91
	21		42	124.3	153.3	8.0	12.1	8.9	26.6	3.85
	19		37	123.5	151.9	7.2	10.7	8.9	23.7	3.80
102 × 152	17	305 × 102	33	102.4	156.3	6.6	10.8	7.6	20.9	4.14
	14		28	101.9	154.4	6.1	8.9	7.6	18.2	4.23
	13		25	101.6	152.4	5.8	6.8	7.6	15.7	4.48
146 × 127	22	254 × 146	43	147.3	129.8	7.3	12.7	7.6	27.6	2.67
	19		37	146.4	128.0	6.4	10.9	7.6	23.7	2.58
	16		31	146.1	125.7	6.1	8.6	7.6	20.0	2.68
102 × 127	14	254 × 102	28	102.1	130.2	6.4	10.0	7.6	18.1	3.25
	13		25	101.9	128.5	6.1	8.4	7.6	16.1	3.35
	11		22	101.6	127.0	5.8	6.8	7.6	14.2	3.49
133 × 102	15	203 × 133	30	133.8	103.4	6.3	9.6	7.6	19.0	2.10
	13		25	133.4	101.6	5.8	7.8	7.6	16.1	2.12

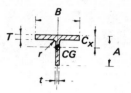

Table 9. Structural tees cut from universal columns -- dimensions for detailing

| Serial size (mm) | Mass per metre (kg) | Cut from universal beam | | Width of section B (mm) | Depth of section A (mm) | Thickness | | Root radius r (mm) | Area of section (cm²) | Dimension C_x (cm) |
		Serial size (mm)	Mass (kg/m)			Web t (mm)	Flange T (mm)			
406 × 178	118	356 × 406	235	395.0	190.5	18.5	30.2	15.2	149.9	3.41
368 × 178	101	356 × 368	202	374.4	187.3	16.8	27.0	15.2	129.0	3.32
	89		177	372.1	184.2	14.5	23.8	15.2	112.9	3.10
	77		153	370.2	181.0	12.6	20.7	15.2	97.6	2.92
	65		129	368.3	177.8	10.7	17.5	15.2	82.5	2.73
305 × 152	79	305 × 305	158	310.6	163.6	15.7	25.0	15.2	100.6	3.04
	69		137	308.7	160.3	13.8	21.7	15.2	87.3	2.86
	59		118	306.8	157.2	11.9	18.7	15.2	74.9	2.69
	49		97	304.8	153.9	9.9	15.4	15.2	61.6	2.50
254 × 127	66	254 × 254	132	261.0	138.2	15.6	25.3	12.7	84.5	2.72
	54		107	258.3	133.4	13.0	20.5	12.7	68.3	2.47
	45		89	255.9	130.2	10.5	17.3	12.7	57.0	2.24
	37		73	254.0	127.0	8.6	14.2	12.7	46.4	2.06
203 × 102	43	203 × 203	86	208.8	111.1	13.0	20.5	10.2	55.0	2.22
	36		71	206.2	108.0	10.3	17.3	10.2	45.5	1.98
	30		60	205.2	104.8	9.3	14.2	10.2	37.9	1.88
	26		52	203.9	103.1	8.0	12.5	10.2	33.2	1.76
	23		46	203.2	101.6	7.3	11.0	10.2	29.4	1.71
152 × 76	19	152 × 152	37	154.4	80.9	8.1	11.5	7.6	23.7	1.55
	15		30	152.9	78.7	6.6	9.4	7.6	19.1	1.41
	12		23	152.4	76.2	6.1	6.8	7.6	14.9	1.43

Table 10. Black bolts and nuts to BS 4190 — range of sizes

Nominal size and thread diameter (mm)	Pitch of thread (coarse pitch series) (mm)	Max. width of head and nut		Max. height of head		Max. thickness of nut		Tensile stress area (mm²)	Minimum distance between centres (mm)
		Across flats (mm)	Across corners (mm)	Black (mm)	Faced on underside (mm)	Black (mm)	Faced one side (mm)		
6	1	10.00	11.5	4.375	4.24	5.375	5	20.1	15
8	1.25	13.00	15.0	5.875	5.74	6.875	6.5	36.6	20
10	1.5	17.00	19.6	7.45	7.29	8.45	8	58.0	25
12	1.75	19.00	21.9	8.45	8.29	10.45	10	84.3	30
16	2	24.00	27.7	10.45	10.29	13.55	13	157	40
20	2.5	30.00	34.6	13.90	13.35	16.55	16	245	50
(22)	2.5	32.00	36.9	14.90	14.35	18.55	18	303	55
24	3	36.00	41.6	15.90	15.35	19.65	19	353	60
(27)	3	41.00	47.3	17.90	17.35	22.65	22	459	67.5
30	3.5	46.00	53.1	20.05	19.42	24.65	24	561	75
(33)	3.5	50.00	57.7	22.05	21.42	26.65	26	694	82.5
36	4	55.00	63.5	24.05	23.42	29.65	29	817	90
(39)	4	60.00	69.3	26.05	25.42	31.80	31	976	97.5
42	4.5	65.00	75.1	27.05	26.42	34.80	34	1120	105
(45)	4.5	70.00	80.8	29.05	28.42	36.80	36	1300	112
48	5	75.00	86.6	31.05	30.42	38.80	38	1470	120
(52)	5	80.00	92.4	34.25	33.50	42.80	42	1760	130
56	5.5	85.00	98.1	36.25	35.50	45.80	45	2030	140

Sizes shown in brackets are non-preferred.

Table 11. Black washers to BS 4320 — range of sizes

Nominal size of bolt (mm)	Flat				Taper
	Form E		Form F		
	Outside dia. (mm)	Thickness (mm)	Outside dia. (mm)	Thickness (mm)	
6	12.5	1.6			
8	17.0	1.6	21.0	1.6	
10	21.0	2.0	24.0	2.0	
12	24.0	2.5	28.0	2.5	
16	30.0	3.0	34.0	3.0	
20	37.0	3.0	39.0	3.0	
(22)	39.0	3.0	44.0	3.0	For taper washers see table 15
24	44.0	3.0	50.0	3.0	
(27)	50.0	4.0	56.0	4.0	
30	56.0	4.0	60.0	4.0	
(33)	60.0	5.0	66.0	5.0	
36	66.0	5.0	72.0	6.0	

Sizes shown in brackets are non-preferred.

Table 12. Manufacturers' recommended range of sizes of black bolts — grade 4.6

Nominal length (mm)	Nominal diameter						
	M6	M8	M10	M12	M16	M20	M24
20	•						
25	•	•	•	•			
30	•	•	•	•	○		
35	•	•	•	•	○		
40	•	•	•	•	○	○	
45	•	•	•	•	○	○	
50	•	•	•	•	△	○	
55			•	•	△	○	
60	•	•	•	•	△	△	○
65			•	•	△	△	
70	•	•	•	•	△	△	△
75			•	•	△	△	
80	•	•	•	•	△	△	△
90	•	•	•	•	△	△	△
100	•	•	•	•	△	△	△
110				•	•	•	•
120		•	•	•	•	•	•
130					•	•	
140			•	•	•	•	•
150						•	
160				•	•	•	•
180				•	•	•	•
200				•	•	•	•
220				•	•	•	•
260				•	•	•	•
300				•	•	•	•

•—Standard thread lengths.
○—Short thread lengths.
△—Available in standard and short thread lengths.

Table 13. HSFG bolts and nuts to BS 4395: Part 1 — range of sizes

Nominal size and thread diameter (mm)	Pitch of thread (coarse pitch series) (mm)	Max. width of head and nut		Max. height		Washer face of head and nut		Max. radius under head (mm)	Tensile stress area (mm²)	Proof load	
		Across flats (mm)	Across corners (mm)	Head (mm)	Nut (mm)	Max. dia. (mm)	Max. thickness (mm)			tonne force (1000 kgf)	kilo-newtons
12*	1.75	22.0	25.4	10.45	11.55	22.0	0.4	1.0	84.3	5.04	49.4
16	2.0	27.0	31.2	10.45	15.55	27.0	0.4	1.0	157	9.39	92.1
20	2.5	32.0	36.9	13.90	18.55	32.0	0.4	1.2	245	14.64	144
22	2.5	36.0	41.6	14.90	19.65	36.0	0.4	1.2	303	18.11	177
24	3.0	41.0	47.3	15.90	22.65	41.0	0.5	1.2	353	21.10	207
27	3.0	46.0	53.1	17.90	24.65	46.0	0.5	1.5	459	23.88	234
30	3.5	50.0	57.7	20.05	26.65	50.0	0.5	1.5	561	29.19	286
36	4.0	60.0	69.3	24.05	31.80	60.0	0.5	1.5	817	42.51	418

*Non-preferred. To be used only for the lighter type of construction where practical conditions, such as material thickness, do not warrant the usage of a larger size bolt than M12.

There are other types of friction grip bolts available and reference should be made to BS 4395: Parts 2 and 3.

Table 14. Length of bolts. The minimum length of a bolt should be calculated by adding to the grip the allowance given in the table.

Nominal size and thread diameter	M12	M16	M20	M22	M24	M27	M30	M36
Allowance to be added to the grip in mm	22	26	30	34	36	39	42	48

These figures allow for the thickness of one nut and one flat washer and for sufficient protrusion of the bolt end. When other washer arrangements (including taper washers) are used, an additional allowance will be required in determining the length of the bolt.

Table 15. HSFG washers to BS 4395: Part 1 — range of sizes

Nominal size of bolt (mm)	Round flat		Square taper		
	Outside diameter (mm)	Thickness (mm)	Length of side (mm)	Mean thickness	
				3° and 5° (mm)	8° (mm)
12*	30	2.8	31.75	4.76	6.35
16	37	3.4	38.10	4.76	6.35
20	44	3.7	38.10	4.76	6.35
22	50	4.2	44.45	4.76	6.35
24	56	4.2	57.15	4.76	6.35
27	60	4.2	57.15	4.76	6.35
30	66	4.2	57.15	4.76	6.35
36	85	4.6	57.15	4.76	6.35

Washers to BS 4395: Parts 2 and 3 are the same as the dimensions given in table 15.

*Non-preferred.

Table 16. Manufacturers' recommended range of sizes of
           HSFG bolts — general grade

Nominal length (mm)	Nominal diameter							
	M12*	M16	M20	M22	M24	M27	M30	M36
30		X						
35		0						
40	0	X	X	0				
45	0	0	0	0				
50	0	X	X	X	X	0		
55	0	0						
60	0	X	X	X	X	0		
65	0	0	0	0				
70	0	X	X	X	X	0	0	
75	0	0	0	0	0	0		
80	0	X	X	X	X	0	0	
85	0	0	0	0	0	0	0	
90	0	0	X	X	X	0	0	
100	0	0	0	X	X	0	0	0
110	0	0	0	0	X	0	0	0
120	0	0	0	0	X	0	0	0
130	0	0	0	0	0	0	0	0
140	0	0	0	0	0	0	0	0
150	0	0	0	0	0	0	0	0
160	0	0	0	0	0	0	0	0
170	0	0	0	0	0	0	0	0
180	0	0	0	0	0	0	0	0
190	0	0	0	0	0	0	0	0
200	0	0	0	0	0	0	0	0
220	0	0	0	0	0	0	0	0
240	0	0	0	0	0	0	0	0
260	0	0	0	0	0	0	0	0
280	0	0	0	0	0	0	0	0
300	0	0	0	0	0	0	0	0

X Stock sizes.
* Non-preferred diameters.

THE DETAILING OF STRUCTURAL STEELWORK ACCORDING TO *BS 449: THE USE OF STRUCTURAL STEEL IN BUILDING*

RIVETS AND RIVETING

51. *a.* **Rivets.** Rivets shall conform to the requirements of BS 4620 for dimensions.

b. **Minimum pitch.** The distance between centres of rivets shall be not less than $2\frac{1}{2}$ times the nominal diameter of the rivet.

c. **Maximum pitch.** (i) The distance between centres of any two adjacent rivets (including tacking rivets) connecting together elements of compression or tension members shall not exceed $32t$ or 300 mm where t is the thickness of the thinner outside plate.

(ii) The distance between centres of two adjacent rivets, in a line lying in the direction of stress, shall not exceed $16t$ or 200 mm in tension members, and $12t$ or 200 mm in compression members. In the case of compression members in which forces are transferred through butting faces this distance shall not exceed $4\frac{1}{2}$ times the diameter of the rivets for a distance from the abutting faces equal to $1\frac{1}{2}$ times the width of the member.

(iii) The distance between centres of any two consecutive rivets in a line adjacent and parallel to an edge of an outside plate shall not exceed 100 mm+$4t$, or 200 mm in compression or tension members.

(iv) When rivets are staggered at equal intervals and the gauge does not exceed 75 mm the distances specified in (ii) and (iii) above, between centres of rivets, may be increased by 50 per cent.

d. **Edge distance.** (i) The minimum distance from the centre of any hole to the edge of a plate shall be in accordance with Table 21.

(ii) Where two or more parts are connected together a line of rivets or bolts shall be provided at a distance of not more

Table 21. Edge distance of holes

Diameter of hole (mm)	Distance to sheared or hand flame cut edge (mm)	Distance to rolled, machine flame cut, sawn or planed edge (mm)
39	68	62
36	62	56
33	56	50
30	50	44
26	42	36
24	38	32
22	34	30
20	30	28
18	28	26
16	26	24
14	24	22
12 or less	22	20

than 40 mm + $4t$ from the nearest edge, where t is the thickness in millimetres of the thinner outside plate. In the case of work not exposed to weather, this may be increased to $12t$.

e. **Tacking rivets.** Where tacking rivets are necessary to satisfy the requirements of *d* (ii) above, such tacking rivets, not subject to calculated stress, shall have a pitch in line not exceeding 32 times the thickness of the outside plate or 300 mm whichever is the less. Where the plates are exposed to the weather, the pitch in line shall not exceed 16 times the thickness of the outside plate or 200 mm whichever is the less. In both cases, the lines of rivets shall not be a greater distance apart than these pitches.

The foregoing requirements shall apply to struts and compression members generally, subject to the stipulations in this British Standard affecting the design and construction of struts.

131

In tension members composed of two flats, angles, channels or tees in contact back-to-back or separated back-to-back by a distance not exceeding the aggregate thickness of the connected parts, tacking rivets, with solid distance pieces where the parts are separated, shall be provided at a pitch in line not exceeding 1000 mm.

f. **Countersunk heads.** For countersunk heads one-half of the depth of the countersinking shall be neglected in calculating the length of the rivet in bearing. For rivets in tension with countersunk heads the tensile value shall be reduced by $33\frac{1}{3}$ per cent. No reduction need be made in shear.

g. **Long grip rivets.** Where the grip of rivets carrying calculated loads exceeds 6 times the diameter of the holes, the number of rivets required by normal calculation shall be increased by not less than $\frac{5}{8}$ per cent per additional 1 mm of grip; but the grip shall not exceed 8 times the diameter of the holes.

BOLTS AND BOLTING

52. *a.* **Pitches, edge distances and tacking bolts.** The requirements for bolts shall be the same as specified for rivets in Subclauses 51*b, c, d* and *e*.

b. **Black bolts (black all over).** The dimensions shall conform to those given for black bolts in BS 4190, 'ISO metric black hexagon bolts, screws and nuts.'

c. **Close tolerance bolts.** The dimensions shall conform to those given for bolts 'faced under the head and turned on shank' in BS 4190.

INSPECTION

55. The purchaser and his authorised representatives shall have access at all reasonable times to all places where the work is being carried out, and shall be provided, by the contractor, with all the necessary facilities for inspection during construction.

STRAIGHTNESS

56. All material, before and after fabrication, shall be straight unless required to be of curvilinear form, and shall be free from twists.

CLEARANCES

57. Care shall be taken to ensure that the clearances specified are worked to. The erection clearance for cleated ends of members connecting steel to steel shall not be greater than 2 mm at each end. The erection clearance at ends of beams without web cleats shall be not more than 3 mm at each end, but where, for practical reasons, this clearance has to be increased, the seatings shall be suitably designed.

Where black bolts are used the holes may be made not more than 2 mm greater than the diameter of the bolts, for bolts up to 24 mm diameter and not more than 3 mm greater than the diameter of the bolts, for bolts over 24 mm diameter, unless otherwise specified by the Engineer.

CUTTING

58. Cutting may be by shearing, cropping, sawing or machine flame cutting. Hand flame cutting may be permitted, subject to the approval of the Engineer.

Sheared or cropped edges shall, if necessary, be dressed to a neat workmanlike finish and shall be free from distortion where parts are to be in metal-to-metal contact.

HOLING

59. Holes through more than one thickness of material for members such as compound stanchion and girder flanges shall, where possible, be drilled after the members are assembled and tightly clamped or bolted together. Punching may be permitted before assembly, provided the holes are punched 2 mm less in diameter than the required size and reamed after assembly to the full diameter. The thickness of material punched shall be not greater than 15 mm.

When holes are drilled in one operation through two or more separable parts, these parts, when so specified by the Engineer, shall be separated after drilling and the burrs removed.

Holes in connecting angles and plates, other than splices, also in roof members and light framing, may be punched full size through material not over 12 mm thick, except where required for close tolerance or barrel bolts.

All matching holes for rivets and black bolts shall register with each other so that a gauge 2 mm less in diameter than the diameter of hole will pass freely through the assembled members in a direction at right angles to such members. Finished holes shall not be more than 2 mm in diameter larger than the diameter of the rivet or black bolt passing through them, for rivet or bolt diameters up to 24 mm, and not more than 3 mm greater than the diameter of the rivet or black bolt for rivet or bolt diameters over 24 mm, unless otherwise specified by the Engineer.

Holes for close tolerance and barrel bolts shall be drilled to a diameter equal to the nominal diameter of the shank or barrel subject to a tolerance of +0.15 mm and −0 mm. Preferably, parts to be connected with close tolerance or barrel bolts shall be firmly held together by tacking bolts or clamps and the holes drilled through all the thicknesses at one operation and subsequently reamed to size. All holes not drilled through all thicknesses at one operation shall be drilled to a smaller size and reamed out after assembly. Where this is not practicable, the parts shall be drilled and reamed separately through hard bushed steel jigs.

Holes for rivets or bolts shall not be formed by a gas cutting process.

BOLTING

62. Where necessary, washers shall be tapered or otherwise suitably shaped to give the heads and nuts of bolts a satisfactory bearing.

The threaded portion of each bolt shall project through the nut at least one thread.

In all cases where the full bearing area of the bolt is to be developed, the bolt shall be provided with a washer of sufficent thickness under the nut to avoid any threaded portion of the bolt being within the thickness of the parts bolted together.

Where a tubular member is drilled to take bolts or studs, provision shall be made to prevent the access of moisture to the interior of the tube. For example, a transverse sleeve can be inserted where a bolt passes through a tube, or grommets can be used under heads and nuts.

WELDING

63. Welding shall be in accordance with BS 5135 Metal-arc welding of carbon and carbon manganese steels.

MACHINING OF BUTTS, CAPS AND BASES

66. Stanchion splices and butt joints of compression members dependent on contact for the transmission of compressive stresses, shall be *accurately prepared to butt* so that the permitted stress in bearing is not exceeded nor eccentricity of loading created which would induce secondary bending in the members. Stanchion caps and bases shall be prepared in a similar manner to the above, and, where this is obtained by machining, care shall be taken that any attached gussets, connecting angles or channels are fixed with such accuracy that they are not reduced in thickness by more than 2 mm.

SLAB BASES AND CAPS

67. Slab bases and slab caps, except when cut from material with true surfaces, shall be accurately machined over the bearing surfaces and shall be in effective contact with the end of the stanchion. A bearing face which is to be grouted direct to a foundation need not be machined if such face is true and parallel to the upper face.

To facilitate grouting, holes shall be provided where necessary in stanchion bases for the escape of air.

MARKING

69. Each piece of steelwork shall be distinctly marked before delivery, in accordance with a marking diagram, and shall bear such other marks as will facilitate erection.

PAINTING

70. All surfaces which are to be painted, oiled or otherwise treated shall be dry and thoroughly cleaned to remove all loose scale and loose rust.

Shop contact surfaces need not be painted unless so specified. If so specified, they shall be brought together while the paint is still wet.

Surfaces not in contact, but inaccessible after shop assembly, shall receive the full specified protective treatment before assembly. This *does not apply* to the interior of sealed hollow sections.

In the case of surfaces to be welded the steel shall not be painted or metal coated within a suitable distance of any edges to be welded if the paint specified or the metal coating would be harmful to welders or impair the quality of the welds.

Welds and adjacent parent metal shall not be painted prior to de-slagging inspection and approval.

Parts to be encased in concrete shall not be painted or oiled.

THE DETAILING OF STRUCTURAL STEELWORK ACCORDING TO BS 5950: PART I: 1985 STRUCTURAL USE OF STEEL IN BUILDING

CONNECTIONS

6.1 General recommendations

6.1.1 General

Connections should be designed on the basis of a realistic assumption of the distribution of internal forces, having regard to relative stiffnesses. Such assumptions should correspond with direct load paths through the elements of connections. It is essential that equilibrium with the external applied factored loads is maintained.

Where members are connected to the surface of a web or flange or a section, the local ability of the web or flange to transfer the applied forces should be checked and stiffening provided where necessary.

Ease of fabrication and erection should be considered in the design of joints and splices. Attention should be paid to clearances necessary for tightening of fasteners, welding procedures, subsequent inspection, surface treatment and maintenance.

The ductility of steel assists the distribution of forces generated within a joint. Therefore residual stresses and stresses due to tightening of fasteners and normal accuracy of fit-up need not usually be calculated.

When different forms of fasteners are used to carry a shear load or when welding and fasteners are combined, then one form of connection should normally be designed to carry the total load except that torqued friction grip fasteners may be designed to share the load with welding provided the bolts are fully tightened after welding.

6.1.2 Intersections

Usually, members meeting at a joint should be arranged with their centroidal axes meeting at a point. Where there is eccentricity at intersections the members and connections should be designed to accommodate the moments which result. In the case of bolted framing of angles and ties the setting out lines of the bolts may be adopted instead of the centroidal axis.

6.1.3 Joints in simple construction

Joints between members in simple construction should be capable of transmitting the forces calculated in design and should be capable of accepting the resulting rotation. They should not develop significant moments adversely affecting members of the structure.

6.1.4 Joints in rigid construction

Joints between members in rigid construction should be capable of transmitting the forces and moments calculated from the design method. For elastic design the rigidity of the joint should be not less than that of the members. For plastic design the moment capacity of a joint at a plastic hinge location should be not less than that of the member and in addition the joint should possess sufficient plastic rotation capacity.

6.1.5 Joints in semi-rigid construction

Joints between members in semi-rigid construction should provide a predictable degree of interaction between members. They should be capable of transmitting the restraint moments in addition to the other forces and moments at the joints. It is important that the connection is neither too rigid nor too flexible to fulfil accurately the assumptions made in design.

6.1.6 Joints subject to vibration and/or load reversal

Where a connection is subject to impact or vibration, pretensioned friction grip fasteners, locking devices or welding should be used.

Where a connection is subject to reversal of stress (unless such stress is due solely to wind) or where for some special reason slipping of bolts is unacceptable, then pretensioned friction grip fasteners or welding should be used.

6.1.7 Splices

6.1.7.1 *General.* Splices should be designed to hold the connected members in place and wherever practicable the members should be arranged so that the centroidal axis of the splice coincides with the centroidal axis of the members joined. If eccentricity is present then the resulting forces should be catered for.

6.1.7.2 *Splices in compression members.* Where the members are not prepared for full contact in bearing the splice should be designed to transmit all the moments and forces to which the member at that point is subjected.

Where the members are prepared for full contact in bearing the splice should provide continuity of stiffness about both axes and resist any tension where bending is present.

The splice should be as near as possible to the ends of the member or points of inflexion. Where this is not achieved account should be taken of the moment induced by strut action.

6.1.7.3 *Splices in tension members.* The splice covers should be designed to transmit all the moments and forces to which the member at that point is subjected.

6.1.7.4 *Splices in beams.* Beam splices should be designed to transmit all the forces and moments in the member at that point and have adequate stiffness.

6.2 Fastener spacing and edge distances

6.2.1 Minimum spacing

The distance between centres of fasteners should be not less than 2.5 times the nominal diameter of the fastener.

6.2.2 Maximum spacing in unstiffened plates

The distance between centres of two adjacent fasteners in a line lying in the direction of stress should not exceed $14t$ where t is the thickness of the thinner element. Where the members are exposed to corrosive influences the maximum spacing of fasteners in any direction should not exceed $16t$ or 200 mm, where t is the thickness of the thinner outside ply.

6.2.3 Minimum edge and end distances

The distance from the centre of a fastener hole to the edge or end of any part should be not less than the value given in table 31. The edge distance is the distance from the centre of a hole to the adjacent edge at right angles to the direction of stress. The end distance is the distance from the centre of a hole to the adjacent edge in the direction in which the fastener bears. The end distance should also be sufficient to provide adequate bearing capacity.

Table 31. Minimum edge and end distances to fasteners

Quality of cut	*Edge and end distance*
For a rolled, machine flame cut, sawn or planed edge	$1.25D$
For a sheared or hand flame cut edge and any end	$1.40D$

D is the diameter of the hole

6.2.4 Maximum edge distances

The maximum distance to the nearest line of fasteners from an edge of any unstiffened part should not exceed $11te$. This rule does not apply to fasteners interconnecting the components of back-to-back tension member.

Where the members are exposed to corrosive influences the maximum edge distance should not exceed 40 mm + $4t$.

6.4 Friction grip fasteners

6.4.1 General

For a parallel shank friction grip fastener the transverse capacity should be obtained from the minimum value given by the slip resistance, the bearing capacity and, where appropriate, the resistance of long joints.

For a waisted shank fastener the capacity should be obtained from the slip resistance only and the bearing and long joint capacities need not be checked.

6.4.6 Holes for friction grip fasteners

6.4.6.1 *General.* Clearance holes should be specified for all friction grip connections unless oversize or slotted holes are required, when consideration should be given to minimum spacing, edge and end distance, bearing strength and tension capacity in order to provide the necessary strength in the connected parts.

6.4.6.2 *Size of holes*

6.4.6.2.1 *General*. The size of holes for friction grip fasteners should not exceed the dimensions given in table 35.

6.4.6.2.2 *Oversize and short slotted holes*. Oversize and short slotted holes may be used in all plies of a friction grip connection provided that a standard hardened washer is positioned over the holes in the outer plies.

6.4.6.2.3 *Long slotted holes*. Long slotted holes should not be used in more than one of the connected plies at any individual faying surface.

Where long slotted holes are used in an outer ply an external plate having sufficient size to completely cover the slot should be provided. Such a washer or plate should be at least 8 mm thick and of structural material but need not be hardened. Hardened washers should also be placed under the turned element.

Table 35. Maximum dimensions of holes

Bolt shank diameter	Clearance hole diameter	Oversize hole diameter	Short slotted hole dimensions		Long slotted hole dimensions	
mm	mm	mm	mm	mm	mm	mm
⩽ 22	$d + 2$	$d + 5$	$d + 2$	$d + 6$	$d + 2$	$2.5d$
24	$d + 3$	$d + 6$	$d + 3$	$d + 8$	$d + 3$	$2.5d$
⩾ 27	$d + 3$	$d + 8$	$d + 3$	$d + 10$	$d + 3$	$2.5d$

d is nominal bolt diameter (in mm)

6.6 Weld detail and design

6.6.1 General

The details of all welded connections should comply with BS 5135.

6.6.2 Details of fillet welds

6.6.2.1 *End returns*. Fillet welds terminating at the ends or sides of parts should be returned continuously around the corners for a distance of not less than twice the leg length of the weld unless access or the configuration renders this impracticable. This detail is particularly important for fillet welds on the tension side of parts carrying a bending load.

6.6.2.2 *Lap joints*. In lap joints the minimum lap should be not less than $4t$ where t is the thickness of the thinner part joined. Single fillet welds should only be used where the parts are restrained to prevent opening of the joint.

Where the end of an element is connected only by longitudinal fillet welds the length of the welds, L, should be not less than the transverse spacing, T_w (see figure 14).

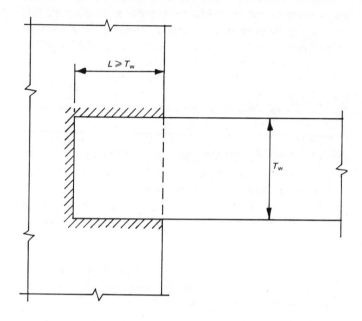

Figure 14 Welded end connections

6.6.2.4 *Single fillet welds*. A single fillet weld should not be subject to a bending moment about the longitudinal axis of the weld.

6.6.2.5 *Intermittent fillet welds*. Intermittent fillet welds should not be used in fatigue situations or where capillary action could lead to the formation of rust pockets.

The longitudinal spacing along any one edge of the element between effective lengths of weld should not exceed 300 mm or $16t$ for compression elements or $24t$ for tension elements, where t is the thickness of the thinner part joined.

Back-to-back struts and ties should have spacing of welds in accordance with **4.7.13** and **4.6.3** respectively.

End runs of fillet welds should extend to the end of the part connected.

6.6.3 Partial penetration butt welds

Partial penetration butt welds should not be used intermittently or in fatigue situations.

6.6.4 Welded details for structural hollow sections

A weld connecting two structural sections end-to-end should be a full penetration butt weld.

A weld connecting the end of a structural hollow section to the surface of another member should be continuous and may be either a butt weld throughout, a fillet weld throughout or a fillet weld in one part with a butt weld in another with a continuous change from one to the other.

6.7 Holding-down bolts

Holding-down bolts should be designed to resist the effect of factored loads determined in accordance with **2.4.** They should provide resistance to tension due to uplift forces and bending moments and shear where appropriate.

Holding-down bolts required to transmit tension should be anchored into the foundation by a washer plate or other load distributing member embedded in the concrete; this plate or member should be designed to span any grout tubes or adjustment tubes provided for the holding-down bolts.

The embedment length of the holding-down bolts and the arrangement of the load distributing assembly should be such that in transmitting the loads from the anchorage to the foundation the load capacity of the foundation is not exceeded.

Rag bolts and indented foundation bolts should not be used to resist uplift forces.

METSEC PURLINS AND SIDE RAILS — SECTION DIMENSIONS AND PROPERTIES

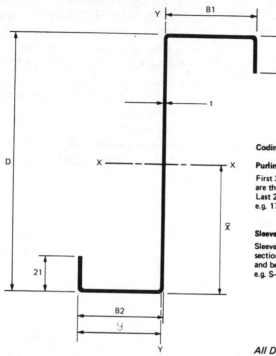

Coding of Sections

Purlins

First 3 digits of section reference number are the depth of the purlin(mm).
Last 2 digits are the thickness (mm x 10)
e.g. 17216 depth of purlin = 172mm
thickness = 1.6mm

Sleeves

Sleeves should be of the same section as the purlin, but used in reverse, and be prefixed S—
e.g. S—17216.

All Dimensions Nominal

Section Ref.	Depth	Top Flange	Bottom Flange	Thick-ness	Wt/M	Area	Ixx	Zxx	Iyy	Ryy	ȳ	x̄	Clm
	D mm	B1 mm	B2 mm	t mm	Kg	cm²	cm⁴	cm³	cm⁴	cm	mm	mm	
12215	122	54	49	1.5	2.96	3.765	87.76	14.18	25.84	2.62	49.42	61.80	0.801
12216	122	54	49	1.6	3.25	4.132	95.96	15.51	28.12	2.61	49.42	61.80	0.833
14215	142	54	49	1.5	3.15	4.018	127.8	17.69	26.58	2.542	49.50	72.26	0.744
14216	142	54	49	1.6	3.46	4.413	140.4	19.43	29.05	2.533	49.43	72.26	0.771
14221	142	54	49	2.1	4.43	5.644	171.6	23.87	35.61	2.512	48.83	71.92	0.848
17215	172	65	60	1.5	3.74	4.784	224.2	25.68	43.55	2.988	60.48	87.29	0.709
17216	172	65	60	1.6	4.12	5.258	246.4	28.23	47.67	2.979	60.40	87.29	0.738
17218	172	65	60	1.8	4.49	5.729	268.5	30.75	51.71	2.969	60.32	87.29	0.742
17225	172	65	60	2.5	6.29	8.014	358.7	41.28	68.90	2.932	59.58	86.91	0.838
20216	202	65	60	1.6	4.50	5.746	359.0	35.06	47.68	2.852	60.30	102.40	0.664
20218	202	65	60	1.8	5.09	6.476	395.9	38.66	52.24	2.840	60.20	102.40	0.686
20221	202	65	60	2.1	5.70	7.283	455.0	44.44	59.61	2.825	60.06	102.40	0.719
20225	202	65	60	2.5	6.88	8.764	524.5	51.45	68.91	2.804	59.51	101.96	0.763
23219	232	76	69	1.9	6.06	7.740	638.3	54.11	82.11	3.224	69.57	118.00	0.669
23224	232	76	69	2.4	7.43	9.482	782.0	66.28	99.38	3.196	69.33	118.00	0.710
26224	262	80	72	2.4	8.19	10.460	1087.0	82.25	120.30	3.353	71.65	132.00	0.693
26229	262	80	72	2.9	9.67	12.350	1275.0	95.62	132.50	3.229	72.22	133.30	0.713

METSEC PURLIN PIERCINGS, SLEEVES AND CLEATS

Sleeved System Single Span Details & Dimensions

Notes

All dimensions in millimetres. All holes 18mm dia. for 16mm dia. bolts.

Clearance between purlins or side rails at joints—6mm.

End fixing holes are supplied as standard. Other holes normally pierced in pairs can be added to suit individual requirements. Maximum length 13.0 metres excluding 122 and 142 Series. 122 and 142 Series max. length of purlin 10.0 metres.

DOUBLE SPAN PURLINS ARE AVAILABLE ON REQUEST.

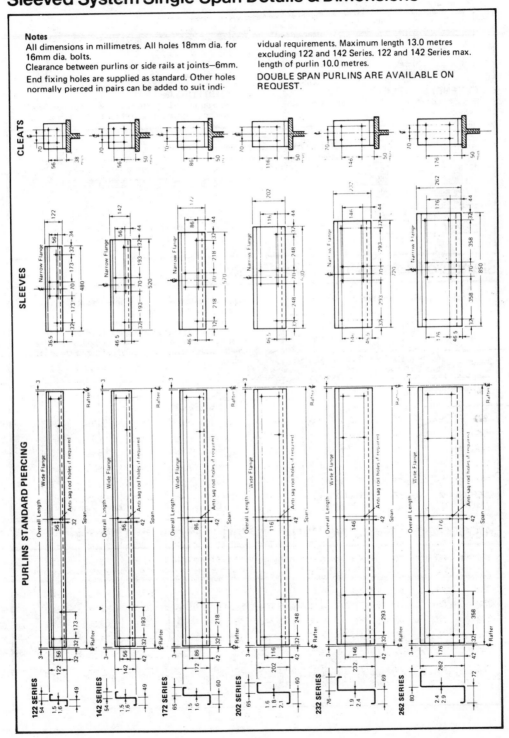

METSEC PURLIN/RAIL CLEATS

Purlin & Side Rail Extensions

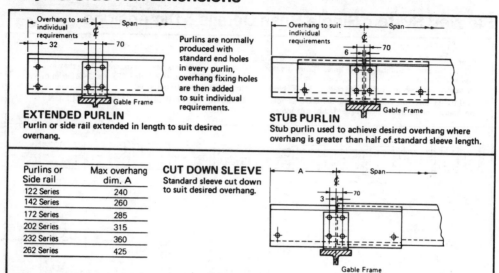

Purlins are normally produced with standard end holes in every purlin, overhang fixing holes are then added to suit individual requirements.

EXTENDED PURLIN
Purlin or side rail extended in length to suit desired overhang.

STUB PURLIN
Stub purlin used to achieve desired overhang where overhang is greater than half of standard sleeve length.

CUT DOWN SLEEVE
Standard sleeve cut down to suit desired overhang.

Purlins or Side rail	Max overhang dim. A
122 Series	240
142 Series	260
172 Series	285
202 Series	315
232 Series	360
262 Series	425

Standard Metsec Purlin/Rail Cleats

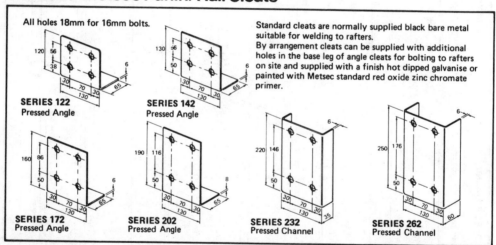

All holes 18mm for 16mm bolts.

Standard cleats are normally supplied black bare metal suitable for welding to rafters.

By arrangement cleats can be supplied with additional holes in the base leg of angle cleats for bolting to rafters on site and supplied with a finish hot dipped galvanise or painted with Metsec standard red oxide zinc chromate primer.

SERIES 122
Pressed Angle

SERIES 142
Pressed Angle

SERIES 172
Pressed Angle

SERIES 202
Pressed Angle

SERIES 232
Pressed Channel

SERIES 262
Pressed Channel

Suggested Alternative Purlin to Rafter Fixing by Others

Metsec Zed Purlins have a plain flat web, therefore any cleat with a flat surface can be used. We show a few examples of alternative cleats a steelwork fabricator can easily manufacture.

Alternative cleats should be of appropriate thickness and not less than those shown for standard cleats above.

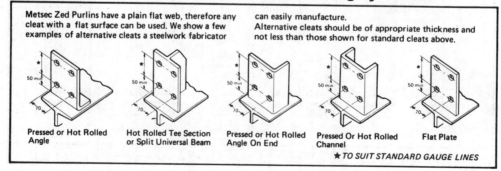

Pressed or Hot Rolled Angle

Hot Rolled Tee Section or Split Universal Beam

Pressed or Hot Rolled Angle On End

Pressed Or Hot Rolled Channel

Flat Plate

★ TO SUIT STANDARD GAUGE LINES

WARD PURLINS

Section Range

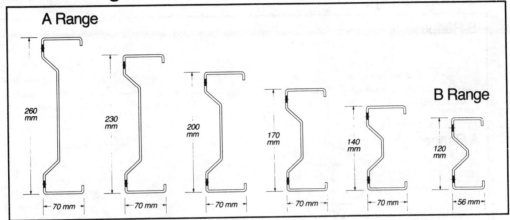

Section Dimensions

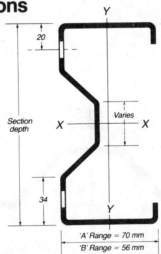

'A' Range = 70 mm
'B' Range = 56 mm

Section Properties

Section	Thickness mm	Area Cm²	Weight Kg/m	Ixx Cm⁴	Zxx Cm³	Iyy Cm⁴	Zyy (min) Cm³	Rxx Cm	Ryy Cm	CLm Factor
B120/150	1.50	3.83	3.08	80.20	13.31	12.03	3.40	4.58	1.77	1.322
A140/155	1.55	4.72	3.79	140.42	19.29	22.90	5.21	5.46	2.20	1.285
A140/165	1.65	5.03	4.04	149.57	20.85	24.46	5.55	5.45	2.21	1.300
A140/180	1.80	5.51	4.42	163.71	23.12	27.21	6.12	5.45	2.22	1.313
A170/160	1.60	5.30	4.25	228.17	25.94	23.20	5.16	6.56	2.09	1.283
A170/170	1.70	5.71	4.57	245.89	28.32	25.83	5.81	6.56	2.13	1.303
A170/180	1.80	6.07	4.86	261.76	30.37	27.79	6.28	6.57	2.14	1.315
A200/160	1.60	5.80	4.65	337.06	32.84	23.61	5.38	7.62	2.02	1.189
A200/180	1.80	6.55	5.24	379.66	37.59	26.74	6.06	7.62	2.02	1.236
A200/200	2.00	7.30	5.83	423.87	42.21	30.02	6.77	7.62	2.03	1.273
A230/180	1.80	7.06	5.65	529.55	45.66	26.59	6.03	8.66	1.94	1.133
A230/200	2.00	7.89	6.30	592.85	51.34	30.02	6.78	8.67	1.95	1.168
A230/240	2.40	9.44	7.52	705.17	61.39	35.09	7.93	8.64	1.93	1.225
A260/200	2.00	8.67	6.93	873.83	64.46	30.02	6.79	10.04	1.86	1.060
A260/240	2.40	10.17	8.10	951.51	73.31	35.96	8.03	9.67	1.88	1.128
A260/270	2.70	11.46	9.11	1071.17	82.63	40.77	9.02	9.67	1.89	1.167
A260/320	3.20	13.61	10.81	1269.94	98.02	48.91	10.67	9.66	1.90	1.233

Values of Ixx and Zxx have been modified in accordance with clause III of Addendum No. 1 to BS 449.

WARD CLADDING RAILS

Section Range

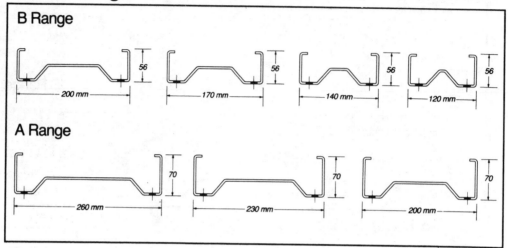

B Range

200 mm — 56
170 mm — 56
140 mm — 56
120 mm — 56

A Range

260 mm — 70
230 mm — 70
200 mm — 70

Section Dimensions

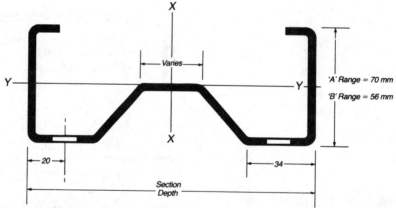

Varies

'A' Range = 70 mm
'B' Range = 56 mm

20   34

Section Depth

Section Properties

Section	Thickness mm	Area Cm²	Weight Kg/m	Ixx Cm⁴	Zxx Cm³	Iyy Cm⁴	Zyy (min) Cm³	Rxx Cm	Ryy Cm	CLm Factor
B120/150	1.50	3.83	3.08	80.20	13.31	12.03	3.40	4.58	1.77	1.322
B140/150	1.50	4.09	3.29	114.65	16.35	11.94	3.41	5.29	1.71	1.317
B140/165	1.65	4.51	3.62	126.24	18.07	13.21	3.76	5.29	1.71	1.321
B140/180	1.80	4.95	3.96	138.42	19.85	14.75	4.14	5.29	1.73	1.323
B170/155	1.55	4.69	3.77	189.42	22.26	12.50	3.63	6.36	1.63	1.307
B170/165	1.65	5.00	4.01	201.73	23.76	13.37	3.87	6.35	1.64	1.316
B170/180	1.80	5.48	4.39	222.15	26.16	14.94	4.26	6.37	1.65	1.323
B200/160	1.60	5.34	4.28	293.20	29.28	13.50	3.90	7.41	1.59	1.201
B200/170	1.70	5.67	4.54	311.54	31.16	14.29	4.13	7.41	1.59	1.219
B200/180	1.80	6.00	4.80	328.39	32.92	15.05	4.35	7.40	1.58	1.237
A200/160	1.60	5.80	4.65	337.06	32.84	23.61	5.38	7.62	2.02	1.189
A200/180	1.80	6.55	5.24	379.66	37.59	26.74	6.06	7.62	2.02	1.236
A200/200	2.00	7.30	5.83	423.87	42.21	30.02	6.77	7.62	2.03	1.273
A230/180	1.80	7.06	5.65	529.55	45.66	26.59	6.03	8.66	1.94	1.133
A230/200	2.00	7.89	6.30	592.85	51.34	30.02	6.78	8.67	1.95	1.168
A230/240	2.40	9.44	7.52	705.17	61.39	35.09	7.93	8.64	1.93	1.225
A260/200	2.00	8.67	6.93	873.83	64.46	30.02	6.79	10.04	1.86	1.060

WARD CLEATS

Cleat Dimensions

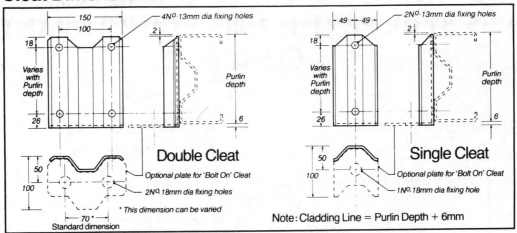

Double Cleat

- 4 N°.13mm dia fixing holes
- 150
- 100
- 18
- Varies with Purlin depth
- 26
- 2
- Purlin depth
- 6
- 50
- 100
- Optional plate for 'Bolt On' Cleat
- 2 N°.18mm dia fixing holes
- * This dimension can be varied
- 70 *
- Standard dimension

Single Cleat

- 2 N°.13mm dia fixing holes
- 49 + 49
- 18
- Varies with Purlin depth
- 26
- 2
- Purlin depth
- 6
- 50
- 100
- Optional plate for 'Bolt On' Cleat
- 1 N°.18mm dia fixing hole

Note: Cladding Line = Purlin Depth + 6mm

Fixes to all types of building

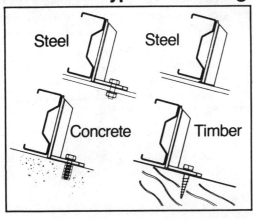

Steel Steel
Concrete Timber

Cleat References

Purlin Section Size	Application			
	Weld On		Bolt On	
	Single	Double	Single	Double
120	CS 12	CD 12	CS 12B	CD 12B
140	CS 14	CD 14	CS 14B	CD 14B
170	CS 17	CD 17	CS 17B	CD 17B
200	CS 20	CD 20	CS 20B	CD 20B
230	CS 23	CD 23	CS 23B	CD 23B
260	CS 26	CD 26	CS 26B	CD 26B

Bolt On Cleats: For hole centres other than those shown, please contact Ward.

THE DETAILING OF REINFORCEMENT ACCORDING TO BS 8110: PART I: 1985 STRUCTURAL USE OF CONCRETE

3.3 Concrete cover to reinforcement

3.3.1 Nominal cover

3.3.1.1 *General*. Nominal cover is the design depth of concrete cover to all steel reinforcement, including links. It is the dimension used in design and indicated on the drawings. The actual cover to all reinforcement should never be less than the nominal cover minus 5 mm. The nominal cover should:

(a) comply with the recommendations for bar size, aggregate size and for concrete cast against uneven surfaces (see **3.3.1.2** to **3.3.1.4**);
(b) protect the steel against corrosion (see **3.3.3**);
(c) protect the steel against fire (see **3.3.6**); and
(d) allow for surface treatments such as bush hammering.

3.3.1.2 *Bar size*. The nominal cover to all steel should be such that the resulting cover to a main bar should not be less than the size of the main bar or, where bars are in pairs or bundles, the size of a single bar of cross-sectional area equal to the sum of their cross-sectional areas. At the same time the nominal cover to any links should be preserved.

3.3.1.3 *Nominal maximum size of aggregate*. Nominal covers should be not less than the nominal maximum size of the aggregate.

3.3.1.4 *Concrete cast against uneven surfaces*. In such cases the specified nominal cover should generally be increased beyond the values given in table 3.4 to ensure that an adequate minimum cover will be obtained. For this reason, the nominal cover specified where concrete is cast directly against the earth should generally be not less than 75 mm. Where concrete is cast against an adequate blinding, a nominal cover of less than 40 mm (excluding blinding) should not generally be specified.

3.3.2 Ends of straight bars

Cover is not required to the end of a straight bar in a floor or roof unit where its end is not exposed to the weather or to condensation.

3.3.3 Cover against corrosion

The cover required to protect the reinforcement against corrosion depends on the exposure conditions and the quality of the concrete as placed and cured immediately surrounding reinforcement. Table 3.4 gives limiting values for the nominal cover of concrete made with normal-weight aggregates as a function of these factors. There may be cases where extra precautions are needed beyond those given in **3.3.4** in order to ensure protection of the reinforcement.

3.3.4 Exposure conditions

3.3.4.1 *General*. The exposure conditions in service listed in table 3.4 are described in table 3.2.

3.3.4.2 *Freezing and thawing and de-icing salts*. Where freezing and thawing actions under wet conditions exist, enhanced durability will be obtained by the use of air-entrained concrete. All concrete lower than grade C50 should contain appropriate amounts of entrained air where surfaces are subject to the effects of de-icing salts.

3.3.5 Concrete materials and mixes

3.3.5.1 *Mix proportions*. Table 3.4 gives maximum free water/cement ratios and minimum cement contents for concretes appropriate for use in given environments with specified covers. The minimum grades will generally ensure that the limits on free water/cement ratio and cement content will be met without further checking. These limits relate to concrete made using 20 mm nominal maximum sized normal-weight aggregates.

Table 3.2 Exposure conditions

Environment	Exposure conditions
Mild	Concrete surfaces protected against weather or aggressive conditions
Moderate	Concrete surfaces sheltered from severe rain or freezing whilst wet
	Concrete subject to condensation
	Concrete surfaces continuously under water
	Concrete in contact with non-aggressive soil
Severe	Concrete surfaces exposed to severe rain, alternate wetting and drying or occasional freezing or severe condensation
Very severe	Concrete surfaces exposed to sea water spray, de-icing salts (directly or indirectly), corrosive fumes or severe freezing conditions whilst wet
Extreme	Concrete surfaces exposed to abrasive action, e.g. sea water carrying solids or flowing water with pH $\leqslant 4.5$ or machinery or vehicles

3.3.5.2 *Permitted reduction in concrete grade.* Where due to the nature of the constituent materials there is difficulty in complying with the concrete grades in table 3.4, the further checking not required in **3.3.5.1** becomes necessary to ensure compliance with the limits on the free water/cement ratio and cement content. Provided a systematic checking regime is established to ensure compliance with these limits in the concrete as placed, the concrete grades C30, C35, C40 and C45 in table 3.4 may be relaxed by not more than 5, that is to C25, C30, C35 and C40 respectively. *This relaxation should not be applied to the mixes permitted in* **3.3.5.5** *and* **3.3.5.6**.

3.3.5.3 *Permitted reduction in cement content.* Where concrete with free water/cement ratios significantly lower than the maximum values in table 3.4, which are appropriate for normal workability, is both manufactured and used under specially well controlled conditions, the cement content may be reduced provided the following requirements are met:

(a) the reduction in cement content does not exceed 10% of the appropriate value in table 3.4;
(b) the corresponding free water/cement ratio is reduced by not less than the percentage reduction in the cement content.
(c) the resulting mix can be placed and compacted properly;
(d) the establishment of systematic control to ensure that the reduced limits are met in the concrete as placed.

3.3.5.4 *Adjustment to cement contents for different sized aggregates.* The minimum cement contents given in table 3.4 relate to 20 mm nominal maximum size of aggregate. For other sizes of aggregate they should be modified as given in table 3.3 subject to the condition that the cement content should be not less than 240 kg/m³ for the exposure conditions covered by table 3.4.

3.3.6 Cover as fire protection

Cover for protection against corrosion may not suffice as fire protection. The values given in tables 3.4 and 3.5 or table 3.5 and figure 3.2 will ensure that fire resistance requirements are satisfied. The tables are based on recommendations given in section four of BS 8110: Part 2: 1985; however, in columns and beams the covers included in the tables have been adjusted to permit nominal covers to be specified to all steel (including links). Minimum dimensions of members for fire resistance are also included in figure 3.2. In some circumstances a more detailed treatment of the design for fire may give significant economies. Section four of BS 8110: Part 2: 1985 gives further information on design for fire, including information on surface treatments for improving fire resistance.

3.3.7 Control of cover

Good workmanship is required to ensure that the reinforcement is properly placed and that the specified cover is obtained. Recommendations for this are given in 7.3.

Table 3.3 Adjustments to minimum cement contents for aggregates other than 20 mm nominal maximum size

Nominal maximum aggregate size	Adjustments to minimum cement contents in table 3.4
mm	kg/m³
10	+40
14	+20
20	0
40	−30

Table 3.4 Nominal cover to all reinforcement (including links) to meet durability requirements (see note)

Conditions of exposure (see 3.3.4)	Nominal cover				
	mm	mm	mm	mm	mm
Mild	25	20	20*	20*	20*
Moderate	—	35	30	25	20
Severe	—	—	40	30	25
Very severe	—	—	50†	40†	30
Extreme	—	—	—	60†	50
Maximum free water/cement ratio	0.65	0.60	0.55	0.50	0.45
Minimum cement content (kg/m^3)	275	300	325	350	400
Lowest grade of concrete	C30	C35	C40	C45	C50

*These covers may be reduced to 15 mm provided that the nominal maximum size of aggregates does not exceed 15 mm.

†Where concrete is subject to freezing whilst wet, air-entrainment should be used (see **3.3.4.2**).

Note. This table relates to normal-weight aggregate of 20 mm nominal maximum size.

Table 3.5 Nominal cover to all reinforcement (including links) to meet specified periods of fire resistance (see notes 1 and 2)

Fire resistance	Nominal cover						
	Beams*		Floors		Ribs		Columns*
	Simply supported	Continuous	Simply supported	Continuous	Simply supported	Continuous	
h	mm	mm	mm	mm	mm	mm	mm
0.5	20†	20†	20†	20†	20†	20†	20†
1	20†	20†	20	20	20	20†	20†
1.5	20	20†	25	20	35	20	20
2	40	30	35	25	45	35	25
3	60	40	45	35	55	45	25
4	70	50	55	45	65	55	25

*For the purposes of assessing a nominal cover for beams and columns, the cover to main bars which would have been obtained from tables 4.2 and 4.3 of BS 8110: Part 2: 1985 have been reduced by a notional allowance for stirrups of 10 mm to cover the range 8 mm (see also **3.3.6**).

†These covers may be reduced to 15 mm provided that the nominal maximum size of aggregate does not exceed 15 mm (see **3.3.1.3**).

Note 1. The nominal covers given relate specifically to the minimum member dimensions given in figure 3.2. Guidance on increased covers necessary if smaller members are used is given in section four of BS 8110: Part 2: 1985.

Note 2. Cases that lie below the bold line require attention to the additional measures necessary to reduce the risks of spalling (see section four of BS 8110: Part 2: 1985).

3.12 Considerations affecting design details

3.12.1 Permissible deviations

3.12.1.1 *General*. The effect of permissible deviations on design and detailing is given in **3.12.1.2** to **3.12.1.5**.

3.12.1.2 *Permissible deviations on member sizes*. In the selection of member sizes allowance should be made for inaccuracy of construction. BS 5606 gives guidance on accuracy and permissible deviations. The degree of permissible deviation specified should be consistent with the structure's fitness for its purpose.

The partial safety factors will, on a design based on nominal dimensions, provide for all normal permissible deviations. When large permissible deviations are allowed for small highly-stressed members, it may be necessary to base the design on net dimensions after allowance for the maximum specified permissible deviation; this would occur rarely.

3.12.1.3 *Position of reinforcement*. Normally the design may assume that the reinforcement is in its normal position. However, when reinforcement is located in relation to more than one face of a member, e.g. a link in a beam in which the nominal cover for all sides is given, the actual concrete cover on one side may be greater and can be derived from consideration of certain other permissible deviations. These are:

(a) dimensions and spacing of cover blocks, spacers and/or chairs (including the compressibility of these items and the surfaces they bear on);

(b) stiffness, straightness, and accuracy of cutting, bending and fixing of bars or reinforcement cage;

(c) accuracy of formwork both in dimension and plane (this includes permanent forms, such as blinding or brickwork);

(d) the size of the structural part and the relative size of bars or reinforcement cage.

3.12.1.4 *Permissible deviations on reinforcement fitting between two concrete faces*. The overall dimension on the bending schedule should be determined for this reinforcement as the nominal dimension of the concrete less the nominal cover on each face and less the deduction for permissible deviation on member size and on bending given in table 3.26.

Table 3.26 Bar schedule dimensions: deduction for permissible deviations

Distance between concrete faces	Type of bar	Total deduction
m		mm
0 up to and including 1	Links and other bent bars	10
Above 1 up to and including 2	Links and other bent bars	15
Over 2	Links and other bent bars	20
Any length	Straight bars	40

These deductions will apply to most reinforced concrete construction. However, where the permissible deviation on member size is greater than 5 mm, 5 mm, 10 mm and 10 mm for the four categories respectively, larger deductions should be made or the cover increased.

3.12.1.5 *Accumulation of errors*. In practice, the positioning of bars within their allotted individual permissible deviations may result in the accumulation of permissible deviations all in one direction. This may lead to reductions in resistance moments exceeding the percentage allowed for in the normal value of the partial safety factors. In the design of a particularly critical member, therefore, appropriate adjustment to the effective depth assumed may be necessary.

3.12.2 Joints

3.12.2.1 *Construction joints*. Careful consideration should be given to the location of construction joints and their position agreed before concreting. They should generally be at right angles to the direction of the member. If special preparation of the joint faces is required, it should be specified.

3.12.2.2 *Movement joints*. The location of movement joints should be clearly indicated on the drawings both for the individual members and for the structure as a whole. In general, movement joints in the structure should pass through the whole structure in one plane. Information on various types of movement joints is given in section eight of BS 8110: Part 2: 1985.

3.12.4 Reinforcement

3.12.4.1 *Groups of bars.* Bars may be in groups of two, three or four, in contact. Where this is done, the bundle or pair should be treated as a single bar of equivalent area for all purposes in section three. In no situation, even at laps, should more than four bars be arranged in contact.

3.12.4.2 *Bar schedule dimensions.* Bars should be scheduled in accordance with BS 4466. Where reinforcement is to fit between two concrete faces, the permissible deviations recommended in **3.12.1.4** should be adopted.

3.12.5 Minimum areas of reinforcement in members

3.12.5.1 *General.* Enough reinforcement should be provided to control, within reason, cracks however caused. The minimum quantities recommended in **3.12.5.3** and **3.12.5.4** should suffice.

3.12.5.2 *Symbols.* For the purposes of **3.12.5** the following symbols apply.

A_c total area of concrete

A_{cc} area of concrete in compression

A_s minimum recommended area of reinforcement

A_{sc} area of steel in compression

A_{st} area of transverse steel in a flange

b breadth of section

b_w breadth or effective breadth of the rib; for a box, T or I section, b_w is taken as the average breadth of the concrete below the flange

f_y characteristic strength of reinforcement

h overall depth of the cross section of a reinforced member

h_f depth of flange

l span of the beam

3.12.5.3 *Minimum percentages of reinforcement.* The minimum percentages of reinforcement appropriate for various conditions of loading and types of member are given in table 3.27.

3.12.5.4 *Minimum size of bars in side face of beams to control cracking* (see **3.12.11.2.9**). The minimum size of bars in side face of beams to control cracking should be not less than $\sqrt{(s_b b/f_y)}$ where s_b is the bar spacing and b the breadth of the section at the point considered (or 500 mm if less).

Table 3.27 Minimum percentages of reinforcement

Situation	Definition of percentage	Minimum percentage	
		$f_y = 250$ N/mm²	$f_y = 460$ N/mm²
		%	%
Tension reinforcement Sections subjected mainly to pure tension	$100A_s/A_c$	0.8	0.45
Sections subjected to flexure			
(a) Flanged beams, web in tension:			
(1) $b_w/b < 0.4$	$100A_s/b_wh$	0.32	0.18
(2) $b_w/b \geqslant 0.4$	$100A_s/b_wh$	0.24	0.13
(b) Flanged beams, flange in tension over a continuous support:			
(1) T-beam	$100A_s/b_wh$	0.48	0.26
(2) L-beam	$100A_s/b_wh$	0.36	0.20
(c) Rectangular section (in solid slabs this minimum should be provided in both directions)	$100A_s/A_c$	0.24	0.13
Compression reinforcement (where such reinforcement is required for the ultimate limit state) General rule	$100A_{sc}/A_{cc}$	0.4	0.4
Simplified rules for particular cases:			
(a) rectangular column or wall	$100A_{sc}/A_c$	0.4	0.4
(b) flanged beam:			
(1) flange in compression	$100A_{sc}/bh_f$	0.4	0.4
(2) web in compression	$100A_{sc}/b_wh$	0.2	0.2
(c) rectangular beam	$100A_{sc}/A_c$	0.2	0.2
Transverse reinforcement in flanges of flanged beams (provided over full effective flange width near top surface to resist horizontal shear)	$100A_{st}/h_fl$	0.15	0.15

3.12.6 Maximum areas of reinforcement in members

3.12.6.1 *Beams.* Neither the area of tension reinforcement nor the area of compression reinforcement should exceed 4% of the gross cross-sectional area of the concrete.

3.12.6.2 *Columns.* The longitudinal reinforcement should not exceed the following amounts, calculated as percentages of the gross cross-sectional area of the concrete:

(a) vertically-cast columns: 6%;

(b) horizontally-cast columns: 8%;

(c) laps in vertically- or horizontally-cast columns: 10%.

3.12.6.3 *Walls.* The area of vertical reinforcement should not exceed 4% of the gross cross-sectional area of the concrete.

3.12.7 Containment of compression reinforcement

3.12.7.1 *Diameter of links for containment of beam or column compression reinforcement.* When part or all of the main reinforcement is required to resist compression, links or ties at least one-quarter the size of the largest compression bar or 6 mm, whichever is the greater, should be provided at a maximum spacing of twelve times the size of the smallest compression bar.

3.12.7.2 *Arrangement of links for containment of beam or column compression reinforcement.* Every corner bar, and each alternate bar (or pair or bundle) in an outer layer of reinforcement should be supported by a link passing round the bar and having an included angle of not more than 135°. No bar within a compression zone should be further than 150 mm from a restrained bar.

3.12.7.3 *Containment of compression reinforcement around periphery of circular column.* Adequate lateral support is provided by a circular tie passing round the bars or groups. The size and spacing of the ties should be in accordance with **3.12.7.1**.

3.12.7.4 *Diameter of horizontal bars for support of small amounts of compression reinforcement in walls.* Where the main vertical reinforcement is used to resist compression and does not exceed 2% of the concrete area, at least the following percentages of horizontal reinforcement should be provided, depending upon the characteristic strength of that reinforcement:

(a) $f_y = 250$ N/mm^2: 0.30% of concrete area;
(b) $f_y = 460$ N/mm^2 or higher: 0.25% of concrete area.

These horizontal bars should be evenly spaced and be not less than one-quarter of the size of the vertical bars and not less than 6 mm.

3.12.7.5 *Arrangement of links for containment of large amounts of compression reinforcement in walls.* When the vertical compression reinforcement exceeds 2%, links at least 6 mm or one-quarter the size of the largest compression bar should be provided through the thickness of the wall. The spacing of links should not exceed twice the wall thickness in either the horizontal or vertical direction. In the vertical direction it should be not greater than 16 times the bar size. Any vertical compression bar not enclosed by a link should be within 200 mm of a restrained bar.

3.12.8 Bond, anchorage, bearing, laps, joints and bands in bars

3.12.8.1 *Avoidance of bond failure due to ultimate loads.* At both sides of any cross section the force in each bar should be developed by an appropriate embedment length or other end anchorage. Provided this is done, local bond stress may be ignored.

3.12.8.2 *Anchorage bond stress.* Anchorage bond stress is assumed to be constant over the effective anchorage length. It may be taken as the force in the bar divided by its effective surface anchorage area. It should not exceed the appropriate value obtained from table 3.28. In beams where minimum links in accordance with table 3.8 have not been provided, the anchorage bond stresses used should be those appropriate to plain bars irrespective of the type of bar provided. This does not apply to slabs.

3.12.8.6 *Anchorage links.* A link may be considered to be fully anchored if it satisfies the following:

(a) it passes round another bar of at least its own size, through an angle of 90°, and continues beyond for a minimum length of eight times its own size; or
(b) it passes round another bar of at least its own size, through an angle of 180°, and continues beyond for a minimum length of eight times its own size.

In no case should the radius of any bend in the link be less than twice the radius of a test bend guaranteed by the manufacturer of the bar.

3.12.8.7 *Anchorage of welded fabric used as links.* A link may be considered to be fully anchored when it has within the length of the anchorage either two welded transverse wires or a single welded wire of a size not less than 1.4 times the size of the wire being anchored.

3.12.8.8 *Anchorage of column starter bars in bases or pile caps.* The compression bond stresses that develop on starter bars within bases or pile caps do not need to be checked provided;

(a) the starters extend down to the level of the bottom reinforcement;
(b) the base or pile cap has been designed for moments and shears in accordance with **3.10**.

3.12.8.9 *Laps and joints.* Connection transferring stress may be lapped, welded or joined with mechanical devices. They should be placed, if possible, away from points of high stress and should preferably be staggered. Laps in fabric may be layered or nested to maintain the lapped bars in one plane.

3.12.8.10 *Joints where imposed loading is predominantly cyclical.* In such cases bars should not be joined by welding.

3.12.8.11 *Minimum laps.* The minimum lap length for bar reinforcement should be not less than 15 times the bar size or 300 mm, whichever is greater, and for fabric reinforcement should be not less than 250 mm.

3.12.8.12 *Laps in beams and columns with limited cover.* Where both bars at a lap exceed size 20 and the cover is less than 1.5 times the size of the smaller bar, transverse links should be provided throughout the lap length. At the lap the links should be at least one-quarter the size of the smaller bar and the spacing should not exceed 200 mm.

3.12.8.13 *Design of tension laps.* The length should be at least equal to the design tension anchorage length necessary to develop the required stress in the reinforcement. Lap lengths for unequal size bars (or wires in fabric) may be based upon the smaller bar. The following provisions also apply:

(a) where a lap occurs at the top of a section as cast and the minimum cover is less than twice the size of the lapped reinforcement, the lap length should be increased by a factor of 1.4;

(b) where a lap occurs at the corner of a section and the minimum cover to either face is less than twice the size of the lapped reinforcement or, where the clear distance between adjacent laps is less than 75 mm or six times the size of the lapped reinforcement, whichever is the greater, the lap length should be increased by a factor of 1.4;

(c) in cases where both conditions (a) and (b) apply, the lap length should be increased by a factor of 2.0.

Values for lap lengths are given in table 3.29 as multiples of bar size.

3.12.8.14 *Maximum amount of reinforcement in a layer including tension laps.* At laps, the sum of the reinforcement sizes in a particular layer should not exceed 40% of the breadth of the section at that level.

3.12.8.15 *Design of compression laps.* The length should be at least 25% greater than the compression anchorage length necessary to develop the required stress in the reinforcement. Lap lengths for unequal size bars (or wires in fabric) may be based upon the smaller bar.

3.12.8.16 *Butt joints*

3.12.8.16.1 *Bars in compression.* In such cases the load may be transferred by end bearing of square sawn-cut ends held in concentric contact by a suitable sleeve or other coupler. The concrete cover for the sleeve should be not less than that specified for normal reinforcement.

3.12.8.16.2 *Bars in tension.* The only acceptable form of full-strength butt joint for a bar in tension comprises a mechanical coupler satisfying the following criteria.

(a) When a test is made of a representative gauge length assembly comprising reinforcement of the size, grade and profile to be used and a coupler of the precise type to be used, the permanent elongation after loading to $0.6f_y$ should not exceed 0.1 mm.

(b) The design ultimate strength of the coupled bar should exceed the specified characteristic strength by the percentage specified in clause 21 of BS 4449: 1978 and clause 21 of BS 4461: 1978.

3.12.8.17 *Welded joints in bars.* For welded joints in bars, the following recommendations apply:

(a) welded joints should not occur at bends;

(b) where possible, joints in parallel bars of the principal tensile reinforcement should be staggered in the longitudinal direction.

3.12.8.18 *Strength of welds.* The following values may be used where the strength of the weld has been proved by tests to be at least as great as that of the parent bar.

(a) *Joints in compression:* 100% of the design strength of joined bars.

(b) *Joints in tension:* 80% of the design strength of joined bars (100% if welding strictly supervised and if at any cross section of the member not more than 20% of the tensile reinforcement is welded).

3.12.8.19 *Design shear strength of filler material in lap-joint welds.* The design shear strength of filler material in lap-joint welds should be taken as 0.38 times its yield or proof stress as given in the appropriate British Standards.

3.12.8.20 *Design of welded lap joints.* The length of weld should be sufficient to transmit the design load in the bar.

3.12.8.21 *Limitation of length of weld in laps.* The length of a run of weld should not normally exceed five times the size of the bar. If a longer length of weld is required it should be divided into sections and the space between runs made not less than five times the size of the bar.

3.12.8.22 *Hooks and bends.* End anchorages in the form of hooks and bends should only be used to meet specific design requirements and should comply with BS 4466.

3.12.8.23 *Effective anchorage length of a hook or bend.* The effective anchorage length of a hook or bend is the length of straight bar which would be equivalent in anchorage value to that portion of the bar between the start of the bend and a point four times the bar size beyond the end of the bend. This effective anchorage length may be taken as follows.

(a) *For a 180° hook:* either (1) eight times the internal radius of the hook with a maximum of 24 times the bar size or (2) the actual length of bar in the hook including the straight portion, whichever is greater.

(b) *For a 90° bend:* either (1) four times the internal radius of the bend with a maximum of 12 times the bar size or (2) the actual length of the bar, whichever is greater. Any length of bar in excess of four bar diameters beyond the end of the bend and which lies within the concrete to which the bar is to be anchored may also be included for effective anchorage.

3.12.8.24 *Minimum radius of bends.* In no case should this be less than twice the radius of the test bend guaranteed by the manufacturer of the bar, nor less than the radius required to ensure that the bearing stress at the mid-point of the curve does not exceed the values given.

3.12.11 Spacing of reinforcement

3.12.11.1 *Minimum distance between bars.* The horizontal distance between bars should not be less than $h_{agg} + 5$ mm, where h_{agg} is the maximum size of the coarse aggregate. Where there are two or more rows:

(a) the gaps between corresponding bars in each row should be vertically in line;

(b) the vertical distance between bars should be not less than $2h_{agg}/3$.

When the bar size exceeds $h_{agg} + 5$ mm, a spacing less than the bar size or equivalent bar size should be avoided.

Section seven. Specification and workmanship: reinforcement

7.1 General

Reinforcement should comply with BS 4449, BS 4461, BS 4482 or BS 4483. Different types of reinforcement may be used in the same structural member.

7.2 Cutting and bending

It is essential that reinforcement (particularly grade 460/425) should not be subjected to mechanical damage or shock loading prior to embedment.

Reinforcement should be cut and/or bent in accordance with BS 4466.

Bends in reinforcement should have a substantially constant curvature. Where the temperature of the steel is below 5°C, special precautions may be necessary such as reducing the speed or bending or, with the engineer's approval, increasing the radius of bending. If necessary, reinforcement may be warmed to a temperature not exceeding 100°C.

Where it is necessary to bend reinforcement projecting from concrete, care should be taken to ensure that the radius of bend is not less than that specified in BS 4466.

Where it is necessary to reshape steel previously bent, this should only be done with the engineer's approval and each bar should be inspected for signs of fracture.

It is permissble to bend grade 250 reinforcement projecting from concrete provided that care is taken to ensure that the radius of bend is not less than that specified in BS 4466. Grade 460 bars should not be bent, rebent or straightened without the engineer's approval.

7.3 Fixing

Rough handling, shock loading (prior to embedment) and the dropping of reinforcement from a height should be avoided. Reinforcement should be secured against displacement outside the specified limits. Unless specified otherwise,

(a) the actual concrete cover should be not less than the required nominal cover minus 5 mm;
(b) where reinforcement is located in relation to only one face of a member, e.g. a straight bar in a slab, the actual concrete cover should be not more than the required nominal cover plus:

5 mm on bars up to and including 12 mm size;
10 mm on bars over 12 mm up to and including 25 mm size;
15 mm on bars over 25 mm size.

Nominal cover should be specified to all steel reinforcement including links. Spacers between the links (or the bars where no links exist) and the formwork should be of the same nominal size as the nominal cover.

Spacers, chairs and other supports detailed on drawings, together with such other supports as may be necessary, should be used to maintain the specified nominal cover to the steel reinforcement. Spacers or chairs should be placed at a maximum spacing of 1 m and closer spacing may sometimes be necessary.

Spacers should be of such materials and designs as will be durable, not lead to corrosion of the reinforcement and not cause spalling of the concrete cover.

The mix used for spacer blocks made from cement, sand and small aggregate should be comparable in strength, durability, porosity and appearance to the surrounding concrete as far as is practicable. Concrete spacer blocks made on the construction site should not be used.

Non-structural connections for the positioning of reinforcement should be made with steel wire, tying devices, or by welding (see **7.6**). Care should be taken to ensure that projecting ends of ties or clips do not encroach into the concrete cover.

The position of reinforcement should be checked before and during concreting, particular attention being directed to ensuring that the nominal cover is maintained within the limits given, especially in the case of cantilever sections. The importance of cover in relation to durability justifies the regular use of a covermeter to check the position of the reinforcement in the hardened concrete.

7.4 Surface condition

Reinforcement should not be surrounded by concrete unless it is free from mud, oil, paint, retarders, loose rust, loose mill scale, snow, ice, grease or any other substance which can be shown to affect adversely the steel or concrete chemically, or reduce the bond. Normal handling prior to embedment in the concrete is usually sufficient for the removal of loose rust and scale from reinforcement.

7.5 Laps and joints

Laps and joints should be made only by the methods specified and at the positions shown on the drawings or as agreed by the engineer.

THE DETAILING OF REINFORCEMENT ACCORDING TO THE RECOMMENDATIONS FOR THE PERMISSIBLE STRESS DESIGN OF REINFORCED CONCRETE BUILDING STRUCTURES (THE INSTITUTION OF STRUCTURAL ENGINEERS 1989) [Referred to in this book as THE NEW CP114]

310. Concrete cover

In addition to durability and fire-protection requirements (see subsections 3J and 3K) the following structural requirements apply:

(i) for reinforcement in a slab, not less than 15 mm nor less than the diameter of such reinforcement

(ii) for longitudinal reinforcement in a beam, not less than 25 mm nor less than the diameter of such reinforcement

(iii) for a longitudinal reinforcing bar in a column, not less than 40 mm nor less than the diameter of such a bar. In the case of columns with a minimum dimension of 200 mm or less whose bars do not exceed 12 mm diameter, 25 mm cover may be used.

For bar bundles, the cover should be taken as not less than the diameter of a single bar of equivalent area or 50 mm, whichever is less.

Requirements for cover are exclusive of plaster or other decorative finishes, and where surface treatment such as bush hammering cuts into the face of the concrete, the expected depth of treatment should be added to the specified cover.

311. Distance between bars

The horizontal distance between two parallel steel bars or bundles of bars should not be less than the maximum size of coarse aggregate plus 5 mm, or the bar size, whichever is greater.

Where there are two or more rows of bars or bundles of bars, they should be arranged vertically above each other and the vertical spacing between rows should not be less than the bar size or two-thirds of the maximum size of coarse aggregate, whichever is greater.

In detailing, the spacing of the reinforcement should be carefully considered in relation to the ease of compaction of the concrete and a space of not less than 75 mm between bars or groups of bars should normally be provided to enable a poker vibrator to be inserted at appropriate intervals, unless other means of compaction are specified and agreed.

In beams the clear distance between bars near the tension face should not exceed 185 mm (f_{st} = 250 N/mm²) or 300 mm (f_{st} < 155 N/mm²) where f_{st} is the steel tensile stress; limits for intermediate stresses may be interpolated. Where the design moment has been reduced by redistribution as permitted in clause 316, the bar spacing should be reduced proportionally. The clear distance between the corner of a beam and the nearest longitudinal bar in tension should not exceed half the above values. Reinforcement should be placed within the side faces of deeper beams if appropriate.

For slabs up to 200 mm thick, the pitch of the main bars should not exceed three times the effective depth, that of distribution bars should not exceed five times the effective depth and neither should exceed 750 mm. These limits also apply to thicker slabs where A_s/bd is less than 0.3%; where A_s/bd is greater than 1%, the recommendations for beams apply, and for intermediate reinforcement percentages the limits may be interpolated.

312. Bond and anchorage

a. BARS IN TENSION. A bar in tension should extend from any section for a distance to the end of the bar such that the average bond stress does not exceed the permissible average bond stress in Table 1. This condition will be satisfied if the length measured from such section is not less than:

the bar diameter $\times \dfrac{\text{the tensile stress in the bar}}{\text{four times the permissible average bond stress}}$

154

The bar should extend at least 12 bar diameters (or the effective depth if this is greater) beyond the point at which it is no longer required to resist stress.

For the purpose of this clause, the length of bar so determined may have deducted from it a length equivalent to the value of the hook as given in subclause 312f, but no deduction should then be made for the length of bar contained in the hook.

b. BARS IN COMPRESSION. A bar in compression should extend from any section for a distance such that the average bond stress does not exceed the permissible bond stress given above for bars in tension by more than 25%. This condition will be satisfied if the length measured from each section is not less than:

$$\text{the bar diameter} \times \frac{\text{the compressive stress in the bar}}{\text{five times the permissible average bond stress}}$$

The bar should extend at least 12 diameters beyond the point at which it is no longer required to resist stress.

c. AVOIDANCE OF BOND FAILURE. Each bar should have adequate anchorage on both sides of any cross section to develop the calculated force. This may be assessed by direct calculation, or it may be assumed to be satisfied if the local bond stress does not exceed the permissible average bond stress by more than 25%.

$$\text{Local bond stress} = \frac{V}{do}$$

where V is the shear force across the section, and
 o is the sum of the perimeters of the bars in the tension reinforcement.

In members of variable depth the effect of change of depth should be taken into account in calculating the bond stress.

d. BEARING STRESSES ON BENDS. The bearing stress calculated from the formula:

$$\frac{\text{calculated force in bar at the start of the bend}}{\text{internal radius of bend} \times \text{the bar diameter}}$$

should not exceed $3p_{cc}$.

For any bar, provided that the bar is not assumed to be stressed more than four diameters beyond the end of the bend, bearing stresses need not be calculated.

e. HOOKS AND OTHER ANCHORAGES. Hooks and other anchorages of reinforcement should be of such form, dimensions and arrangement as will ensure their adequacy without overstressing the concrete or other anchorage material.

f. DIMENSIONS OF HOOKS. Where hooks are used they should be of the U-type or L-type shown in Fig. 4. In both types, for high yield bars:

(i) the internal radius of the bend should be at least three times the diameter of the bar or four times the diameter of the bar for bars of 25 mm diameter and greater.

(ii) the length of straight bar beyond the end of the curve should be at least four times the diameter of the bar.

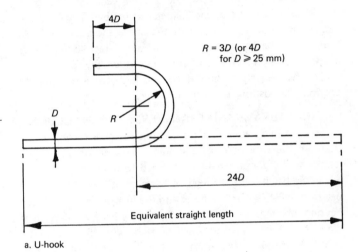

a. U-hook

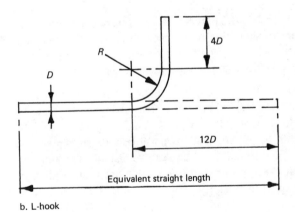

b. L-hook

Figure 4 Standard hooks for high yield bars

g. EFFECTIVE ANCHORAGE LENGTHS FOR U-HOOKS AND L-HOOKS: HIGH YIELD BARS. The effective anchorage length of hooks and bends as shown in Fig. 4 may be taken as:

(i) U-hooks: 24 times the bar diameter, or the actual length of bar in the hook, including the straight portion, whichever is the greater.

(ii) L-hooks: 12 times the bar diameter, or the actual length of bar in the hook, including the straight portion, whichever is greater.

The bearing stress should be checked when the straight portion exceeds four times the diameter.

h. EFFECTIVE ANCHORAGE LENGTHS FOR U-HOOKS AND L-HOOKS: PLAIN BARS. When hooks are formed in plain round mild steel bars, the internal radius of the bend should be at least twice the diameter of the bar. The length of straight bar beyond the end of the curve should be at least four times the diameter of the bar and effective anchorage lengths may be taken as 16D for U-hooks and 8D for L-hooks.

The bearing stress should be checked when the straight portion exceeds four times the diameter.

i. LINKS IN BEAMS AND TRANSVERSE TIES IN COLUMNS. Notwithstanding any of the provisions of these recommendations, in the case of links and transverse ties complete bond length and anchorage may be deemed to have been provided when the bar is bent through an angle of at least 90° round a bar of at least its own diameter and the link or tie is continued beyond the end of the curve for a length of at least eight diameters or, through an angle of 180° with the link or tie continued beyond the end of the curve for a length of at least four bar diameters.

j. SHEAR REINFORCEMENT. All bent-up bars acting as shear reinforcement should be fully anchored in both flanges of the beam, the anchorage length being measured from the end of the sloping portion of the bar nearest to the anchored end.

k. GENERAL REQUIREMENTS FOR CONNECTING REINFORCEMENT. All connections transferring stress may be lapped, welded or joined with suitable mechanical devices. Laps should be placed, as far as possible, away from points of high stress and should be staggered. Welded joints should conform with the appropriate Code of Practice, but welding of bars is not recommended where loading is predominantly cyclical.

Where the smaller bar at a lap is larger than 20 mm diameter and the cover is less than 1$\frac{1}{2}$ times the bar size, links should be provided throughout the lap length. The spacing of the links should not exceed 200 mm and their diameter should be not less than one-quarter of the smaller main bar diameter.

Where lapped bars are of different diameters, the length of the lap may be based on the diameter of the smaller bar.

The minimum lap for bar reinforcement should be 15 diameters or 300 mm, whichever is greater, and for fabric reinforcement not less than 250 mm.

l. TENSION LAPS. For bars in tension, the length of lap should not be less than

$$\text{the bar diameter} \times \frac{\text{the tensile stress in the bar}}{\text{four times the permissible average bond stress}}$$

The following recommendations also apply to tension laps:

(i) Where a lap occurs in the top of a member as cast and the minimum cover is less than twice the size of the lapped reinforcement, the calculated lap length should be increased by 40%.

(ii) Where a lap occurs at the corner of a section and the minimum cover to either face is less than twice the size of the lapped reinforcement, or where the clear distance between adjacent laps is less than 75 mm or six times the size of the lapped reinforcement, whichever is greater, the calculated lap length should be increased by 40%.

(iii) In situations where both (i) and (ii) apply, the calculated lap length should be doubled.

At tension laps, the sum of the reinforcement sizes in a particular layer should not exceed 40% of the breadth of the section at that level.

m. COMPRESSION LAPS. For bars in compression the length of lap should not be less than

$$\text{the bar diameter} \times \frac{\text{the compressive stress in the bar}}{\text{four times the permissible average bond stress}}$$

n. ANCHORAGE BOND AND LAP LENGTHS. Values for minimum anchorage bond and lap lengths for fully stressed bars as multiples of bar size are given in Table 5 for grade 30 concrete. For other concrete strengths, these values should be multiplied by the modification factors given in Table 5A.

o. EFFECTIVE PERIMETER. The effective perimeter of a single bar may be taken as π times its nominal diameter.

p. GROUPS OR BUNDLES OF BARS. The effective diameter of a group or bundle of bars may be taken as the diameter of a bar of equal total area. For calculation of bearing stress under subclause 312d, the effective diameter may be taken as the diameter of a bar of equal area. At laps between bundles of bars at no point should there be more than four bars in contact.

313. Joints, crack control and minimum reinforcement requirements

Consideration should be given to the extent of cracking of the structure and finishes arising from the effects of thermal and shrinkage movements in the concrete. Some structures, such as basements, are relatively well protected against seasonal temperature effects, and in such cases, the principal cause of cracking is likely to be drying shrinkage, the bulk of which takes place in a relatively short period after casting and can often be controlled by leaving sections of concrete for casting after the concrete on either side has matured for a period (shrinkage bays). Shrinkage effects reduce with time and stable conditions eventually occur; however for 'summer casting' conditions, where the effects of drying shrinkage and thermal contraction may be additive, enhanced provisions should be considered.

Table 5. Anchorage bond and lap lengths as multiples of bar size for fully stressed bars

reinforcement type	grade 250	grade 460		fabric (see clause 306)
	plain	deformed type 1	deformed type 2	
	concrete grade 30			
tension anchorage and lap length (see subclause 3121)	36	44	35	49
compression anchorage length	25	30	24	34
compression lap length	31	38	30	42

Note: The values are rounded up to the next whole number, and the lengths derived from these values may differ slightly from those calculated directed for each bar or wire size.

Table 5A. Modification factors for various concrete grades

concrete grade	20	25	30	35	40	45	50
factor	1.20	1.06	1.00	0.90	0.86	0.82	0.75

Thermal movements are of greater importance for exposed concrete structures, unprotected within a building envelope, such as external retaining walls, and while movements predominantly produced by shrinkage can often be largely accommodated by shrinkage bays and specified casting sequences, significant thermal movements require the provision of permanent movement joints. The effects of all movements tend to concentrate at weak points such as abrupt changes of section, and the location of joints should be considered in relation to their probable effectiveness and their impact on the overall design of the building and finishes. The design and detail of permanent joints should be such as will permit movements to occur without detrimental effects on stability, watertightness, durability, fire resistance or other essential functions of the structure.

The question of the provision and spacing of joints is left to the discretion of the designer in view of the large number of factors involved, but if joints are provided their design should be carefully considered in relation to their probable performance over the lifetime of the structure. Generally, if permanent joints can be avoided (which may be the case where movements are predominantly due to shrinkage) this may be regarded as desirable. Other non-structural elements such as brickwork, blockwork, mosaic finishes, etc. will require to be jointed at considerably more frequent intervals than is necessary in a concrete framed structure. Special consideration should also be given to structures where the vertical supporting elements are of loadbearing masonry which has less flexibility and capability of accepting horizontal movement of the floor slabs due to shrinkage and thermal effects than would be the case in a fully framed structure.

The provision of joints may also be necessary to accommodate movements due to differential settlement or other anticipated causes producing vertical or horizontal effects on the structure.

SUBSECTION 3B: BEAMS AND SLABS

314. General

a. EFFECTIVE SPAN. The effective span, l, of a beam or slab should be taken as the lesser of the two following:

(i) the distance between the centres of bearings, or
(ii) the clear distance between supports plus the effective depth of the beam or slab, the effective depth being the distance between the centre of tension and the edge of the compression section.

b. SLENDER BEAMS. The clear distance between restraints should not exceed:

(i) simply supported or continuous beams: the lesser of $60b$ or $250b^2/d$
(ii) cantilevers with lateral restraints only at support: the lesser of $25b$ or $100b^2/d$.

where b is taken as the breadth of the compression face, at midspan in case (i) and at the support in case (ii).

d is the effective depth, which need not be taken as more than the minimum value required to resist the design loads without compression reinforcement.

c. MINIMUM REINFORCEMENT. The minimum area of high-yield reinforcement provided in tension should be as follows (areas of mild steel are given in parentheses). The area is expressed as a percentage of the gross concrete area in the case of solid sections and as a percentage of the rib area ($b_r h$) in the case of T- or L-beams:

Solid slabs, solid beams, flanged beams with webs in tension and b_r/b at least 0.4	0.13% (0.24%)
Flanged beams with webs in tension and b_r/b less than 0.4	0.18% (0.32%)
T-beams with flange in tension (continuous support)	0.26% (0.48%)
L-beams with flange in tension (continuous support)	0.20% (0.36%)

d. COMPRESSION REINFORCEMENT IN BEAMS. The compression reinforcement should be effectively anchored in two directions at right-angles over the distance where it is required to act in compression, at points not further apart, centre to centre, than 12 times the diameter of the anchored bar or 300 mm, whichever is less. Links used for this purpose should pass round, or be hooked over, both the compression and tension reinforcement.

The amount of steel in compression should preferably not exceed 4%, but if it does, only 4% should be allowed for in the calculation of the resistance moment of the beam. This percentage should be calculated as follows:

(i) in rectangular beams, on the total cross-sectional area
(ii) in T-beams or L-beams, on an area equal to the total depth multiplied by the width of the rib.

Where compression reinforcement is needed, the area should not be less than 0.2%, except in the case of webs to T- and L-beams, where it should not be less than 0.4%.

SUBSECTION 3E: COLUMNS

346. Reinforcement in columns

a. LONGITUDINAL REINFORCEMENT. A reinforced concrete column should have longitudinal steel reinforcement, and the cross-sectional area of such reinforcement should not be less than 0.8% nor more than 8% of the gross cross-sectional area of the column required to transmit all the loading in accordance with these recommendations.

It should be noted that the use of 8% of steel may involve serious practical difficulties in the placing and compacting of concrete and a lower percentage would be recommended. Where bars from the column below have to be lapped with those in the column, the percentage of steel should usually not exceed 4%.

A reinforced concrete column having helical reinforcement should have at least six bars of longitudinal reinforcement within this helical reinforcement. The longitudinal bars should be in contact with the helical reinforcement and equidistant around its inner circumference.

For laps in longitudinal bars see clause 312.

The bars should be not less than 12 mm in diameter.

b. TRANSVERSE REINFORCEMENT.

(i) *General.* A reinforced concrete column should have transverse reinforcement so disposed as to provide restraint against the buckling of each of the longitudinal reinforcing bars. Every corner bar and each alternate bar in a column near the face should be properly linked by having at least one link with a change of direction at that bar. The ends of such transverse reinforcement should be properly anchored. No longitudinal bar within a compression zone should be further than 150 mm from a restrained bar.

(ii) *Pitch.* The pitch of transverse reinforcement should be not more than the least of the three following distances:

(a) the least lateral dimension of the column
(b) 12 times the diameter of the smallest longitudinal reinforcement in the column
(c) 300 mm.

(iii) *Helical reinforcement.* Helical reinforcement should be of regular formation, with the turns of the helix spaced evenly, and its ends should be anchored properly. Where an increased load on the column on account of the helical reinforcement is allowed for under subclause 347a(ii), the pitch of the helical turns should be not more than 75 mm or more than one-sixth of the core diameter of the column, nor less than 25 mm nor less than three times the diameter of the steel bar forming the helix. In other cases the requirements of (ii) above should be met.

(iv) *Diameter.* The diameter of the transverse reinforcement should be not less than one-quarter the diameter of the main rods, and in no case less than 5 mm.

SUBSECTION 3J: DURABILITY AND RESISTANCE TO CHEMICAL ATTACK

358. Durability

a. GENERAL. In a reinforced concrete design one of the most important aims is the production of a durable structure. To produce it requires the integration of all aspects of design, materials and construction.

Much of the damage to reinforced concrete structures arises from water penetration to the reinforcement causing rusting and subsequent cracking and spalling of the concrete cover, but the effects of other potentially deleterious substances need also to be considered.

To prevent such damage, it is necessary that the cover specified is adequate for the conditions applying, that the concrete is of a suitable quality and that it is correctly placed to give a dense impermeable whole.

b. DRAINAGE. Care should be taken that surfaces exposed to water are laid to adequate falls or other appropriate measures taken to avoid ponding.

c. WATER/CEMENT RATIO. For low permeability, it is necessary that a concrete mix should have an adequate cement content and a sufficiently low water/cement ratio and be fully compacted.

d. CHLORIDE CONTENT OF MIXES. Chlorides in concrete increase the risk of corrosion of embedded metals and may adversely affect the sulphate resistance of the concrete. The total chloride ion content of the constituents of each mix, expressed as a percentage by weight of cement (including ggbfs or pfa if used) in the mix, must not exceed the following:

concrete made with cement complying with
BS 4027 or BS 4248   0.2%
concrete containing embedded metal and made
with cement complying with BS 12, BS 146,
BS 1370, BS 4246 or combinations with
ggbfs or pfa   0.4%

Calcium chloride and chloride-based admixtures should never be added in reinforced concrete, prestressed concrete and concrete containing embedded metal.

e. ADMIXTURES. Where admixtures are used their effect on the durability of the concrete and the risk of corrosion of the reinforcement should be considered. The chloride ion content of admixtures must not exceed 2% by mass of the admixture or 0.03% by mass of the cement.

f. AIR ENTRAINMENT. Air-entraining agents are of value where severe frost conditions are likely to occur. The agent and dosage used should be such that the air content can be readily maintained within the limits specified at the time of placing.

When concrete lower than grade 50 is used, the average air content by volume of the fresh concrete at the time of placing should be:

7% for 10 mm nominal maximum sized aggregate
6% for 14 mm nominal maximum sized aggregate
5% for 20 mm nominal maximum sized aggregate
4% for 40 mm nominal maximum sized aggregate

All concrete lower than grade 50 should contain appropriate amounts of entrained air where surfaces are subject to the effects of de-icing salts.

g. REQUIREMENTS FOR DURABILITY OF CONCRETE. Table 22 gives recommended maximum free water/cement ratios and minimum cement contents for various conditions of exposure and nominal cover for reinforced concrete using 20 mm nominal sized aggregate. Clause 359 gives recommendations for concrete mixes used below ground.

Table 22 Durability and concrete cover

Conditions of exposure	Nominal cover to all reinforcement for durability (mm)			
Mild (Internal concrete)	25	20	20*	20*
Moderate (Sheltered from severe rain and freezing whilst saturated with water)	—	35	30	25
Severe (Exposed to driving rain, alternate wetting and drying, occasional freezing or severe condensation)	—	—	40	30
Very Severe (Exposed to seawater spray, de-icing salts, corrosive fumes and severe freezing while wet)	—	—	50	40
Maximum free water–cement ratio	0.65	0.60	0.55	0.50
Minimum cement content, kg/m^3	275	300	325	350

*These covers may be reduced to 15 mm provided that the nominal maximum size of aggregate does not exceed 15 mm.

Notes 1 For work against earth faces, the cover should not be less than 40 mm for all reinforcement in concrete cast against forms or protected by blinding. For concrete cast directly against earth faces, cover should not be less than 75 mm.
2 Where concrete is subject to severe freezing when wet, air entrainment should be used.
3 Where the face of the concrete is protected by a suitable coating, it may be reasonable to vary these recommendations.
4 In no case should the cover to the main bars be less than the diameter of such reinforcement.

Table 23 gives adjustments to minimum cement contents where other sized aggregates are used. However, any adjustment made is subject to the condition that the minimum cement content should not be less than 240 kg/m^3.

502. Reinforcement

a. SPECIFICATION. Reinforcement should comply with current British Standards.

b. CUTTING AND BENDING. Reinforcement should be cut and bent in accordance with BS 4466. Rebending of reinforcement should be done only with the engineer's approval.

c. FIXING. All reinforcement should be placed and maintained in the position shown on the drawing. Unless otherwise specified, the actual concrete cover should be not less than the specified cover minus 5 mm. Spacers, chairs or other supports should be used to maintain the reinforcement in its correct position. Spacers should be of such materials or designs as will be durable, not lead to corrosion of the reinforcement or cause spalling of the concrete cover. Spacer blocks made from cement, sand and small aggregate should match the mix proportions of the surrounding concrete as far as is practicable.

d. SURFACE CONDITION. All reinforcement should be free from loose mill scale, loose rust, oil and grease, snow and ice or other harmful matter immediately before placing the concrete.

e. WELDING. Welding on site should be avoided if possible, but where suitable safeguards and techniques are employed, and provided that the types of steel have the required welding properties, it may be undertaken. All welding should be carried out in accordance with the relevant British Standards and the recommendations of the reinforcement manufacturers, and only with the engineer's prior approval.

f. MECHANICAL SPLICES. Butt joining of reinforcement with mechanical splices or couplers of approved design is permissible, but the cover to any sleeve should not be less than that specified for normal reinforcement. Mechanical couplers should be used in accordance with the manufacturer's recommendations, and for bars in tension they should satisfy the following criteria:

(i) When a test is made of representative gauge length assembly comprising reinforcement of the size, grade and profile to be used and a coupler of the precise type to be used, the permanent elongation after loading to $0.6\,f_y$ should not exceed 0.1 mm.

(ii) The design ultimate strength of the coupled bar should exceed the specified characteristic strength by the percentage specified in BS 4449.

MEASUREMENT OF BENDING DIMENSIONS OF BARS FOR REINFORCED CONCRETE — PREFERRED SHAPES (FROM BS 4466)

Shape code	Method of measurement of bending dimensions	Total length of bar (L) measured along centreline	Dimensions to be given in schedule
20		A	Straight
32		$A + h$	
33		$A + 2h$	
34*		$A + n$	
35*		$A + 2n$	
37*		$A + B - \frac{1}{2}r - d$	
38*		$A + B + (C) - r - 2d$	
41*		$A + B + (C)$	
43*		If angle with horizontal is 45° or less $A + 2B + C + (E)$	

r = Standard radius of bend unless otherwise stated.
* For this shape L should be rounded up to a 25 mm multiple.

Shape code	Method of measurement of bending dimensions	Total length of bar (L) measured along centre line	Dimensions to be given in schedule
51		$A + (B)$ $-\frac{1}{2}r - d.$ If r is minimum use shape code 37	
6		$2(A + B) + 12\,d$	
62		If angle with horizontal is 45° or less $A + C$	
82		$2A + 3B + 18\,d$	
77	Other shapes 	$2A + B + 20\,d$	
85		$A + B + 0.57C$ $(D) - \frac{1}{2}r - 2.57d$	
99	All other shapes	To be calculated A dimensional sketch shall be drawn out over schedule columns A to E. Every dimension shall be specified and the dimension that is to allow for the permissible deviations shall be indicated in parenthesis, otherwise the fabricator is free to choose which dimensions shall allow for the tolerance. If a shape that is given in this table or in table 1 is required but a different dimension is to allow for the permissible deviations, the shape shall be drawn out and given the shape code 99 and the free dimension shall be indicated in parentheses. The tolerance given in table 4 also apply.	

The dimensions in parentheses are free dimensions.

STEEL FABRIC REINFORCEMENT TO BS 4483

Made by welding steel wire into a rectangular mesh. Wire may be plain round, indented or otherwise deformed, welded or inter-woven.

BS ref.	Pitch		Bar size		Description
	Main	Cross	Main	Cross	
A 393			10	10	
A 252			8	8	
A 193	200	200	7	7	Square mesh
A 142			6	6	
A 98			5	5	
B 1131			12	8	
B 785			10	8	
B 503	100	200	8	8	Structural mesh
B 385			7	7	
B 283			6	7	
B 196			5	7	
C 785			10	6	
C 636			9	6	
C 503	100	400	8	5	Long mesh
C 385			7	5	
C 283			6	5	
D 98	200	200	5	5	Wrapping fabric
D 49	100	100	2.5	2.5	

Note that BS reference is area of main steel per metre width.

Quality of steel: Hard drawn steel wire to BS 4461
                    Tensile strength 460 N/mm².
Standard sizes: Sheets 2.400 × 4.800
                    Rolls 2.400 × 48.000
                    Rolls 2.400 × 72.000.
Ordering procedure: BS 4483
                    Reference number
                    Type of material and process of manufacture
                    Number and size of sheets or rolls.

BIBLIOGRAPHY

British Standards

BS 4: Part 1: Structural steel sections
BS 308: Engineering drawing practice
BS 449: Part 2: The use of structural steel in building
BS 499: Part 2: Symbols for welding
BS 1192: Construction drawing practice
BS 1579: Connectors for timber
BS 4190: ISO metric black hexagon bolts screws and nuts
BS 4320: Metal washers for general engineering purposes
BS 4395: Part 2: High strength friction grip bolts
BS 4449: Hot rolled steel bars for the reinforcement of concrete
BS 4461: Cold worked steel bars for the reinforcement of concrete
BS 4466: Bending dimensions and scheduling of bars for the reinforcement of concrete
BS 4482: Hard drawn mild steel wire for the reinforcement of concrete
BS 4471: Part 1: Sizes of sawn and planed timber
BS 4483: Steel fabric for the reinforcement of concrete
BS 4620: Rivets for general engineering and shipbuilding purposes
BS 4848: Part 2: Structural hollow sections
BS 4848: Part 3: Equal and unequal angles
BS 4978: Timber grades for structural use
BS 5268: Part 2: Structural use of timber: code of practice for permissible stress
             design, materials and workmanship
BS 5268: Part 3: Structural use of timber: code of practice for trussed rafter roofs
BS 5328: Methods for specifying concrete, including ready-mixed concrete
BS 5950: Structural use of steel in building
BS 8110: Part 1: Structural use of concrete in building

BCSA and SCI publications

Structural steelwork handbook
Metric practice for structural steelwork
Structural steelwork fabrication
Connections in structural steelwork for buildings (F.H. Needham)
Site connections to BS 5400: part 3 (F.H. Needham)

Concrete Society Technical Report No 2 — Standard method of detailing reinforced concrete

Designed and Detailed (J.B. Higgins and M.R. Hollington) British Cement Association.

The Institution of Structural Engineers

Recommendations for the permissible stress design of reinforced concrete building structures

INDEX